Sensational Subjects

The WISH List
(Warwick Interdisciplinary Studies in the Humanities)

Series editors: Jonathan Bate, Stella Bruzzi and Thomas Docherty

In the twenty-first century, the traditional disciplinary boundaries of higher education are dissolving at remarkable speed. The last decade has seen the flourishing of scores of new interdisciplinary research centres at universities around the world and there has also been a move towards more interdisciplinary teaching.

The WISH List is a collaboration between Bloomsbury Academic and the University of Warwick, a university that has been, from its foundation, at the forefront of interdisciplinary innovation in academia. The series aims to establish a framework for innovative forms of interdisciplinary publishing within the humanities, between the humanities and social sciences and even between the humanities and the hard sciences.

Also in The WISH List:

Reading and Rhetoric in Montaigne and Shakespeare, Peter Mack
The Public Value of the Humanities, edited by Jonathan Bate
Raising Milton's Ghost: John Milton and the Sublime of Terror in the Early Romantic Period, Joseph Crawford
Open-space Learning: A Study in Transdisciplinary Pedagogy, Nicholas Monk, Carol Chillington Rutter, Jonothan Neelands and Jonathan Heron
Confessions: The Philosophy of Transparency, Thomas Docherty
Dress, Law and Naked Truth: A Cultural Study of Fashion and Form, Gary Watt
Joseph Cornell Versus Cinema, Michael Pigott
The Constitution of English Literature: The State, the Nation and the Canon, Michael Gardiner
Sympathetic Sentiments: Affect, Emotion and Spectacle in the Modern World, John Jervis

Sensational Subjects

The Dramatization of Experience in the Modern World

John Jervis

Bloomsbury Academic
An imprint of Bloomsbury Publishing Plc

B L O O M S B U R Y
LONDON • NEW DELHI • NEW YORK • SYDNEY

Bloomsbury Academic
An imprint of Bloomsbury Publishing Plc

50 Bedford Square	1385 Broadway
London	New York
WC1B 3DP	NY 10018
UK	USA

www.bloomsbury.com

BLOOMSBURY and the Diana logo are trademarks of Bloomsbury Publishing Plc

First published 2015

© John Jervis, 2015

This work is published subject to a Creative Commons Attribution Non-Commercial No Derivatives Licence. You may share this work for non-commercial purposes only, provided you give attribution to the copyright holder and the publisher. For permission to publish commercial versions please contact Bloomsbury Academic.

John Jervis has asserted his right under the Copyright, Designs and Patents Act, 1988, to be identified as Author of this work.

No responsibility for loss caused to any individual or organization acting on or refraining from action as a result of the material in this publication can be accepted by Bloomsbury Academic or the author.

British Library Cataloguing-in-Publication Data
A catalogue record for this book is available from the British Library.

ISBN: HB: 978-1-4725-3563-4
PB: 978-1-4725-3559-7
ePub: 978-1-4725-3564-1
ePDF: 978-1-4725-3565-8

Library of Congress Cataloging-in-Publication Data
A catalog record for this book is available from the Library of Congress.

Typeset by Fakenham Prepress Solutions, Fakenham, Norfolk NR21 8NN

Contents

List of Illustrations		vi
A Note to the Reader		vii
Acknowledgements		viii
Foreword		ix
1	Introduction	1
2	Sensation and Sensationalism	13
3	Sensational Processes	43
4	The Aesthetics of Sensation	67
5	The Distractions of the Modern	95
6	Cinematic Sensation: The Sublime and the Spectacle	123
7	Sensational Affect	141
8	The Melodrama of the Modern	159
Notes		183
Index		225

List of Illustrations

Chapter 4, p. 77:
Francis Bacon, *Reclining Woman* (1961)
London, Tate Gallery
© The Estate of Francis Bacon. All rights reserved. DACS 2014

Francis Bacon, *Study after Velázquez's Portrait of Pope Innocent X* (1953)
Des Moines, Des Moines Art Center, p. 79
Bridgeman Art Library
© The Estate of Francis Bacon. All rights reserved. DACS 2014

Bridget Riley, *Current* (1964), p. 89
New York, Museum of Modern Art
© Bridget Riley. All rights reserved, courtesy Karsten Schubert, London

Bridget Riley, *Static 1* (1966), p. 90
New York, Coll. Hannelore B. Schulhof
© Bridget Riley. All rights reserved, courtesy Karsten Schubert, London

Chapter 6, p. 124:
John Martin, *The Destruction of Sodom and Gomorrah* (1852)
Newcastle, Laing Art Gallery
© Laing Art Gallery/Bridgeman Art Library

A Note to the Reader

As a wide-ranging cultural and historical study, this book poses challenges for readers, who may approach it from differing educational and academic backgrounds, and levels of expertise. It is an unavoidable consequence of the scope and ambition of the book that it should pose these challenges, since part of its aim is to further the development of a theoretically integrated framework for grappling with issues raised by text, image and cultural practice in the context of modern experience as it has come down to us over two centuries or so. Specialists can doubtless look after themselves, but for non-specialists it may be helpful to suggest that although all chapters include some tricky theory discussion, Chapters 1–3 and 8 may prove most accessible, and Chapters 5–7 are likely to be most difficult. In particular, Chapter 7 (a critique of contemporary affect theory) can certainly be skipped by non-specialists. Some care has been taken with the index, which may prove a useful additional resource. Ultimately, the book is intended to be thought-provoking rather than in any way definitive, and hopefully the reader will enjoy it in that spirit.

Acknowledgements

I would like to thank Jo Collins for stimulating discussions and for helpful comments on early drafts of the book; her enthusiasm and encouragement have been invaluable. I would also like to thank Mary Evans for her unswerving support and friendship over the many years of this project. And above all I would like to thank Naoko, for being an endlessly delightful source of distraction (see Chapter 5).

An array of cafés and teashops, in Canterbury and London, have also played an important role as congenial sites for discussions between the aforementioned and myself – but there are too many to list …

Foreword

The reader of this and John Jervis's companion volume, *Sympathetic Sentiments*, holds in their hands a veritable challenge to the iconoclastic tradition of Western cultural aesthetics. But 'iconoclastic' here is used quite literally to describe those modes of critical inquiry in the humanities and social sciences that are weary of the image, of the icon, and, with that, are weary of sensorial experience as a source and resource for understanding. Indeed, I might go so far as to suggest that Jervis's volumes are a challenge to the methodological pursuit of understanding in the social and human sciences. In this respect, these works aren't transdisciplinary efforts in the same manner as the other volumes in Bloomsbury's The WISH List series. To be sure, Jervis addresses and draws from a variety of political, aesthetic, cultural and social disciplines, and his engagements will prove crucial to scholars in a diverse range of fields from political science to cultural studies; from geography to film studies; from literary studies to economics. But although Jervis's work is informed and informs these diverse areas of human and social science inquiry, it isn't born from any one of them. Rather, in *Sensational Subjects* and *Sympathetic Sentiments*, Jervis's ambition is to unsettle our expectations regarding the outcome of inquiry itself – namely, comprehension. Jervis puts pressure upon our inherited common sense that a critical attitude begins with establishing the proper distance between subject and object of inquiry so as to achieve comprehension. In short, the issue regards our faith in the existence of mediation, and the collective trust we put in both the temporal and spatial distance of spectatorship.

The concept of mediation has had a plethora of names and representations throughout the Western tradition of aesthetic criticism. Plato's cave shadows mediate access to knowledge; as do the statues described by Augustine that attract our eyes and lead us into temptation; John Locke feared that the mediatory effects of typographical marks – the sentence, verse and chapter breaks inserted in the Bible – would inaugurate a second Babel; while Theodor Adorno held out little to no hope for the mediatory effects of moving images. In most, if not all of these and similar cases, mediation is morally dangerous. Hence the intervention of critical judgement, or dialectical thinking, or critique, that will organize and dispose of objects and sensations so that sense may be made of them. This operation is what Jervis means when, in this volume in particular, he isolates melodrama as a great unifying force that renders diverse registers of experience (practical, moral, aesthetic) intelligible. Melodrama is the mood of modern critical thought, Jervis affirms.

Jervis's challenge, then, is this: the critical impulses of iconoclasm and melodrama need to be put aside. The reason for this is at once simple and devastating: cultural aesthetics postulates an experience that is irreducible to either subjectivity or objectivity. Thus, the capacity to easily assign functions and effects to mediation is undeterminable to such a degree that the methodological ambition of understanding is ultimately, and persistently, undermined.

Consider, in this regard, Jervis's treatment of sensation as a 'cultural configuration'. He begins by affirming the realism of experience, and by undermining the values of heuristics and explanation. What we are prepared to engage, he asserts, is circuits of sensation that are real, not merely heuristically useful for understanding cultural phenomena. There is an ontological realism, as well as a radical empiricism, at work in Jervis's project that troubles most of our inherited intuitions about the kinds of access we can have to the worlds we occupy. Traditionally, we assume that direct access to experience is impossible – this, once again, is because experience is always-already mediated by intervening forces, objects and peoples. But Jervis's work in *Sensational Subjects* forces us to come to terms with the limits of the conceptual assumptions around mediation in order to explore the disjunctive jolts that intervene between cause and effect, and it does this by putting pressure on our experience of immediacy – what Jervis calls 'shuddering', or the 'immediate involuntary sensation of the body in its very being' (p. 16). There is nothing more immediate than shuddering, and shuddering's immediacy points to a domain of experience that is not implicated in the temporal and spatial dimensions of mediation. This is not to say, then, that we should do away with mediation as a critical concept. It is to say, rather, that our current critical and conceptual vocabularies have done away with the experience of immediacy; or, at the very least, have denied shuddering its rightful place as a corporeal experience of cultural aesthetics.

What Jervis ultimately asks of his reader is to come to terms with the limits of understanding – not as a theoretical proposition, nor as a heuristic device, but as an ambition of critical thinking. And this, I submit, is the most challenging dimension of Jervis's radical empiricism and of his realism. It is a challenge grounded in the possibility – indeed, the *fact* – of immediate experience, of jolts plucking on nerves. In this regard, the reader of *Sensational Subjects* and *Sympathetic Sentiments* will find little room for a repose of thought. She will be persistently disturbed at the uncanniness of her response – a response characterized by a simultaneous turning away and holding on to the insights, challenges and conclusions Jervis draws. Indeed, I hazard to say that the reader will not be persuaded by Jervis's argument, because persuasion is not his ambition. It is quite the opposite – namely, the affronting and confronting of what cannot be avoided: the fact of experience and its diffusiveness in the immediacy of the moment.

Davide Panagia
University of California, Los Angeles

1

Introduction

My work originally grew out of thinking about the notion of sensation, and being intrigued by whether, or how, the two meanings of the term – as sensory feeling, and as media event – might be connected. On further investigation, I found the links to be quite strong, and this in turn brings into play important controversies over whether sensationalism distorts our ability to acquire self-knowledge, to understand events around us and to relate to others, controversies that have been around for at least two centuries. In probing this, it seemed important to get beyond tired academic debates about the interests of powerful groups and their capacity for ideological manipulation, so as to gain a sense of the matrix out of which such individuals and groups develop their sense of their 'interests' in the first place. In this book, then, the development of this culture of sensation is explored by examining the dynamics of sensation as experience, as encountered in the embodied effects of shock and the dramatic impact of media events, and in doing this we are drawn to the idea of a 'circuit of sensation'. This is conceptualized in terms of forces, fields and flows, of energy and intensity, that can be variously glossed in the language of 'nerves' and nervous energy (from early on in the period), or of electrical and electromagnetic energy (from rather later), all amounting to a distinctive vision of the connections between the sensory experiences that both connect and separate us, and that can be reinforced by the intensity of media sensationalism. In effect, we display the relations between some of the terms whereby the modern world tries to make sense of the experiences that it does, itself, produce, often in unforeseen ways and with unexpected consequences, hence producing and reproducing the distinctive cultural configuration of 'sensationalism'.

This configuration turns out to have wide ramifications. It suggests, for example, that any notion of isolating 'high art' from these cultural currents, resting as it does on a notion of sensation purified of contamination by popular culture and the mass media, is not only unrealistic but shows a misunderstanding of the way art is itself embedded in these currents. Film, in particular, has had an engagement with 'sensation' from the start, raising the possibility that this is not just a matter of film content but of the cinematic experience itself, encapsulating the dynamic relation between concentration and distraction that is central to the experience of modern life. For a further example, developed later in the book, the intriguing contemporary revival of interest in 'evil' is addressed, and it is argued that the distinctive conjunction of sensationalism and sentimentalism present here enables us to position this in terms of a theory of melodrama, which helps cast light on reactions to contemporary phenomena like 9/11.

Main themes

Sensational events, sensational experiences: we variously enjoy them, suffer them, are overwhelmed by them; but what makes them count as *sensational*, and what is 'sensational' in sensation, is not something we reflect on much. It is apparent that the modern world presents each of us with a plenitude of 'sensational moments', concentrations of experience that are already potentially public, poised for further intensification through media reproduction, and a potent, arguably fundamental, resource for exploration in the arts. And it seems likely that such events and experiences help to construct us as subjects, able to endure, survive and even seek out such experiences. We experience sensations, just as we are presented with them through the media. 'Sensational subjects' are produced and reproduced in modernity both as the agent having the experience and as the topic experienced, both subjective and objective dimensions of the modern spectacle.

It is not so easy to avoid this, either. In a culture of hyperbole, even the normal has to become extraordinary if it is to be noticed, and no problem is worth announcing, no misfortune worth proclaiming, unless one can claim to have been traumatized by it. Nor does trying to be resolutely ordinary and inconspicuous, creeping through life in a humble station, necessarily work. If striving to make an impact can indeed make it all the more likely that you will succeed, there is no escape the other way: straining to avoid this fate can have the same effect – the media will find you anyway. We all have some 'other side', we all have some secret; and secrets revealed, transgressing the boundary into the glare of publicity, become sensational. Besides, the very ordinariness of the ordinary, and ordinary people, can be rendered spectacular, hence enhancing and dramatizing that very ordinariness, reminding us that this is, after all, the age of reality television, and the logic of celebrity. 'Sensational subjects' indeed.

This already suggests that there may be a relationship between the two senses of the term 'sensation' – as embodied feeling and as dramatic media event – and indeed this becomes the central theme of the book. The association had become very clear by the time of the 'sensation novel' of the 1860s, when sensational events in the stories were troublingly translated into symptomatic responses in the body of the reader – physical signs of excitement and distress, nervous palpitations – and such 'sensationalism' had already become controversial in the culture. But we can perhaps point to a rather different response by the reader here. This response can be one of sympathy with the plight of the hero or heroine, whether in these fictional adventures or in real-life scenarios. This sympathetic engagement also involves the feelings, but is more nuanced, involving mind and emotion as well as the immediacy of feeling. This response is more other-oriented, whether through strong identification or imaginative involvement, and assumes a degree of distance even as it seeks to overcome it.

These responses are not mutually exclusive, or at least can both be present in quick succession. Initial reactions to viewing the unfolding drama of the terrorist attack of 11 September 2001 tended to run along 'sensational' lines; but sympathy – and alternative responses that could occupy the same emotional 'space', such as anger – could kick in quickly thereafter. Nevertheless, these responses point in different directions, and have different cultural forms, implications and histories. So 9/11 reminded us of Hollywood special effects, of disaster movies, just as it reminded us of other dramatic 'spectacles', encountered by most of us primarily as media events, such as volcanoes, earthquakes and battles. In the broad sense, such spectacles are thereby treated as *engrossing*, even entertaining when presented explicitly in these terms, as in film, but always implicitly so, too; often in ways that make us feel queasy or guilty (tourists at volcanoes, drivers slowing down when passing a road accident to see it better …). In these cases, it is as though the aesthetic sense short-circuits the moral one, whereas when our engagement is primarily sympathetic, it is the other way around. As these examples show, all this presents problems for us in the age of mass media spectacle: one may wonder to what extent sympathetic engagement is still possible, for example.

Here, it is important to mention that it is only the 'sensation' strand that will be considered in this book; the other strand, relating to sympathy, is discussed in a second book, to be published simultaneously, entitled *Sympathetic Sentiments: Affect, Emotion and Spectacle in the Modern World*. The two books stand on their own, but there are of course links and overlaps. It is also necessary to add that while *Sensational Subjects* traces the history of the sensational back to the early nineteenth century, the sources of this strand can be found in eighteenth-century 'sensibility', which is also the source of the 'spectacle of sympathy', and the ramifications of this originating cultural pattern are explored in the other book, which also examines some of the problems of relating the two strands in their subsequent development through the nineteenth century and beyond.

Returning to this book, we can already see, with the Gothic, how 'sensation' could indeed be 'sensational', aligning feelings of the self with events beyond; one also sees that if this is one pole into which sensibility fractures, the other pole is constituted by the emergent cultural experience of the sentimental, reconstructed as a sensibility 'to excess', available for critique and denunciation. Gender politics is implicated here, together with a not unconnected interest in exploring the presuppositions of rational action and the factors – both cultural and psychological – that could inhibit it. 'Affect', now reconstructed as recalcitrant, a threat to rationality, and in need of discipline, is indulged and controlled in the domestic sphere yet is also allowed a problematical role in fantasy, in Gothic and its successors (although even here an attempt is made to recuperate the rational-scientific model by providing 'answers' to the mysteries). Here, and concentrating henceforth on the sensation strand, we find that boundaries between 'reality' and 'fantasy' are always troublesome, in that 'fantasy' must in some sense be part of reality, despite being set up as 'opposed' to it; and in the nineteenth century, an age increasingly influenced by the mass media, these boundaries become threatened by the media's capacity to appropriate and magnify real-life events.

These events classically include physical violence, notably murder – and it is above all here that the era of mass sensationalism is born, always carrying with it this link to the fundamentally *embodied* nature of experience. The body is now positioned decisively as the site, or switch-point, of a 'circuit of sensation' that exists on the cusp of the relation between physiology and culture, implicitly questioning their mutual independence in a world that is increasingly media-inflected, with channels of communication increasingly seen as structuring and 'mediating' these ostensibly separate spheres. And it is the body in its most gruesome form, both threatening and abject, that constitutes the pulsating heart of this cultural transformation. Overall, then, we can say that this distinctive cultural configuration involves quasi-physical circuits of both continuities and breaks, manifest in shocks, and defences overwhelmed, seen as producing a culture that encompasses both restless energy and nervous stress, linked to tension, but also pleasure and release. Sensations involve processes, and indeed cycles, with a tendency to inflation: yoked together with the impact of consumerism, one is constantly in search of 'newer' or 'better' sensations. Sensation engages us as organic and physical beings, through energy, force and flow, but these are also processes that are channelled through culture, shaped by it and grasped reflexively *as* cultural.

The ramifications of all this work themselves out through the later decades of the nineteenth century. By then, it was widely assumed that the shocks and jolts of everyday life, both literal and metaphorical, the endless new sensations and stresses of modern city life, constituted a threat of ill-health, of 'nervous exhaustion' (neurasthenia), but that consciousness itself could constitute a defence mechanism, a kind of 'stimulus shield'. Consciousness could register shock while diminishing its impact, making everyday experience manageable while building up a submerged layer of impressions and images that had escaped this, or been repressed, hence constituting an unconscious, existing as a potent resource for neurosis but also for artistic creativity. A corollary was that for something to be truly 'sensational' it needed to break through the shock defence altogether – but in this case, it is always potentially traumatic. As it cannot be merely 'filed away', in safe form, and is beyond any control by the subject, it is always liable to 'unmotivated' returns, as devastating as the initial impact.

While it is the potential of the 'mass spectacle' to transmit 'unconscious' influences that tends to be emphasized by psychoanalytical and other critics, there is a subtly different angle. That the audience should 'pay attention', at least to some extent, would seem to be a necessary presupposition for all this, after all; and that the sensational 'grabs our attention' is crucial to how it works in normal contexts, where it can be dramatic without being traumatic, as it were. 'Attention' has indeed been of considerable cultural interest since late nineteenth-century psychology positioned it as an issue. People can pay too much attention, or too little, and not necessarily to the right things; our attention can become 'distracted', both by losing concentration and by wandering to 'distractions'. One can, indeed, pay more attention to the 'distractions' of popular culture, to which indeed a 'distracted consciousness' may be better suited. By implication, such 'distraction' contrasts with the 'absorption' that allegedly characterized the attention we pay to great art, but we may that find that the implications of the relation between distraction and attention subvert conventional distinctions between 'high' art and 'popular' or 'mass' culture.

All this in turn focuses our own attention on those distinctive sites of cultural transmission, particularly film and television, where audiences are positioned in 'concentrated' fashion to experience 'distraction'; places where the bombardment of stimuli, now reconfigured as the reception of currents and waves in the form of messages and images, offers possibilities for proactive response, for degrees of involvement and choice by the experiencing subject – an arena of opportunities that could be used to navigate through the interpenetrating worlds of leisure, entertainment and even work. This zone of diffusion and concentration thus includes the technologies of mass communication and broadcasting whereby sounds, images and messages are dispersed through space and time, available for concentration in specific sites but always existing beyond these, hence transforming our experience of space, time and presence, indeed transforming 'communication across distance' so that it entails 'co-presence', thus forcing us to rethink boundaries of public and private, virtual and real. It is on this terrain that we increasingly encounter the subtly reconfigured relations between sensation, spectacle and the possibility of sympathetic engagement. In the light of this, we can also ponder the possibility that the contrast between shock or sensation, on the one hand, and the everyday world of routines, on the other, suggests two modes of experiencing the world of modernity and modern individuality: intensity and concentration, the visceral experience of the body, yet linked to the risks and hopes of insight and artistic inspiration; and distraction, diffusion, expansiveness, relaxation, perhaps with a certain superficiality, or the risk of boredom.

That sensationalism does indeed become more 'spectacular' seems clear enough, as we move again towards emphasizing the contemporary. Indeed, in everyday parlance 'spectacular' and 'sensational' are barely distinguishable; and they are frequently conjoined in cultural criticism as twin pathologies of the modern, twin embodiments of the pervasive power of the mass media. In the contemporary world, we can certainly be aware of a 'spectacle of sensation', always straining for greater impact, for dramatic new effects, always desperate to escape the death of submergence back into the sea of the undifferentiated, the boredom and inertia of a world where 'too much' can also become boring, where consumerism both feeds on sensation, in the endless promises, shocks and spills of the new and the transgressive, along with the dreams of pleasure and plenitude these can encompass, just as it subverts their realization in the drabness of the everyday.

In these possibly postmodern times, when rationalist ideologies of social transformation have fallen away, we are left with media-influenced hunts for scapegoats, for someone or some group to blame; and we can see, looming into view, another mode of presenting, experiencing and reacting to these events that has actually been around since the early nineteenth century – namely, melodrama. This is a culminating form of the 'spectacle of sensation', engaging the audience's sympathetic response to the necessarily innocent victim, together with anger at the villain, but in a context of sensationalism and the spectacular: it is about moral absolutes, battles of good and evil, in an arena of 'special effects' that incorporates the full resources of visual technology. This, again, offers a perspective on 9/11. Melodrama seems to have become a crucial factor in shaping our contemporary perceptions, corresponding as it does to the sense of diffuse threats and conspiracies, the imperative to blame, the escalation of moral dilemmas to simplified moral absolutes, the stigmatization of unacceptable otherness, and the sense of excess that have become central to mediated culture. The great promise of melodrama is that of a unification of experience in its practical, aesthetic and moral registers: melodrama reacts to the profound contingency of the world by attempting to render it intelligible as *drama*, as cosmic struggle and resolution. Its 'over the top' quality both reinforces its impact, helps to hold it together, and papers over the instability of its own fusion of forms. Exploring this, we can say that our world comes to present *itself* in ways that invite characterization as melodrama; it doesn't require much help from newscasters, novelists or film-makers (though doubtless gets it anyway).

Briefly, then, the implications of my argument can be summarized as follows. There is no point in harking back, or looking forward, to a golden age in which sensation, sensationalism and spectacle would no longer corrupt our rational appraisal of the world, which they allegedly do either by distorting the content of what is being said or shown, or by overcoming our defences against the overflow of undisciplined feeling. Since the eighteenth century, Western modernity has been deeply embedded in a body-focused culture of spectacle and sensation; they appear as inherent concomitants of mass literacy and the mass media, and have evolved with them, being present from very early on in the way we both conceive of, and experience, our relations with each other and the wider world. They are not inherently good or bad, but they are *there*. Of course, there are important issues to be confronted, 'culture wars' and important political battles to be fought, over power, inequality, exploitation and discrimination, but these have to be fought out on *this* terrain, and using its weapons, not somewhere else – for this is inescapably the world in which we now live.

General approach and assumptions

This book is a multi-layered history of modern experience as it has been 'sensationalized' over the period since the nineteenth century, and subjected to theoretical reflection. It draws on literature, art, film and other cultural resources, including the ideas of Benjamin and Deleuze, to develop a distinctive cultural framework for understanding these controversies and their contemporary implications; through drawing on a range of disciplinary perspectives, the hope is that this will further the development of a historically informed theoretical framework for cultural studies. Such a 'cultural aesthetics' would complement the study of socio-economic processes, and the discipline-focused study of the specific arts, with an emphasis on 'culture' as inclusive, refusing any constitutive distinction between 'high' and 'mass' culture, and on 'aesthetics' as incorporating the whole dimension of 'feeling' as a response to the world that includes the sensory but also the sense of reaction and orientation to – and in – a world we encounter yet which also encompasses us, hence an orientation that necessarily includes the embodied imagination. This would entail an approach to 'mind', 'body' and 'culture' that would be evocative of that relatively undifferentiated flux of ideas and impressions that constituted early modern culture before the Enlightenment philosophers began tidying it up. Academically, if this is an 'interdisciplinary' study, then it seeks to establish that the 'inter' would necessarily be a reference to the 'culture' that is the implicit, missing term in all this.

There is much here that could do with further elaboration – and to some extent this is done in the introduction to *Sympathetic Sentiments* – but enough has been said to make it clear that this is *not* a book about sensationalism as media manipulation, or 'mass culture' as reflecting the interests of competing groups, and underlying socio-economic processes, although there is plenty here that would be *relevant* to such sociological concerns, important as they are. Rather, the emphasis here is on the underlying patterns of meaning and experience embedded in cultural practices and products wherein and out of which emergent individuals and groups can situate themselves in the ideological debates of the time, whether the options offered by everyday consumerism or the 'grand narratives' of overarching meaning; and it is only in terms of these that notions like 'interest' make sense. In their anxiety to relate power to pre-constituted socio-economic or psychological interests, there is always a risk with these other approaches that they miss these underlying dimensions that constitute culture as irreducible, as a distinctive perspective *on* the world, rather than simply a part or product *of* it. This is not to say that this book is uncritical; indeed, if cultural aesthetics necessarily involves an orientation, a positioning, *within* culture, it is hardly possible to avoid the fact that such positioning will have implications, and will be embedded in controversies. That is to be welcomed.

We now need to consider more explicitly the idea of sensation as a 'cultural configuration'. As has been suggested, a study of the way 'sensation' works, whether in discourse, experience, or postulated as an underlying physiological reality, suggests the concept of a 'circuit of sensation'. The term is not, however, intended merely as an organizing concept or heuristic device that helps us to understand the world but does not really refer to entities or processes within it. Rather, it refers to ostensibly 'real' processes, linking bodies, minds, technologies and 'others': it is a 'cultural' reality that points to and attempts to incorporate discursive *and* physical dimensions. Only if we make such strong, and potentially troublesome, claims can we be true to the place 'sensation' occupies, the role it plays, in modern culture and experience. This does, after all, seem to converge with, or reflect, a powerful strand of thought from the eighteenth century onwards, namely that there are indeed currents, running through 'nerves', and manifest in 'feelings', that serve as real-enough, quasi-physical circuits, as linkages between minds and bodies and other minds and bodies. Notions of 'contagion' are encountered frequently here. Of course, within this, the concepts have shifted significantly over the period: scientific understanding has evolved in various ways, organic and electrical metaphors come and go, and the idea of media as *themselves* being physical objects or channels that can intervene in these circuits, even be significantly constitutive of them, has become widespread since the mid-nineteenth century. In our time, all this has been shifting again, with new theoretical perspectives opening up as we try to make sense of cyberspace and digital media.

But we need to be careful here. To write *wholly* from within this language of physical circuits, the world appropriated within a specific and changeable scientific discourse, is to allow oneself to treat the latter as unquestioned resource, rather than as part of the topic being investigated. This is an important reason for the critique of central strands of contemporary 'affect theory' offered later in this book, where we find that currently fashionable forms of scientific discourse (such as 'neuroscience') are extended into new areas in a rather dogmatic and uncritical way, rather than finding that this development *itself* is treated as a fascinating subject for cultural reflection. The challenge is to inhabit some branch of science (or other area of culture) while simultaneously indicating a degree of distance from it – that characteristically 'modern' position that is also a constitutive stance of any adequate cultural study.

We find, then, that just as the modern world has presented us with these diffuse but interrelated experiences of mental, organic and physical entities interacting within conventional spatio-temporal coordinates, making sense in everyday terms, so it has also provided us with shifting concepts and metaphors for figuring these, in a range of discourses and representations, through the arts and sciences. Our 'sensational' metaphors (burn with passion, melt with pleasure, freeze with terror) are not random individual products but both reflect and manifest this process of figuration whereby the cultural imaginary constructs and reconstructs the world of experience through the framing that makes it meaningful; and it is *within* this that questions of ontology, of reality and truth, are situated and debated. This is why the concept of 'figuration' is useful: it incorporates the figurative, the literary use of tropes, but has the potential to go beyond this, able to question or transgress even the most basic ontological boundaries, such as those that define reality itself, and the coordinates through which we pin it down. It is, for example, misleading to place the circuit of sensation simply within a conventional framework of space and time, since, as process, it has an explosive, fracturing potential that positions time as relative to it, and space as constructed by it; in these respects, it suggests 'modernist' (scientific and aesthetic) articulations of space–time disjunctions.

One aspect of this can be developed here. This book reconfigures the contemporary within the modern, and displays the modern *as* contemporary. If the contemporary is the horizon of the present, hence ever-shifting, ever disappearing and reappearing as we move on, it cannot be *identified* with the modern: rather, the latter is that very process of change and stasis itself, both occurring *in* time, time which thereby becomes history, and as the *pattern* of conjunctions and disjunctions that subverts any sense of a single, uniquely identifiable overall process – a process that would ignore the reflexive movement whereby one simultaneously makes sense of it *and* institutes the distance of difference itself in the heart of the same. It is this that enables these patterns to have consequences, to be causes and have effects; but, as patterns, they cannot themselves *have* causes, since patterns only exist as appropriated or figured through reflexive cultural practices. One can add that the implication here of a possible gap between cause and effect, a disproportion, is itself a theme in modern discussions of science and history, just as it occurs in the argument of this book in the context of sensation: any circuit of sensation seems to involve the language and imagery of shocks, disjunctions, jolts and jumps. Always there is this reflexive gap, inherent in grasping something the subject is involved in, belongs to; and the impossibility of secure knowledge of these currents and feelings that swirl in and around the self, for example, is not due to some mystery of the individual, some irreducible uniqueness of the person, but testifies to the impossibility of reducing reflexive appropriation to causation, in whatever context.

Relative to outcome, the sense of linear development in history has to be grasped as a process of increasing complexity; but relative to origin, this is rather to be seen as diffusion, dispersion. Movement is outwards, as well as onwards, the sense of pattern, of structure, emerging as centrifugal (although individual structures can of course entail depth, as in the model of the self composed of conscious and unconscious 'layers'). All this gives a sense of repetition, of continuity, as well as change: the origin, the impossible first moment, reflexively constitutive of the series, is grasped in and as repetition, but repetition as difference, through diffusion. Such a reflexive grasp of time is a move out of time, projecting it, as figuration or breaking it up, constituting it as pattern in the very act of attempting to grasp it – the reflexive mode of the modern. And we return to the circuit of sensation: this is given reflexively, as a theoretical concept that develops out of these processes and purports to mirror aspects of them; but it can only do this if it also, in a sense, partakes of them, continues them by other means. It can only reflect the real if it reflects the homologies of pattern and process, present in the gaps and disjunctions that *also* constitutes it in its *distance* from the real. As such, the concept attempts to theorize the cultural configuration that suggests it, accepting that it cannot avoid the possibility that it also subtly contributes to it, perhaps indeed to its 'dispersion'. Ultimately, then, through 'sensation', this book rejoins the very processes it reflexively articulates, manifest in its own structure, and the possibilities it thereby opens up …

2

Sensation and Sensationalism

The extension of meaning whereby sensation as media event develops out of sensation as feeling, from the eighteenth through the nineteenth centuries, corresponds to a real cultural process, one in which the conjunction of feeling, media and modern experience reveals a 'culture of sensation' that is fundamental to popular culture and modernity itself. In this culture of sensation, the body is always already mediated, and the media embodied, in a process of mutual constitution.

'Sensation' refers both to the mark of experience on the body, as 'feeling', and to a spectacular, challenging happening, experienced as such. An important aspect of the culture and experience of modernity is the relation between these: the sense in which sensations do indeed become 'sensational', and the conditions under which this conjunction or transformation occurs. Sensation in the first sense marks the experience of experience, our physical, embodied awareness of experience as such. In the second sense, it marks experience as always potentially spectacular: as experience becomes mediated, it becomes dramatic, with a public aspect; it thereby gains a voice, becomes known. As sensation becomes sensational, we become voyeurs both of our own and of others' experiences. In both senses, 'sensation' refers to experience in its excessive and unpredictable modes, carrying the message that time is not just that of rational project but is also that of rupture, interruption, chance or fate. It embodies both an ethos and an ontology, mapped in a language whereby the unpredictable passivity of sensation-as-experience draws on notions of nerves, nervousness, energy flows, circuits, connections, 'influences'.

A sensational case

At the beginning of Edgar Allan Poe's story 'The Facts in the Case of M. Valdemar', the narrator tells of his unease at 'going public' with his extraordinary tale. He had wanted to keep it quiet while further scientific investigations were pursued, but the case has already 'excited discussion', and a 'garbled or exaggerated' account has 'made its way into society', resulting in 'many unpleasant representations'. Hence, he has chosen to give his own account now.

We have heard all this before – because we have heard it so many times since. It recurs eternally, as a foundational rationale for the sensational media story: 'setting the record straight', or, conversely, anticipating 'misleading' versions by 'telling the truth now'. Several features of this are worth commenting on. One might wonder, initially, about the reference to 'society'. This could have a slightly antique ring to it: 'society' as 'polite society', the elite. But one's suspicion that the real concern lies elsewhere is confirmed by a further reference near the other end of the story, mentioning 'unwarranted popular feeling' about the events described.[1] So here we have it, then; the real object of fear is the mass public, which refers as much to a process as a readership: the process whereby dissemination is always already corruption, so that to pass on the news is already to distort, exaggerate, misrepresent – in short, sensationalize – it. The mass public as reception, and the mass media as circuit of communication, are mutually implicated in this process, indeed really only exist as complementary products or moments of it. And we see how the true and the false become interlocked in the production of the sensational as the barely credible, the (almost) incredible. Indeed, 'truth' and 'falsity' become nebulous here; what really matters is exploring the boundaries of the credible, producing 'excited' discussion. Nor indeed do 'facts' contradict sensation; rather, they are grist to its mill.

And then, the narrator himself – his position is disingenuous, to say the least. Who does *he* address? It is clearly not written as a personal letter; indeed, it is evidently written for some public or other. And it is an account that is sensational enough in form, quite apart from content; an account structured, crafted, to produce the maximum sensational impact. It is hardly a medical report, though cunningly has something of this aura about it; it is ostensibly in lieu of such a report (which can only come 'later'). In short, it is guaranteed to contribute to the sensationalism it purports to distance itself from: the cure for sensation, it appears, is further sensation. It carries, embodies, the sensationalism it ostensibly disavows. Actually, the story, as written by Poe, was published originally in an American magazine – so Poe, like his narrator, writes for a public audience. But for Poe, of course, the dilemma, while still present, is less pressing. He may have aspired to a reputation among the literary elite, but was clearly not averse to a popular readership. Indeed, his 'sensationalism' has made him an author who has been controversial, difficult to 'place', ever since: he is both in the canon, and exiled from it, the difficult presence who questions the boundary itself, insisting on sensationalism both *in* and *as* literature.

If we return to the narrator, we can see him, also, as a key figure in this foundational media story: for he is the eyewitness, the person who guarantees presence, who was *really there*; his is the 'first person' account. Thus is the naive empiricism of 'facts' reinforced by that of 'witness', together producing the authority of 'total presence', the source of unmediated truth. And he, the narrator, embodies it twice over, because here the medical discourse plays its full part. He himself was present throughout this 'medical experiment', the attempt to mesmerize his dying friend; but so, too, were various doctors and nurses, along with a medical student, who took notes. So although we are not *quite* offered an official medical report, it is presented as the next best thing, with the narrator as the ultra-reliable witness. All of which, in turn, serves of course to reinforce the sensationalism …

As really, physically, *there*, however, the narrator not only has the truth of what he has *seen* to offer us; there is the truth of his whole body. For this is an account that presents us not just with the truth of the visual sense, but also of smell, of touch, of sound; it is a synaesthetic truth, a truth truly 'sensational', of the body as receptive to sensation. And M. Valdemar can be introduced here; for what we are told about him qualifies him, too, as a sensational subject. He is dying of phthisis (tuberculosis), a disease with suitably wide-ranging, gross – and graphically described – physical symptoms and effects. And we are told, further, that his temperament was 'markedly nervous', hence making him a 'good subject for mesmeric experiment'.[2] 'Nervous' is a term that has a resonance across both the physical and the psychological registers: to be 'nervous' is a physiological state, engendered by over-active nerves; yet it also designates a personality type, someone sensitive, in a positive sense, more than usually open to 'sensation' and 'feeling', but also likely to be 'temperamental', have mood swings, indispositions, possibly liable to hysterical or depressive episodes. Such a person has an 'affinity' for mesmerizing magnetism (as she later would for the hypnosis of Charcot and Freud).

And so the experiment proceeds. The dying Valdemar is duly mesmerized. This is known to have succeeded because the 'glassy roll' of the eye was changed for 'that expression of uneasy *inward* examination' that is apparently characteristic in such cases.[3] In looking 'inward', the dying man looks in to the depth of the self, towards that paradoxically physical location of the non-physical: he is already 'elsewhere'. His eyes are now closed; but he can continue to respond, with difficulty, to questions. He is left in this state for a few hours, and the decision is then taken to let him die. The narrator, however, wants to try one last question. An excessive question produces a suitably excessive response to match. The skin assumes a 'cadaverous hue', the upper lip 'writhed away' from the teeth, and the lower jaw fell open, revealing a 'swollen and blackened tongue', from which a 'hideous' voice came forth, 'unearthly', as if from a vast distance, from a vast cavern, but a voice that also impressed the narrator, in a way he admits is difficult to describe, as 'gelatinous or glutinous matters impress the sense of touch'. This voice, then, comes from the depths, from elsewhere, from far away; but it is also tactile, viscous, here and now, in unearthly, terrifying proximity.

This truly figures the sensational, poised as it is between distant event or cause and proximate, physical manifestation or response, an ambiguity mapped also in the media sensation, referring simultaneously to the mediated event and to its effect on the audience. And indeed the narrator describes his own response as one of 'unutterable, shuddering horror'.[4] 'Shuddering' is a deeply embodied response, an immediate involuntary sensation of the body in its very being; again, both a surface effect (affect), but also one that engages the self, the dimension of depth. There is a circuit of sensation here, from Valdemar to his friend and witness, just as surely as the media circuit identified previously: an involuntary language of the body, its feelings and responses, just as the more apparent language of the media which, in its own way, also registers and transmits a body, the social body. And this circuit incorporates *us*, as readers, in our own immediate, affective response: we, too, can shudder. 'It is as though the story itself had become horribly corporealized before our very eyes', as Jonathan Elmer puts it. Thus do the textual and the affective merge in the sensational. And Elmer comments on the mixture of pleasure and threat in this encounter: on the one hand, 'a masochistic pleasure arising ultimately from the reading body's own submission to invasion', that of being 'mastered by affect'; but at the same time, it is a 'threatening encounter', to be recoiled from.[5]

Valdemar is then left in this apparently suspended, corpse-like state, for some months, while kept under observation. Finally, they try to question him once more, and awaken him. This repeated excess – doubly excessive – again meets its appropriate response. An 'ichor', a viscous fluid, issues from his eyelids, with a 'highly offensive' odour. The same 'hideous voice', repeating the same message as last time, breaks out. The words conclude: '*I say to you that I am dead!*' And the story reaches its climax: '… amid ejaculations of "dead! dead!" absolutely bursting from the tongue and not from the lips … his whole frame at once … shrunk – crumbled – absolutely rotted away … Upon the bed, before the whole company, there lay a nearly liquid mass of loathsome – of detestable – putridity.'[6]

Here, at the core of Poe's sensationalism, in that obsession with the possible instability of the most important boundary of all, that dividing life and death, we encounter a frenetic, desperate abundance of language in its attempt to capture the impossible presence of the sensational moment in all its transgressive splendour, fracturing the very categories of our attempt to communicate it. In the climactic scene, these incessant, dramatic, cumulatively punched out superimpositions of sensory description, sensory images, serve to incorporate and emphasize *all* the senses, including smell, that lowest and least tolerated of the senses in the refined, 'civilized' world of the modern West, and touch, present here as the viscous, neither truly liquid nor solid, hence as slime, signifier of the unutterably abject. All serve to produce a suitably sensational 'climax' in which a dead, black tongue ejaculates spasms of paradoxical, self-refuting meaning. This is indeed a scenario of 'body-horror', of the kind identified by Karen Halttunen as fundamental to sensationalism.[7] And this excess of the senses in sensationalism is complemented by the excess of meaning, as though all the conceivable registers of interpretation must be called on to be simultaneously present, reinforcing the impact: so an impossible male ejaculation from a dead tongue issues out of the equally impossible surface/depth of the female/maternal throat/birth canal, in a birth of meaning that is inseparable from its death, all reinforcing this sense of a ghastly, sensationally grotesque body, a transfiguration of the 'grotesque body' of Carnival[8] into a register of *simultaneous* life and death, disconnected from any mooring in the cycles of death, rebirth and renewal, and made all the more grotesque by the mediated incorporation of the taboos and disavowals of the modern world.

Sensations challenge us – and always return. Nor, as we have seen, does their status as sensational depend unduly on their status as 'real' rather than 'imaginary', a distinction they do not necessarily respect. Before moving on, then, let us visit an episode from May 1995, when the Ebola virus was ravaging the population of Zaire. This disease causes internal haemorrhaging, the organs go soft and spongy, the skin dissolves, and uncontrollable spasms and seizures are triggered. 'The surface of the tongue goes soft and pulpy and is spat out or swallowed ... Death often comes after one final seizure, during which virus-laden blood is spewed over anyone and everything nearby.' This was given huge press coverage: it was gruesome, mysterious, 'a horrible way to die', 'the big one', a 'doomsday disease', as Susan Moeller puts it, adding that 'When the admittedly sensational Ebola is represented in such a sensationalized fashion by the media and by Hollywood, other diseases pale by comparison'. In one television report, scenes from the fictional movie *Outbreak* were spliced in, only acknowledged as such at a late point in the news item.[9] It could as well have been M. Valdemar ...

From sensation to sensationalism

Writing in 1863, in one of the first books on advertising, William Smith refers to – and defends – what he calls '"sensation" advertising', explaining that 'the modern appetite for "sensation" is manifest even in advertisements'.[10] The use of quotation marks around 'sensation' is of interest here, suggesting that he is using a word that will be intelligible to his readers but is as yet relatively new, at least in this usage. Two specific examples of the word in his book are worth mentioning. He refers to a mining accident, in which several hundred miners died, which 'caused a widespread sensation'; as a result, charity donations flowed in, including one from the Queen, who included a letter of 'most touching sympathy'. Certainly disasters, along with accidents, murders and battles, could count as startling or shocking public events that could appropriately be called 'sensations'; and that such sensations seem inseparable from a response in terms of feeling or emotion shows how an older use of the word remains central to it. The other emergent use of the term comes out in this quote: 'For those delighting in what are now called "sensations", Monsieur Blondin has been risking his neck on the top of a very high rope at the Crystal Palace ...' Here, a 'sensation' is a spectacular entertainment, a performance, which could incorporate any out-of-the-ordinary episode of magic, circus or theatre. Put together, these become twin aspects of the mass culture spectacle, disseminated through the media, and with close links to consumerism, since as Smith reminds us, 'any matter which can be advertised with reference to any great public event should not be neglected'.[11]

Not that this is the beginning. In the British context, we encounter a use of the term in a report in *The Times* upon the attempted assassination of Queen Victoria in 1840. It suggests that 'the sensation produced by this diabolical attempt upon the lives of Her Majesty and her illustrious consort ... may well be imagined'. The term is nicely ambiguous here, referring to both the feeling and the event, and it shows that a sensation is *produced*, as a kind of mass subjective effect – or affect – and is thereby also *appropriated*, in part through the imagination. Then again, *The Times* referred in May 1847 to the big impact made by Jenny Lind, the Swedish soprano, in her first London performance, which showed how 'that wondrous thing, a new sensation was actually created'.[12] Thus does sensation involve not just producing an effect, but is also a production that must involve novelty.[13]

Inevitably, though, we are drawn deeper into the world of media sensationalism when we consider crime and crime reporting. A sign of things to come was the bludgeoning to death of a fellow-gambler by one John Thurtell in 1823, precipitating extensive newspaper interest and 'sensational' coverage, along with a huge turnout to see him executed.[14] The savage murder of Eliza Grimwood in the slum areas around Waterloo in 1838 created tremendous public interest, stirred up by graphic accounts in the press. Even 50 years later, at the height of the hunt for 'Jack the Ripper', the horror of the Whitechapel murders was brought home by comparing them with this iconic case. There is also an intriguing literary reflection of this: it has recently been argued, with some plausibility, that the gory murder of Nancy by Bill Sikes in *Oliver Twist* (1837–8) was based directly on the descriptions of Eliza's murder that appeared in the press.[15] Switching now to America, and concentrating on the same decade, Halttunen suggests that a key moment came in 1836, when the axe murder of a beautiful young woman of dubious repute resulted in two months of extensive press coverage of the trial of the alleged murderer, and the newspapers most involved, which took opposed positions on the likely guilt of the accused, found their circulations dramatically expanded. It is not clear from Halttunen's account whether the word 'sensation' was actually used here, but clearly it could have been, and within a few years undoubtedly would have been, for this is what may be the first clear example, on any scale, of the mass media appropriation and reproduction of an event as 'sensational'.[16]

Shelley Streeby in turn notes that the now largely forgotten Mexican-American War of 1846-8 – as a result of which the United States hugely increased in size by the acquisition of New Mexico, Southern California, Texas and Arizona – was the first clear example of 'sensationalism in the service of U.S. empire'. The print revolution, along with the extension of the penny press, and the invention of the telegraph, ensured the rapid diffusion of news from the front, on a virtually daily basis; and in his mass circulation stories, based on the war, the popular novelist Lippard made 'a sensational appeal to his readers, an appeal that records a visceral, mass response to war'. Overall, the graphic depiction of events, both in text and pictures, brought the intensely physical presence of war into people's lives, making it all the more vivid and dramatic, and showing how 'nationalism as mediated by print capitalism' depends on 'thrilling sensations of embodiment'.[17] Enough has been said to suggest that the 'if it bleeds, it leads' principle of news sensationalism today has deep roots, just as Keith Tester's claim that, when geared to the human interest dimension, contemporary journalism will 'tend to emphasize sensation, bolstered by an attempt to represent the inner feelings of the journalists and victims themselves' has long been true, along with his conclusion: 'Sensational journalistic practice is sensational in both senses of the word.'[18]

Origins are misty – both conceptually and empirically – but suggestive. One can consult the *Shorter Oxford Dictionary* to bring these questions into clearer focus. In effect, there are two main clusters of meaning around the term 'sensation'. It can refer to the 'subjective element' in the operation of the senses, the feeling itself, either in relation to the physiological response or to the more mental side, including the emotional response (hence 'sensation of distress', 1755). And it can refer to 'a condition of excited feeling produced in a community by some occurrence' (1779), which can in turn be linked to 'the production of violent emotion as an aim in works of literature or art'. Taken together, we can see how these two clusters of meaning can come to interpenetrate, defining the terrain on which 'sensation' as a facet of modern culture, a cultural configuration, will come to operate. And we can see the tensions and instabilities here, the sliding between subjective and objective, individual and social, the ordinary and the extraordinary, the physical and the psychological, the active and the passive, the public and the private; just as we also notice, in these definitions, an absence, the lack of any explicit reference to the mass media, which will later become so crucial as the site of these tensions and the mode of their transmission, intensification and modification.

It is also worth remembering that implicit in this archaeology of the 'modern sensation' is the reconstruction of selfhood as interiority in the eighteenth century, with the resultant distinctively modern nexus of issues around mind, self and embodiment, along with the difficulties this posed for communication between members of society as networks of such individuals. When Klaus Theweleit tells us, with reference to the medieval period, that 'paprika and silk' were once words for 'new sensations',[19] he is not only pointing, again, to the links with commerce, but to the idea that sensations were once as much an attribute of the *object* as of the subject, rather as 'awe' had once been an attribute of God, or 'fear' a quality of events, as sudden or unexpected.[20] For them to be relocated, as internal to the self, a new experience of selfhood has to be produced whereby 'emotion' and 'feeling' can be read as having a crucially subjective reference, while operating as mediators, through embodiment, to the 'outside' world, potentially problematical features of interpersonal relations, always difficult to place. Hence 'sensation', as feeling, points both ways, becoming liable to slide or oscillate, a feature essential for its capacity to be read in both subjective, psychological terms, and to exist as a public, cultural phenomenon, an 'extraordinary event'.

And this also reminds us that, to this extent, sensationalism and sentimentalism both originate in eighteenth-century discourses that 'ground the social tie in the movements of "sympathy", the dynamics of identificatory affect',[21] a grounding that also helps us to understand the origins of the tendency towards 'the representation of social problems as affective dilemmas', as Ann Cvetkovich puts it.[22] If we add the Gothic fusion of horror and mystery, along with the interest in the battle of good and evil central to early nineteenth-century melodrama,[23] we have the main components of 'sensation' as a cultural phenomenon in place. Indeed, by the turn of the century we find Wordsworth protesting at the pandering to public excitement, the 'craving for extraordinary incident' that he linked with the pressure of life in the modern city,[24] an aspect of what Halttunen refers to as 'a popular voyeuristic taste for scenarios of suffering'.[25]

It is the 1860s, though, that is the decade that has been seen as central to the generalizing of 'sensation' as a key feature of modern culture; it is also the decade in which the word 'sensationalism' comes to be recorded. It refers both to a philosophical programme that emphasizes 'sensation' either as the epistemological core of our knowledge of the world (John Stuart Mill) or as the basic constituent of its ontology (Ernst Mach, writing a decade or two later), and also to the better-known sense, glossed by the dictionary as 'addiction to what is sensational in literature'. Here, the reference to addiction, to a repetitive pattern of behaviour, is significant, but so is the fact that this doesn't quite capture the full range of the modern term, referring as it does to the production, reception and cultivation of 'sensation' as a central aspect of modern culture. Thus Tom Gunning claims: 'Around 1860 the term "sensation" migrated from its primary meaning of the evidence of the senses to describe the centre-piece of a new form of theatrical drama.' While the first part of this may be misleading – as we have seen, 'sensation' had been 'migrating' for decades, indeed, almost since its inception – certainly the 1860s is the decade of the 'sensation scene' in melodrama, a scene whose 'spectacular appearance and technical virtuosity was devised precisely to thrill the audience'. Hence, sensation referred to 'a particularly intense, even overwhelming experience', and it addressed itself 'directly to the body and the senses'.[26] Ben Singer in turn comments on the role of sensationalism in popular melodrama, emphasizing 'action, violence, thrills, awesome sights, and spectacles of physical peril'.[27] Michael Diamond adds that eventually 'sensation scene' referred to 'any lavishly mounted sequence in a melodrama which took the audience's breath away, or any scene of intense emotional upheaval'.[28] The 'lavishly mounted sequence' would characteristically involve the simulation of some terrible accident or natural disaster, so that the conjunction of disastrous event and emotionally intense reaction mapped the way 'sensations' were also perceived – and experienced – in the extra-theatrical dramas of everyday life.

Distinguishing between 'classic' literature, a genteel 'sentimental-domestic' genre, and the sensational 'low' texts (including dime novels and crime pamphlets), David Reynolds suggests that in America the proportion the latter category took of the whole had reached 60 per cent by 1860.[29] Best known, of course, is the 'sensation novel' itself. Lyn Pykett characterizes the sensation novel as 'a catholic mixture of modes and forms, combining realism and melodrama, the journalistic and the fantastic, the domestic and the romantic or exotic'.[30] Surprising events, extraordinary coincidences and disturbing secrets were relied on for effect, with character being subordinated to incident and plot. She adds that the sensation novel was seen as 'the characteristic fictional form of a modern, high-speed, industrialised culture',[31] adding that it was widely denounced as 'both cause and symptom of the depravity of contemporary morality and the modern sensibility'.[32] Parodying the sensation 'product' as 'devoted to Harrowing the Mind, making the Flesh Creep' and 'Giving Shocks to the Nervous System', *Punch*, in the 1860s, thus neatly encapsulated the relation between mind, feeling, body and the influence of the media, that many contemporaries found so disturbing.[33] Overall, Cvetkovich makes a big claim for the sensation novel's significance: 'The appearance of the Victorian sensation novel in the 1860s marks the moment at which sensations became sensational.'[34] Again, one might respond that sensations had been 'sensational' for quite a while, but it certainly seems that by the 1860s we can refer to a whole *culture* of sensation, and the sensation novel both indicates this and contributes to furthering its development.

'Sensation' seemed everywhere: newspapers, the theatre, popular novels and – later – films, drew on 'sensational' techniques and installed them at the heart of popular culture. Thomas Boyle cites a newspaper editorial from 1861, on a schoolmistress charged with beating and mistreating a pupil: finally, we are told, 'to enjoy a new sensation, she submitted the young girl to indescribably bestial insults'.[35] Here, body and mind, loss of control and exercise of authority all converge, sweeping aside older uses that keep 'sensation' as a term strictly contrasted with 'thought', reinforcing the unease produced by the sensation novel. Thus we are not surprised to encounter the sensationalizing of the body in another area: that of sex. In the UK, W. T. Stead's famous mud-raking exposé of a 'white slave trade' in the *Pall Mall Gazette* in 1885, followed by the Oscar Wilde trials of 1895, were both sensational media events in themselves and also established sexual codes and their transgression as central to sensationalism. One finds, observes John Sloan, that 'sensationalism and moral rectitude made hypocritical bed-fellows'[36] – indeed a potent combination that has recurred frequently since. Rendering 'public' the very 'privacy' of sex both sensationalized sexuality and continued a tension between these spheres that was already central to their development.[37] By the later decades of the nineteenth century, then, a 'culture of sensation' has become established as a key component of the modern world. Gunning indeed concludes: 'One could argue for the term being one of the key words of the popular culture of modernity.'[38] Sensationalism can even threaten to overwhelm realism: discussing 'the sensational use of the male body in pain' in war reports, documentaries and films, Cvetkovich refers to the difficulty of separating the two,[39] a difficulty that suggests there may be no real distinction here. Violation of the body, its integrity and its boundaries, is after all a precipitate of 'sensation', and it is difficult to see anything other than a faint difference of degree between the 'realistic' and the 'sensational' here, a situation that indeed poses challenges for representation in general and for artists such as Francis Bacon who are drawn to the challenge.

As recently as 1998, the word itself could still be linked to the capacity to shock: 'Sensation' was the name given to the 'Young British Artists' exhibition at the Royal Academy, precipitating the usual mix of fascination, outrage and incomprehension, the reaction neatly encapsulating the duality of sensation as subject matter, the artist's perception, and as the subject of reception, of media frenzy – a duality that is played on both in the title and in the art itself. In his introduction to the catalogue, Norman Rosenthal claimed: 'The greatest images are those that invoke both reality and sensation.'[40] While ostensibly referring to the artworks, this could also be taken as a more general comment on the power of sensational images *as* intensification or transformation of reality.

Shock, pleasure: sensation can give both. Let us end this section with Diamond's conclusion to his study of Victorian sensations, where he chooses to accent the positive: 'They lingered in the minds of everyone who lived through them. They provided a common experience and then a common memory for whole generations, something to talk about at the time and something to refer back to. Sensations offer no greater pleasure than this.'[41]

The sensational and the sentimental

Links between the sensational and the sentimental are suggested by several authors. Pointing to the moment in Dreyer's 1931 film *Vampyr* when a dying sister suddenly revives, her eyes turning towards the other sister with vampiric lust, Elmer claims this illustrates how 'the sensational – the moment of shock, or horror, or revulsion – erupts from within the sentimental', adding that every popular-culture death scene seems to come in these two versions, sentimental and sensational. Thus, in their respective treatments of 'the spectacle of the death of the other' we can see how 'the sentimental and the sensational are complementary mass-cultural modes, dependent on each other for their own proper functioning'.[42] Poe's own story, indeed, is a kind of hideous inversion of the sentimental deathbed scene; and if Valdemar's *'I say to you that I am dead!'* is clearly a sensational version of what Eve Sedgwick has called the 'impossible first person', this example of hers comes from a lyric that falls rather on the sentimental side, albeit with a strong hint of the uncanny: 'She walks these hills in a long black veil, / Visits my grave when the night winds wail'.[43]

The term 'sentimental' emerges in the eighteenth century, out of the already complex range of meanings of 'sentiment' and 'sensibility', evolving from physical and sensual awareness (sensation) to include mental alertness, feeling, taste and understanding.[44] And just as sentimentality evolves in a degree of tension with sensibility, so in turn does sensationalism, just as they are in tension with each other, as parallel modes of excess, relatively unacceptable 'others'. Hence Raymond Williams characterizes the sentimental in terms of a 'conscious opening to feelings, and also a conscious consumption of feelings',[45] thus indicating how the latter could lay the notion open to criticism. If the emergence of 'sentimentalism' out of 'sentiment' or 'sensibility' is marked, for its critics, by display, excess, 'self-indulgence' and theatricality, so is the emergence of 'sensationalism' out of sensation and feeling; and both manifest a crucial relation with the public sphere, with issues of communication, media and 'publicity'. Streeby makes a direct comparison of the two as 'structures of feeling': 'sentimentalism generally emphasizes refinement and transcendence, whereas sensationalism emphasizes materiality and corporeality, even or especially to the point of thrilling or horrifying readers.'[46] Authors could indeed combine both modes, or write both, for separate audiences; or, as in the case of Louisa May Alcott, evolve from one to the more respectable other.[47] Halttunen also suggests that the privatization and moral elevation of the family is significant here; popular accounts of domestic murder could be read as 'cultural nightmares of the new sentimental domesticity', so this sentimental background 'sharpened the horror' of the sensation.[48] Implicit in sentimentalism as excess is that emotion can *insist* on its expression, burst through the constraints of language and aesthetic form. The sentimental *in* the narrative can enforce a response *to* the narrative, all the stronger if this eruption into the narrative takes a dramatic, startling or transgressive form. We are in a circuit of sensation, and sentimentalism slides into sensationalism. One notes also the availability of both for appropriation as melodrama, which was indeed broadly contemporaneous with them in its emergence and development.

To take this further, we need to place these developments in the experience of embodiment, display and representation more clearly in the context of the cultural politics of the time, by examining the impact of 'publicity', and the development of the public sphere. Thus Bruce Burgett refers to the eighteenth-century promise of a politics 'grounded in the autonomy of every body's sensations', and points to how descriptions of intimate body sensations, whether in the novel or journalism, serve to mediate between the individual and the body on the one hand, and social regulation and political life on the other, through the very fact of publication itself. Such 'publicity' renders the 'private' body, foundation of the public sphere, only vicariously private; hence, the body itself is transected by these tensions. One can observe here that 'every body' is indeed singular, the individual body, yet 'everybody' can also be abstracted from this, dematerialized. Hence Burgett refers to the 'sentimental abstraction of the body'[49] as the grounding for civil society and the accompanying politics: only thus can 'every body' become collective, the 'everybody' of the public sphere. Indeed, sentimentalism itself implies a kind of dematerialization. It aspires to a purification of the body, a transcendence of the body *through* purification; thus Elizabeth Barnes refers to the aim of sentimental literature as the 'successful conversion of the material body into the immaterial soul'.[50] Yet of course sentimental fiction is inevitably and deeply 'embodied', especially when the tears flow, and Karen Sánchez-Eppler tells of how the effect of reading 'radically contracts the distance between narrated events and the moment of their reading, as the feelings in the story are made tangibly present in the flesh of the reader'.[51] This sentimental dematerialization thus suffers shipwreck in the very fact of reading, again reinforcing the sense of a tension arising from publicity itself – a tension that propels this fiction, and its reading, into the circuit of sensation.

Just as the modern body is subjected to the imperatives of the civilizing process, and its processes of purification and individualization, so collective ideas and ideals are increasingly 'embodied' in disembodied notions like 'the people', which evolves as the distinctively political subject, along with 'the mass', the subject of popular culture and its critics, and 'society', as the object of social and political policy. And Elmer points to the tension here: 'The impermeable self and the figures of the social – the masses, the nation, the sovereign people – are reciprocal constructions, mutually determining fictions.' We, as individuals, are separate from these abstract collectivities; yet we also belong to them: apart, but also part. And these disjunctions are joined, in their very disjunction, by 'the ambivalence of affect, the unavoidable experience of being taken out of oneself into another, an unmasterable affection by the otherness internal to the self …'.[52] Hence the 'circuit of sensation' both maintains us in our separateness and marks our unavoidable presence in this social other, which in turn exists as 'other bodies' similarly linked. Michael Warner's comment that mass culture is 'dominated by genres that construct the mass public's impossible relation to a body'[53] thus seems highly apposite, as does Elmer's further reflection that these two genres, the sentimental and the sensational, provide 'the two most enduring and efficacious modes of imagining and experiencing the "impossible" body of mass culture'.[54]

What we are seeing here is how the reconstruction of social life along the lines of the public/private distinction and the emergence of the idea, and the institutions, of 'publicity' itself contribute crucially to the conditions under which sensationalism can emerge. This public/private distinction runs between, and through, bodies and texts, reminding us that 'text', too, is afflicted by a binary that is suggestively parallel to that of the individual body and 'the mass'. 'Text', after all, points both ways: to the transcendent abstraction of disembodied language, floating into immaterial, invisible thoughts and ideas; and to the written object, the written-upon object, the materiality of the commodity, whether book, newspaper, or letter, body among bodies. And Elmer suggests that we perceive here 'the very inextricability of text and body, reading and affect'[55] that sentimentalism and sensationalism both draw on and focus on, in their differing yet complementary and overlapping ways.

The mediation of publicity between private bodies – inherent in the combination of public regulation, a public language for expression, and the public communication of experience through the written word – thus has the effect of incorporating the public within the corporeal, making the body a scenario for the expression of these tensions, frequently pushing it towards the hypochondria and hysteria that would become part of the experience of sentimentalism and the terms in which it was (and is) denounced. Clark thus refers to the problematical evolution of sentimentality from 'that which is the basis of the social to that which threatens the social',[56] which suggests that for critics of sentimentalism the paradox whereby the excess of the body – tears and emotional display – serves as a signifier of purity of feeling becomes rather a symptom of danger to the health of both individual and society. For sensationalism, on the other hand, this is precisely the starting point: in an age of 'publicity', the excesses of the body – excesses which are, as we have seen, arguably inherent in the modern construction of the autonomous body as locus of individuality and affect – can be given an immediacy, a vividness, an intensity that carries significance in and of itself, whether as drama or horror, and which can in turn be reproduced in the moral universe of melodrama, further intensifying the vicarious experience of sensation, sensation *as* vicarious experience. And this circuit of sensation challenges the purification and autonomy of the body in and through the very violence of its dismemberment in sensational narrative, suggesting that the individual body is threatened *in* these very attempts at purification; it thereby insists on the revenge of the expelled and the unacceptable, the very excess, the ugliness and otherness of life that sentimentalism aspires to transcend. The abjection of the body, implicit in sentimentalism, becomes explicit in sensationalism: the body as object, as object of disgust, yet also recalcitrant and resistant, endlessly wallowing in the contradictions of its own embodiment. And, magnifying the 'vices' of sentimentalism, sensationalism can in turn become subject to a parallel critique from the defenders of the social order and of cultural/aesthetic respectability …

The sensational thus takes up the tension in sentimentalism between transcendence and purification on the one hand, and bodily experience and emotion on the other, just as it takes up the tension in sentimentalist politics between the individual, corporeal body and the abstract body of the political community. Thus Streeby points to how the American war narratives of the 1840s – whether in popular fiction or the popular press – show how nationalism works by 'particularizing and foregrounding bodies rather than simply abstracting from them and decorporealizing them',[57] thus correcting Benedict Anderson's influential, rather abstract model of nation and community;[58] and the sensational events, the mangled bodies, may indeed be meshed with sentimental elements (the soldier's wife at home, now alone …). The sensational takes up these tensions in the context of the further paradox generated by the public/private distinction, which intersects the others, with the result that texts and bodies are endlessly torn between the dualisms of individual/mass, material/abstract, restraint/excess, constituted as such through a circuit of sensation in which text and affect are simultaneously embedded and reproduced. The sensational *figures* these tensions, through dramas that enact them; hence this eruption of the inexpressible, that which exceeds, challenges representation, reflecting the unresolvable tensions through making their figuration 'larger than life', thereby abolishing distance, and insisting on immediacy, without hope of transcendence. Hence Poe's sensational bodies, uncertainly dead and/or alive, but desperately material, materialized; or the mangled, mutilated bodies and wreckage of media-reported disasters, the staple of sensationalism ever since. Through this transfiguration of the body as grotesque, transgressive, excessive, the vampire of sensation feeds on the publicity that is its lifeblood, its energy, maintaining the circuit in being, returning endlessly to wreak its havoc as the vicarious collective body, the impossible corporealization of 'everybody' as 'every body'.

Sensational violations

These tensions between the private and the public – a distinction that both engenders the sensational and thereby also ensures its own subversion – can be explored further through the notion of 'violation'. It will be seen that the violation of this distinction – and others – is itself figured as sensational violation in the texts themselves, and in the relation between text and reader.

D. A. Miller suggests that the fundamental value that the novel aspires to uphold, as a cultural institution, is privacy, the autonomy of the 'secret' self; yet, he adds, 'this privacy is always specified as the freedom to read about characters who oversee, suspect, need, and rape one another'. Hence we enjoy our privacy 'in the act of watching privacy being violated, in the act of watching that is already itself a violation of privacy'; we thereby subscribe to the liberal fantasy of our own emancipation from the surveillance that we nonetheless see as omnipresent. And it is after all the body through which these violations and these fantasies alike are acted out. Miller suggests that with the sensation novel, we get undeniable evidence that we are *perturbed* by what we see: if we are, or think we are, unseen, we are certainly not untouched. Hence the sensation novel 'renders the liberal subject the subject of a *body*, whose fear and desire of violation displaces, reworks and exceeds his constitutive fantasy of intact privacy'. The themes that we ordinarily define ourselves *against*, through reading *about* them, are here inscribed in or on the 'reading body' itself.[59]

The theme of mystery – central to the sensation novel, and significant for sensationalism more generally – can be related to this violation of the body.

Thus Cvetkovich informs us that characters are alerted to the presence of a mystery by their own bodily responses, their sensations of fear, suspense and excitement, thus constituting a 'hermeneutics of suspicion' in which everything that precipitates sensation merits investigation.[60] A sensation in the reader's body is a clue to what is sensational in the novel. And when a character in one of these fictions, Eleanor Vane, asks: 'Had every creature a secret, part of themselves, hidden deep in their breasts … some buried memory, whose influence was to overshadow all their lives?',[61] she is vividly conveying a sense of the self as secretly embedded in the body, and in turn possessing secrets that resonate far beyond the body. The secret can of course be given a powerful social interpretation, as in Elaine Showalter's suggestion that the power of sensationalism derives from 'its exposure of secrecy as the fundamental enabling condition of middle-class life'.[62] In whatever context or register, then, sensationalism forces the invisible to become visible, propels the hidden depths to the exposed surfaces. Far from being superficial – or 'merely' superficial – sensationalism can only exist through engaging with the profound, indeed constantly reproduces it as its own enabling condition of existence. The profound can thus be interrogated, subverted, destroyed, reinvented. And the 'high culture' critics of sensationalism have grasped a half-truth, for this process of displacing depth to surface is hardly a means of treating the former with respect. If we return to the body-horror theme, after all, it can be said that sensationalism turns the body inside out, displays the defenceless body as surface, dismembered, bloody, endlessly available for mutilation – and thereby confronts the 'liberal subject' with the vicarious pleasure that can be taken in this spectacle of the abject body, just as this can, and generally does, coexist with the sense of horror.

This spectacle of the body is, all too clearly, a spectacle of the body in pain, or the body that results from the infliction of pain; and all this emerges at a time when pain itself, as the most dramatic aspect of our experience of embodiment, has become increasingly an experience to be avoided. By – and during – the eighteenth century, the body of the civilizing process became increasingly a body that had to be protected from damaging experiences. It was no longer sufficient to see pain as inherent in life; it was becoming ever more intolerable.[63] Increasingly, pain provoked fear and dislike; and this is the context in which the rise of sensationalism becomes both intelligible yet also challenging, deeply puzzling. Popular narratives forced a confrontation with pain; the agonies of murder victims and the battlefield dying were luridly described and imaginatively embellished, revealing and encouraging a prurient fascination. Halttunen refers to a 'pornography of violence' here, feeding the taste for body-horror.

She points to the moral dilemmas inherent in this, how nineteenth-century murder literature set up 'a very troubled relationship between the violence of murder and the reader as imaginative spectator to that violence', so that although the murderer was presented as 'monstrous moral alien', ultimately the reader could not escape being implicated in the guilt; inevitably, voyeurism emerges as morally suspect. And this moral paradox of sensationalism is present just as strongly for the producer of sensational images and the writer of sensational texts. Halttunen observes that 'the more sensationalistic murder literature became, the more its authors and editors formulaically denied their own sensationalism'; then, as now, they claimed merely to respond to public alarm and anxiety, not generate it.[64] Studying press images from later in the century, characteristically linked to narratives denouncing the pressures and dangers of 'modern life', Singer describes these images as 'both a form of social critique and, at the same time, a form of commercialized sensationalism, a part of the very phenomenon of modern hyperstimulus the images criticized'.[65] In this paradox of moral distance, the distancing remains part of what it ostensibly seeks to be distant from; one cannot use, display or criticize the sensational effectively – through quoting it or displaying it – without falling back into it, remaining complicit with it.

This tension between proximity and distance, involvement and detachment, is fundamental to sensationalism and resonates beyond the moral conundrum alluded to. Sensations, as feelings, indicate the immediacy of embodiment, and the emphasis on immediacy carried over into attempts to make sense of sensationalism itself. Neatly linking the experience of sensation and its literary or theatrical appropriation is a quote from the *Quarterly*, from the 1860s, discussing the sensation novel: 'Proximity is, indeed, one great element of sensation. It is necessary to be near a mine to be blown up by its explosion; and a tale which aims at electrifying the nerves of the reader is never thoroughly effective unless the scene be laid in our own days.'[66] 'Electrifying the nerves': as will be shown later, this clearly draws on a distinctive nexus of scientific, physiological assumptions which, in this context, involve a fundamental continuity between sensation as 'outer', the external cause, and as 'inner', the subjective effect. Yet there is also a *dis*continuity here, in that the sensation is 'mediated', exists at one remove, produced by the book. So although this was a world in which 'the new prevalence and power of immediate gripping sensation' defined a new era, the era of 'modern experience',[67] it was also a world of new forms of entertainment to accompany and convey it. Hence, for Gunning, the sensation drama 'presents the modern environment as a series of shocks, filled with assaults on the senses',[68] and this relation between mediated reality and experience was clearly becoming a constitutive element of experience *as* modern.

The sensational thus emerges as *mediated* experience, or experience as always potentially media-inflected; it inserts a distance into the immediacy, or reminds us that distance is always implicated in this experience of immediacy. The sensational both invites us in, and pushes us away; it is about being a witness, rather than a participant, just as it invites us to be 'almost, but not quite' a participant. Sensationalism is the experience of the minimal distance in modern experience as we grasp it; it insists on the incorporation of a minimum distance into presence itself. Sensationalism as representation presents representation *as* experience, that is, suggests a sense in which representation aspires to abolish its own distance from experience, the distance that is constitutive of the possibility of representation in the first place. Thus does sensationalism make a crucial contribution to the production of the *vicarious* as a fundamental mode of modern experience, that mode in which the distinction between representation and experience threatens to break down: the world of, or as, *mediated* experience. This is the scenario on which the tension between distance and proximity, involvement and detachment, is played out, dramatized and managed.

All this gives us significant clues to the widespread unease with sensationalism and the sensation novel in the 1860s and 1870s, and its denunciation by many critics (then and later). Pykett suggests it was 'improper' as it was a form of 'writing the body';[69] for Cvetkovich, it represented the serious threat of a reader 'reduced to a body reacting instinctively' to a text, hence at the mercy of 'appetite' or 'craving'. There is, in short, a crucial slippage here, between the content of the novel and the effect produced, a violation of appropriate boundaries: 'the content has the effect of "exciting" the reader, and what keeps moving is as much the reader's nerves as the novel's plot', as Cvetkovich puts it; hence 'the ambiguity of the term "sensation" novel, which can refer either to the sensational events in the texts or the responses they produce'.[70] And this feeling produced, in its immediacy, can be overwhelming, threatening not just the descriptive powers of language but the very integrity of the self. The threat of dissolution, of lack of control, can be present both for characters in the novel, and for writer and reader, in a wave of contagious sensation that threatens to sweep away all barriers, all restraints. Thus Jenny Taylor comments on the way these connections are formed through 'physiological metaphors, as symptoms which themselves had, principally, physiological effects',[71] and Pykett adds that the 'melodramatic excess' so characteristic of the style 'is an irruption into narration of that feeling (particularly the erotic feeling) which is repressed in the narrative'.[72]

The reference here to 'erotic feeling' is of course another clue: for the violation of the conventional boundary between text and affect suggests a close proximity to the ways the pornographic text (or film) are thought to work their problematical effects (affects). The sensual overload in pornography, the assault on the senses, the dyamics of arousal and/or disgust, raise similar issues of controversy and cultural response. While Burke's aesthetics allows for a link between sensual and 'higher' pleasures, and Helvétius could claim that the object of art and literature is 'to give pleasure and thus to excite in us sensations, which although not painful, are nonetheless strong and vivid',[73] with Kant a firm line is drawn between the sensual pleasures, which can at best be 'agreeable', and the pleasures of art, involving the contemplation of the beautiful. The Kantian tradition in aesthetics requires distance from the object, contemplation according to the norms of 'good taste', detachment rather than desire. Kantian 'distance' allows for 'the separation of the *representation* from the object to be contemplated by the subject without any (interested) relation to the object itself', as Pasi Falk puts it; conversely, 'the loss of distance breaks the rules of representation – necessary for aesthetic reflection and contemplation – and tends to transform the experience into something unrepresentable'.[74] Pornography thus destroys – or threatens – representation in the immediacy of its presence and effect. And as has been seen, this is central to the nature of sensationalism, to its appeal – and its threat. Indeed, it could be said to be more generally true of the pleasures of the text, or indeed the arts as such: the involvement of the body can never sink to zero. Jean Marie Goulemot hence suggests, provocatively, that reading 'licentious works' is, in fact, 'exemplary for all other forms of reading and, indeed, beyond that, for all writing', and that one could even argue that 'it represents all that is not said in a reflection on writing, reading and the actual effects produced by artistic representation'.[75]

Halttunen points to the roughly contemporaneous development of the interest in 'body-horror' and pornography in the eighteenth century, defining pornography as 'the representation of sexual behavior *with a deliberate violation of moral and social taboos*', and arguing that 'the growing violence of it in this period is attributable to the new shock value of pain within a culture redefining it as forbidden and therefore obscene'.[76] This therefore returns us to the issue of pain and its apparently perverse appeal. The emphasis in the works of the Marquis de Sade on the *intensity* of sensation – and it is pain that provided the most intense sensations, after all – certainly seems to reflect the preoccupations of his age; and, referring to his ideas, Simone de Beauvoir argues that if vice is locked firmly into sensation, this is because 'sensation is the only measure of reality, and if virtue arouses no sensation, it is because it has no real basis'.[77] The route to pleasure – and self-identity – is through the magnification and intensification of perverse sensation. Sade is indeed very significant here, conjoining as he does the nascent discourses of sensation, pornography and science, since he seems to have been well-read in the latter.[78] Thus Justine is instructed that all life depends on nerves: 'All sensations, knowledge of ideas, derive from it.' Any 'intense inflammation' of the nerves excites the 'animal spirits', producing pleasure via 'mental sensation'; hence, 'the sphere of one's sensation can be remarkably extended'.[79] One notes here that sensation is already difficult to 'place': it already seems to slide uncertainly between body and mind, the subjective and the objective. It is hardly surprising that the Romantics, too, showed a strong interest in this area; most graphically, perhaps, we find Lord Byron proclaiming that 'the great object of life is Sensation – to feel that we exist – even though in pain'.[80]

Conversely, writing of 'disgust', Kant claims that this 'singular sensation' reflects a situation where the object 'is represented as it were obtruding itself for our enjoyment, while we strive against it with all our might'. Hence 'the artistic representation of the object is no longer distinguished from the nature of the object itself in our sensation, and thus it is impossible that it can be regarded as beautiful'.[81] But if this could be said to suggest an aspect of our response to pornography, the challenge to representation also reminds us of the sublime. What is sublime takes us *beyond* representational distance, into the transcendence of nature over us, its splendour as awesome, even terrifying; conversely, the pornographic takes us *beneath* representational distance, into the body, the immanence of nature in us, its threat to our sense of self, identity and culture, hence the body as abject, object of disgust (and desire). And the sensational? It is clearly not reducible to either, though can overlap with both. In one sense, it is a popular culture version of the sublime, in which nature and culture can become grand media spectacles that engage, enrage and amaze us; but it can also involve a fascination with disasters, murders, the gruesome, the body abjected as flesh. The sensational swings uneasily between subject and object, refusing the rigidity of the boundary that our intellect inserts between them, testifying to the way experience itself is thus placed uneasily within this distance/proximity dynamic, and is therefore recalcitrant to conventions of aesthetic representation that rest on distance and contemplation. Nor is sensation primarily about desire (or disgust), though a 'culture of sensation' can certainly encourage our search for, or even addiction to, the sensational; rather, it addresses that moment of unexpected intensity in experience itself, *subsuming* desire, revulsion or release, rather than *resulting* in them.

We can also observe another sense of violation in play here, namely the way sensation violates normal expectations of meaning, particularly sensation considered in its very *immediacy*. Writing of the sensation novel, Miller suggests that 'sensation is felt to occupy a natural site entirely outside meaning, as though in the breathless body signification expired',[82] pointing out, conversely, that of course there is a sense in which signification *never* expires. It is however true – especially with the more unexpected sensations – that meaning can be rather *post hoc*, and in this way sensation always poses a challenge. That is, after all, crucial to its being a sensation in the first place. Cvetkovich indeed suggests that it may be only after the event, through repetition, that the 'unrepresentable sensation' can be named.[83] Even here, though, it may be that there has to be a certain readiness, a certain receptiveness; thus Miller characterizes surprise as 'the recognition of what one "never suspected"'. He summarizes the tension well: 'Thus, if every sensation novel necessarily provides an interpretation of the sensations to which it gives rise in its readers, the immediacy of these sensations can also be counted on to disown such an interpretation.'[84]

A further aspect of this is that sensation always threatens narrative: it implies a certain rupture, a discontinuity. Each 'sensation' has to be both a high point, a dramatic intervention, yet *also* a contribution to a story, continuous with the rest of it. This tension can also emerge in newspaper sensationalism, where it tends to be mapped on to the contrast between image and text: the image 'carries' the sensation, catches the eye, engages the feelings; the words then expand, situate and 'explain', both repeating yet also altering, and perhaps diminishing, the impact. And the story *as a whole* – whether in novel or newspaper – has to be 'sensational'. Thus there are sensational moments, high points, within a totality that is also coded as 'sensational'. There is 'progress' towards a goal – the *overall* impact – yet also repetition. And here, again, there is a certain resemblance to pornography, which accumulates and repeats climaxes – hence replacing beginnings and middles – yet also culminates in climax. In the case of the sensation novel, though, it must be added that there tends to be a certain winding-down (an anti-climax?) in the later part of the novel, as explanation, rationalization and 'resolution' become more prominent …

Sensational catastrophe

The catastrophe is the ultimate sensation; and, in an age of mass media spectacle, sensation drives towards catastrophe, feeds on it, just as such catastrophe is always reproducible, whether in the real, or in media representation, or in entertainment, as simulation. The role of technology becomes increasingly significant, not merely as the mode whereby catastrophe is disseminated, reproduced, and indeed magnified, but as a significant part of a modern world that is increasingly seen as 'catastrophic' in its implications, as being always potentially catastrophe-inducing.[85] Yet the modern capacity to achieve technological domination of the world is also seen as the ultimate prophylactic, bearing the promise to abolish the realm of the catastrophic, the realm of natural disasters. Catastrophe signifies the failure of the modern project, but also a spur to its further development – which in turn produces further catastrophes.[86] If 'catastrophe' comes from the Greek – the roots meaning 'over-turn' – then what is 'overturned' by catastrophe is both the direction, and the hope, of Progress, the modern ideal of endless development framed as betterment. Catastrophe is the dystopia of progress, 'the always unexpected interruption of this forward movement', as Mary Anne Doane suggests; and, in its dramatic incursion, breaking through the conventional forms of the everyday, it calls for *coverage*, reproduction as spectacle, and the media urge us to 'obsessively confront catastrophe, over and over again'.[87] This simultaneous uniqueness, and endless capacity for reproduction, also reminds us that catastrophe itself becomes subject to the process described as the cycle of sensation, just as it becomes the ultimate instance of the mass cultural reproduction of sensation.

This pattern is clearly in place by the late nineteenth century. By then, 'a hunger for sensational disasters was becoming a prominent feature of everyday American life', as Kevin Rozario puts it.[88] Just as train crashes provided more than their share of sensational catastrophes in the second half of the century,[89] so these were taken up by the amusement parks that spread rapidly during the 1890s, and retained their pre-eminence until the 1920s, when film and cinematic spectacle took over. Tens of thousands of Americans paid to watch locomotives crash into each other at staged train wrecks.[90] In 1906, the huge Coney Island amusement park was awash with disaster shows, all purporting to be reproductions of specific events (floods, hurricanes, volcanoes). When Steeplechase Park at Coney Island burned down in 1907, spectators treated the blaze as one of the attractions, and the owner began charging customers to tour the ruins.[91] Thus did disaster become commercial entertainment in which the whole idea, suggests Rozario, was 'to disorientate and excite the senses';[92] Lubin adds that the visitor 'was encouraged to lose him or herself in the overwhelming plenitude of spectacle and sensation'.[93]

We can sharpen up the implicit contrast here. News of the Lisbon earthquake of 1755 was widely disseminated throughout Europe, but there was little evidence of 'sensational' treatment of the news.[94] It was very different with later episodes, with public curiosity and hunger both for information *and* spectacle feeding off and reinforcing the eagerness of the media to provide it; thus Rozario claims, of the great San Francisco earthquake of 1906, that 'Much of the "information" about the disaster took a sensationalistic form, exaggerating the horrors of an already dreadful event …'.[95] Of course, for some who were present, the 'real' earthquake was sensational enough, as experience, not to need further layers of sensationalism. Visiting Stanford University in the San Francisco area in April 1906, the psychologist William James experienced the full tremors as the earthquake struck. Furniture crashing around him, he reported 'glee and admiration … I felt no trace whatever of fear', and summed it up as a 'memorable bit of experience'.[96] Rozario concludes that sensational accounts, pictures and performances of these events brought the victims' sufferings to everyone's attention, and established 'vicarious, but powerful bonds between spectators and sufferers …', reflected in massive public charitable donations. As for the 'performances', we learn that a theatre in Minneapolis was staging a reproduction of the earthquake just a few months after the event,[97] a 'restaging' that is perhaps not so different from the endlessly repeated television images of the Twin Towers disaster a century later.

Just a few years later, in 1912, the sinking of the *Titanic*, destined to become an iconic instance of catastrophe, in turn reproduced endlessly as spectacle through film and other media, enables us to tease out two further features of catastrophe: scale, combining size and speed of occurrence, hence maximizing the overall impact; and the intense, *mediated* sense of presence. The ship was indeed huge, the largest moving structure ever built, and taller than any hitherto existing building, all of which can be mapped into the film *Titanic* (Cameron, 1997), the biggest blockbuster in American film history, vastly expensive and hugely profitable. Then there is the ship's speed, both as capacity and as actual speed at the time of the disaster. Stephen Kern writes: 'This generation had a strong, confident sense of the future, tempered by the concern that things were rushing much too fast. The *Titanic* symbolized both.'[98] As an instance of the technological sublime, the ship's fate nonetheless showed that the ocean's sublime power could trump any technology, the speed of the ship being more than matched by the speed and impact of the collision with the iceberg. Richard Howells reveals that the myth of the ship's 'unsinkability' only really arose *after* the ship had gone down,[99] as if to emphasize a moral drama – hubris as the cause of nemesis.

The second aspect of this, the transformed sense of presence, was due to the impact of the new technology of wireless. Within a few minutes, a dozen ships were aware of the disaster, and by next day, the news had been transmitted round the world. With this new, intensified sense of the present, the priority of single local events gave way to a simultaneity of multiple distant events,[100] and there can be a tension between this sense of presence, of immediacy, and the sense of linear, sequential development over time, contributing to crises in the concept of 'progress' referred to above. As Jeffrey Sconce argues, radio contributed strongly to the sense that catastrophe was a permanent presence in the modern world, always liable to erupt. If this suggested 'an intimate connection between radio and catastrophe',[101] one might add that this has become true of television too, and media more generally: subjected to the logic of sensationalism, catastrophe can always be sought for, by media and public alike, and always found. We can see how Doane can describe catastrophe as 'the ultimate drama of the instantaneous', and can point to its suitability for television and its mode of operation, condensing the sense of immediacy, presence and discontinuity that are central to it, preserving and intensifying its shock effect while subtly attempting its subordination, through narrative commentary – until the next time.[102] It is this sense of the instantaneous and the simultaneous that provides both for an intensification of the sensational and for its transfiguration in the form of spectacle, thereby permitting the 'mediation' of sensation to occur in a spectacular form that enhances rather than diminishes its effect, hence subtly transforming, even negating, the distance that remains 'present'. And we can briefly return to the film, to the scene of the ship foundering in the darkness, described by David Lubin as 'a sumptuous, iconic rendition of historical disaster as awesome spectacle'.[103]

That 'awesome spectacle' can have another dimension for us in a world that witnessed the September 2001 destruction of the Twin Towers and the 2003 Iraq War hardly needs saying, but the way in which the sensational can be both political and economic, and political economy can be sensational, is worth sharpening up here. Naomi Klein has pointed to the significance of the 'Shock and Awe' doctrine, originally promulgated in a Pentagon paper that served as a blueprint for the Iraq War, arguing that 'shock and awe' had been features of political and economic policies for decades. In what she calls 'disaster capitalism', catastrophic events become 'exciting market opportunities';[104] the catastrophes can range from natural disasters to man-made, military and economic ones, but the subsequent logic of intervention and appropriation remains the same. The initial destructive shock obliterates pre-existing structures – natural, social and institutional – and enforces reconstruction by multinationals and pro-business political elites. One of the most disturbing aspects of her thesis – and particularly relevant to the argument here – is her claim that the widespread use of torture in the political examples of 'shock and awe', from Pinochet's Chile onwards, can be seen as model and metaphor for the political and economic experiments enforced on subject populations, such as the spectacular bombing displays and the mass destruction of civilian targets in the Iraq War, explicitly intended as acts of terror to destroy any will to resist.[105] In other words, the sensationalism of all this, the existence of these catastrophes as media spectacle, is not an accidental by-product; it is central to what they are *as* events. One could say that there is a powerful homology between these apparently separate chains of events, revealing the way the awesome sensations of the body become appropriated as media sensation, thereby 'sensationalized' as spectacle. The sensations of the tortured body, existing as spectacle in the torture chamber, can be mapped onto the sensations of the bodies of those afflicted by military shock, in turn appropriated and magnified through media sensationalism.[106]

Consuming sensation

What is the nature of the spectatorial fascination in all this? We find that some useful observations were made by a commentator on the disaster shows at amusement parks in 1907, R. L. Hart. He identified three types of pleasure at these: wonder, vicarious terror and the 'close shave'. As for the sense of wonder, it could be characterized as a combination of awe, as the submission to the unexpected as spectacle, and 'disinterested' curiosity, curiosity not disciplined by any conscious or unconscious self-interest. As for 'vicarious terror', this seems to refer either to a situation where the spectator witnesses disaster from a position of known safety, or to the exposure to a real-enough representation of such disaster, whereas the 'close shave', or 'brush with death', was geared to give the spectator 'an interval of dazzling, astounding self-revelation' such that 'Out of his littleness, he rises to momentary greatness – feels himself terribly, almost epically, alive'.[107] In effect, we encounter the 'popular sublime'. Something of the latter seems to be implicit in the reaction of William James to the earthquake, though it is not quite the same: *finding* oneself in a life-threatening situation, unexpectedly, is not the same as *choosing* to put oneself into a life-threatening situation.

The latter situation is intriguing. Hart seems to be hinting at something that has become discussed again in our own time: the interest in, and pursuit of, 'extreme' experience. Writing in the 1960s, Susan Sontag characterized ours as an 'age of extremity', when we swing between 'unremitting banality and inconceivable terror',[108] and a theme in her work is the paradoxical appeal of the latter. More recently, Dave Boothroyd finds that contemporary Western societies reveal 'a widespread fascination bordering on obsession with all things extreme', experiences of 'extreme conditions, situations, sensations', manifested in and spread through a 'vicarious consumption' of images of extremity.[109] At the same time, it would be wrong to exaggerate the novelty of this interest in the extreme, which, as already hinted, seems to have deep roots in the modern. 'Exploration', as it was familiar to the nineteenth century, both as reality and as representation – as a favourite theme in boy's adventure fiction, for example – always had a whiff of the extreme: West Africa, the 'white man's grave', justified its reputation; and, closer to our contemporary notion of 'extreme sports', mountaineering cost many lives. 'Testing the self', rites of passage: in an age that cultivates selfhood and self-development as a central ideal (and pressure), the simultaneous proof of individuality and maturity involves experiences that stretch and test the boundaries of capacity and endurance. For most, the vicarious spectacle of involvement may suffice; for others, this is not enough: intensity of self must confront intensity of the real. It is as though the extreme becomes the intended 'cure' for the vicarious. Only through 'authentic' experience can the sense of identity as *reality* be validated. In the extreme, the real is experienced as risk, exists only through risk – and the only risk that ultimately counts is the risk of death, the ultimate catastrophe. An 'extreme' sport, after all, is one where a mistake, *any* mistake, anything going wrong, means the probability, even the certainty, of death.[110] At these limits, as in all these encounters with the sensational, we find, again, the centrality of the body. In Doane's words: 'Catastrophe is at some level always about the body, about the encounter with death.'[111]

In the light of this, we can return to Lubin, writing of the film *Titanic*. He reminds us of the view looking from afar at the doomed ship, from the lifeboat: it is 'like watching others screaming in terror on a giant amusement park ride; you're in sympathy with them, but relieved not to be in their boat'.[112] This quote might make us pause. It rather slides over the difference between finding oneself in an unsought life-threatening situation, and choosing to put oneself into a *simulated* life-threatening situation. Yet in doing this, he reflects the whole drift of modern culture, in which the simulation has to be pushed as close as possible to the real so as to deepen, 'realize', the experience: the amusement park ride has to *feel* like a brush with death if it is to do its job, as it were. Hence the sense in which the mediated experience of the sublime in the age of mass popular culture necessarily involves the *vicarious*, the quality of experience as it becomes 'real enough', indeed preferably 'real enough' to trouble any distinction between authentic and inauthentic experience.[113] There is always, in principle, a degree of negotiation over 'degrees of reality' here, and we might now consider another, contemporary, example.

A new attraction for 2008 at the London Dungeon – though 'not recommended for those of a nervous disposition' – was *Extremis: Drop Ride to Doom!* Based on what purports to be historical accuracy, like the other gruesome 'attractions' on show, the publicity pamphlet's description of this is worth quoting in full:

> At the mercy of the hangman, you are at the very point of death and the end is drawing near ... Taste the fear and feel the adrenaline pump as the trapdoor opens and your heart shoots into your throat as you drop, screaming, into the darkness below ...

And this is accompanied by a picture of five 'terrified' teenagers about to suffer this fate, the nooses dropping round their necks and the void opening up beneath ... Now, like much else in the London Dungeon and similar 'entertainments' this seems parasitic on the 'horror film' experience, though that, in turn, has deeper cultural roots. The all-too-obviously fake expressions of terror on the faces reminds one of similar depictions in nineteenth-century popular journalistic representations of murder scenes, including the Jack the Ripper killings, and posters of early film melodramas. Some of this may simply be the relative incompetence of the artist – the face in terror is not an easy subject to capture – but it may also indicate a shying away, a point of 'so far but no further', a mark of the ultimate difference or distance between the representation and the reality, the latter as not only too difficult to grasp practically but too horrible to grasp morally and aesthetically as well. From this point of view, it is important both to thrill the potential teenage 'victims' and subliminally convey reassurance. They will, actually, survive the sensation, the 'point of death', and the drop; and afterwards, no doubt, will be super-cool and dismissive about the whole thing, skating over the fact that *some* of them, at least, will have screamed, and *some* of the screams, at least, will have been real, or 'real enough' ...

None of these refinements and qualifications are needed with the horror film; here, the 'face in terror' is going to be as real as it can be made to appear to be, as it were. 'Reality' is of the essence, and violence is unredeemed and relentless. This is aptly summarized by Jonathan Crane: 'Special effects are now mobilized around human evisceration not only to terrify the audience but also to give credence to the fact that to be human is to suffer spectacular abominations.' When 'the only *object* of terror is the body' splatter films respond to the challenge, aiming 'to unfold the body in exacting surgical splendour and render the human corpse *in toto* through the indecency of unremittingly refined detail'. Nor can this be effective without the involvement of the audience: 'Films will not work if we refuse to involve the body in the spectacle', putting our own flesh at risk, as it were.[114] Horror films may come into the category Robert Solomon calls 'art horror', but as he rightly observes, 'Horror is, first of all, a very real emotional experience, whether or not it is provoked by very real horrors'.[115] Carol Clover concludes that 'horror and pornography are the only two genres specifically devoted to the arousal of bodily sensation. They exist solely to horrify and stimulate …'[116]

What all these examples have in common is the suggestion that both the reality of sensation, and the sensation of reality, are closely bound up together, with a resulting instability of ontological status. Of the libertine, Simone de Beauvoir writes: 'Sensation is the only measure of reality …',[117] but we can see that it is not just the libertine who is prey to this. We encounter an intriguing collusion between the modern emphasis on a self that is both separate from the body, 'inside' it, simultaneously threatened by the drives of the body and dependent on the body for its security, and the postmodern world of image and simulation; for both of these carry with them profound insecurities over the boundaries between real and unreal, uncertainties over the actual, the real, the virtual, and the imaginary. Since this simultaneously affects (and afflicts) the relation between self and other, necessarily mediated through the body, there is the potential for sensation both to break through this embodied separation, and to experience, and hence affirm, the recalcitrant boundary that ensures it. These links between physical sensation and the problematic status of the real, linking in to tensions around the sense of personal identity, have widespread ramifications in our culture, providing a perspective on phenomena such as trauma and self-harm. 'Cutting' is how those who are often described as engaging in 'self-mutilation' tend to describe what they do. The incision into the flesh marks it, redesigns it: the flesh becomes subject to control and open to meaning, the scar a visible reaffirmation of the embodied self through the intensity of blood and pain, as if such identity, in its very insecurity, can only exist through transcending itself, deploying nature in the very attempt to go beyond it.[118] In short, sensation becomes the hope, the promise, of a cure for its own disease, the *intensity* of an experience that flashes across an unbridgeable gap.[119]

Zygmunt Bauman suggests that consumer culture produces a subject who is a 'sensation gatherer',[120] and we can see why this might be so by further examination of the relation between pleasure and desire in sensation. Desire always contains an element of self-discipline, subordination to a specific goal: it condenses the diffuse longings and distractions of everyday life into something more specific and achievable, but also something that requires a reference outside or beyond the self. In moving from the diffuse, the vague, the daydreams and distractions, to the relative specificity of desire, the failure of the latter to bring full satisfaction is also guaranteed. Sensation, in its fusion of active and passive – we may seek it out, but must then submit to it – addresses this gap, providing the unexpected element that is necessary to the *intensity* of experience. Sensation can provide the interface between desire and the outer world that is lost in the 'detached' consumption associated with routine consumerism; yet, by this very fact, consumerism drives us towards sensation, as the ultimate experience of the real *as* consumable. Here, consumerism meets the drive of the self to 'realization', to break out of its protective shell and 'manifest' itself. Locked in its thoughts and fantasies, the inner self craves reality, the reality of flesh and blood, the rawness of experience. Sensation has become central both to advertising the objects and experiences of consumer culture, and to the promise they themselves seem to offer.[121] The sensationalism of aspiration, in which a hoped-for fusion of diffuse imaginings, specific fantasies embedded in images, and embodied experiences never quite achieves realization, but has 'real enough' consequences, proves a potent mix as we increasingly find ourselves subject to the 'globalization of sensation' in the contemporary world.

3

Sensational Processes

To the extent that we are indeed encountering a 'culture of sensation' here, it is clear that the term does not have to be restricted to the popular sensationalism of the sensation novel and the newspapers; beyond this, it corresponds to a distinctive orientation to, and experience of, the world of modern experience and the refraction of this through modern culture generally. We can pursue this by tracing the further ramifications of the part played by repetition in the culture of sensation, along with the modes whereby sensation is manifested, through enactment and figuration, and the resulting controversies – over sensationalism itself – that have been central to this culture. All this will serve to strengthen a sense of sensation as involving *process*, whereby cycles of sensation, and the means whereby sensation is transmitted, permit us to locate the notion of a 'circuit of sensation' in more detail.

Repetition, transmission, manifestation

If we take repetition, this has been seen as a central feature of the culture of sensation – and, as such, frequently denounced. Thus a commentator from the 1860s referred to 'the violent stimulant of serial publication' with 'its necessity for frequent and rapid recurrence of piquant situation and startling incident'.[1] Readers revealed an 'appetite' for such fiction, 'devoured' it, succumbed to 'addiction'. Sensationalism was of a piece with consumerism. Any specific sensation, after all, rapidly ceases to be sensational, and the 'high', if there has been one, must be sought for anew. This reminds us of Campbell's point that it is 'changes to monitored sensations which yield pleasure rather than anything intrinsic to their natures',[2] again showing a continuity between the physiology of sensation and its cultural dynamics. The plots of the novels were declared to be 'merely vehicles to sustain the reader's interest so that constant and rapid consumption would be guaranteed': stimulating the body thus became an important aspect of marketing. Cvetkovich adds that the reader's body thereby 'becomes a machine hooked into the circuit of production and consumption'.[3] Through this paradoxical repetition of 'novelty', sensation became ever more deeply 'embodied', apparent both as an enactment of the new kinds of experience and a manifestation of possible underlying stresses and strains, whether coded as social, psychological or physiological.

Nevertheless, we must be careful here. It would be wrong to map the idea of 'linear development', an important component of ideologies of modernity as progress, onto sensationalism, as if the latter involves a remorseless unilinear drive towards ever greater, ever more sensational sensationalism. If the restraints of civility do not appear to restrain sensationalism overmuch, neither do we encounter a steady build-up of increased drama or more intense horror, as measured by some absolute standard. Rather, there are *cycles*, as with fashion, and it is the 'interior' of the cycles that does indeed involve the drive to the ever more sensational. Since this is what we tend to notice, it can indeed seem as if the process has an absolute, linear quality. Then, when a certain point in the cycle is reached, a point of near-saturation, of excess becoming excessive, the attention of both producers and consumers is attracted, or distracted, elsewhere. If any one particular cycle is defined in terms of the sensationalism of a particular content, this can develop in a linear way, but there is no overall linear process of which this is a stage; what is involved is more a matter of intrinsically unpredictable outbursts or manifestations of the sensational, each of which develops in a relatively repetitive way. And if sensationalism necessarily produces a response, the nature of this response cannot be guaranteed, which contributes to the uncertainty over both the origin, and the ending, of any particular cycle of sensation.[4]

In moving from the theme of repetition towards considering the modes of transmission and manifestation of sensation we can begin with a consideration of the place of enactment or dramatization in these processes. It is useful to take a specific case, that of Washington Irving Bishop. By the time his career climaxed, in the 1880s, he had become 'the most extraordinary of the performers working at the interface of entertainment, science, and magic', as Simon During puts it. He was a mind reader, performing in public arenas, always with an eye to his media appeal; he did not claim extraordinary powers, rather 'the ability to receive thoughts or sensations via undiscovered psychological capacities',[5] the ability that would in due course come to be christened 'telepathy'. One of his most popular routines was a crime reconstruction he called 'Imaginary Murder'. He would be blindfolded while the audience enacted, in mime, a 'crime' they had planned beforehand, involving a murderer, a victim and a weapon; then, still blindfolded, he would grasp the hands of one or two members of the audience and try to identify the murderer and the victim, ostensibly drawing on the clues offered by involuntary muscular movements and the other involuntary aspects of behaviour whereby people 'give themselves away'. He himself was intensely involved in the process, doing all this at speed: pale, fraught, tense, gesticulating, he would not infrequently collapse, exhausted, at the end. In short, claims During, he was 'acting out an image of exceptional "nervous energy"', precisely in the terms that 'nervous energy' was described by one of the leading contemporary experts on it, the physician Beard, who indeed suggested that this mix of hypersensitivity and exhaustion – neurasthenia – was caused by the shocks, speed and stress of modernity.

Furthermore, by 'enacting nervousness so extravagantly',[6] Bishop simultaneously enacted it as a media spectacle: his career was organized round the print media, rather than the stage, often putting on special performances in public arenas where they were more likely to be well reported, and always taking care to ensure the maximum presence of reporters and photographers. The 'live' quality of his acts – which of course was central to their 'sensational' appeal – was enhanced by the very real possibility of failure; even if, as seems likely, he used confederates, he could at times fail to 'read' the clues. Thus his mind-reading performances, laden with suspense, unfolded in real time, making them all the more dramatic and attractive to the media. And here again we encounter the sense in which the enactment is repetitive, with the sensational body being doubled as sensational media event, the enactment of sensation as both embodied and mediated, and the repeated performances that were never quite identical, hence repeatedly sensational through their separate enactments on different occasions, keeping audience and media hooked.

Miller's presentation of the sensation novel suggests some continuity with this, in that 'its particular staging of nervousness remains cognate with that of many of our own thrillers, printed or filmed', hence demonstrating the continued significance of the 'nervous state' in modern culture. The excitement of the sensation novel renders our bodies 'theatres of neurasthenia',[7] whereby our sensational response becomes a physiological enactment. Anson Rabinbach adds that neurasthenia is a 'cacophony of complaints that replicate "real" illness', an 'unstable mimesis', and a kind of 'corporeal text'; thus we see 'a second order of modernity in neurasthenia beyond its modern etiology, a modernism of the symptoms and the narrative of the illness itself'.[8] Here we encounter the way the sensation novel elaborates 'a fantasmatics of sensation' in which our reading bodies are immediately implicated in a 'hysterical acting out' through physiological response.⁹ This pattern of 'deep meaning', both 'expressing' personality and projecting it as 'surface enactment', marks the modern body as quite deeply hysterical.

These problems and paradoxes of the modern body necessarily and notoriously involve gender. The gender-coding is less obvious in the now little-used 'neurasthenia' but has always been in play in 'hysteria'. Michelle Henning points out that, in the late nineteenth century, ideas about bodily sensation were articulated in terms of 'feminine vulnerability', hence assuming that 'an openness to and absorption in sensation is related to passive acceptance'. Conversely, masculinity involved a kind of closing-down of the senses; men should 'refuse' sensation, maintain strong barriers, since an excess of sensation, in shock, would lead to breakdown.¹⁰ Hence a 'culture of sensation' presented pressures and dilemmas for both sexes: for women, already attuned to sensitivity, sensationalism was a logical extension, though one that threatened either 'nervous exhaustion' or hysteria; for men, the passivity of exposure to sensation threatened a kind of emasculation, especially if the defences of 'male armour' were overcome, producing trauma and, in war, 'shell-shock'.¹¹ In this context, then, 'sensationalism' represents a contagious over-sensitivity to sensation that can potentially incapacitate women and men alike. In the context of reading, if the response is 'hysterical', hence the 'acting out' of a female sensation, then, as Miller points out, the male reader is effectively positioned as the 'female soul in a male body' that was one of the earliest formulations – from the 1860s – of what would in due course come to be identified as 'homosexuality'; and the male reader can become all the more 'nervous' in that 'his experience of sensation must include his panic at having the experience at all'.¹² We can also observe a certain process of circularity here, in that the relative deadening of the senses required for 'normal' masculinity could also result from an excess of sensation. The sensation novel – like other forms and contexts of sensation – can play on these tensions of projection and identification, thus heightening the sensational effect. And we should remember that a *positive* response to these situations could produce pleasure as much as trauma: Emilie Altenloh's celebrated early study of audience response to film (1914) showed women to be particularly ready to be involved in sensory immersion, receptive to the new stimuli of the challenging new medium, eager for experience as 'cinematic subjects'.¹³

Via the theatre, 'enactment' also returns us to questions of aesthetics. The modern theatre has generally been comfortable with the aesthetics of distance, in which the actor 'represents' the role, at some distance from it. Even if the actor who is convincingly playing a role feels the 'appropriate' emotion this still leaves us with the problematic of dissimulation that is implicit in the aesthetics of distance in this context, familiar since Diderot's formulation of the paradox of acting in the eighteenth century.[14] Artaud's modernist theatre reveals a break with this. His aim is presence, not representation; his advocacy of 'nonacting' over acting implies a 'carnalisation' of acting, whereby shared, immediate experience is enacted, and thereby intensified. This production of the body, as ritual, is a theatre of sensation which readily becomes a theatrics of the sensational, a 'theatre of cruelty' in which the 'enactment' of the body displays it in its carnal, and often distressed state.[15] Artaud's theatricality is thus 'anti-theatrical' in being anti-text, opposing gesture, colour and movement to the abstraction and distance of language, requiring language to return to the body, so that language becomes physical too, 'communicating as pure sound and sensation rather than through abstract correspondence'.[16] If, as Michael Fried argues, 'What lies between the arts is theatre',[17] advocating as he does a modernist programme that emphasizes the autonomy of the arts, then a 'modernist theatre' would seem a contradiction in terms. But Artaud takes up and explores this paradox of modernist theatre; his intensification of the theatrical experience, his theatre of sensation, is an articulation not of what lies 'between' the arts so much as what lies 'beneath', what is always implicitly there (as in the sensation novel), now made overt. To 'sensationalize' experience is thus to intensify it, but also testifies to the 'intensity' that is always potentially there in experience anyway – and to shape, form and 'enact' the sensation brings this out. In the theatre, the sensationalism of this also manifests itself in the privilege of the occasion, the actual performance, over the work (as written), thus implicitly (and often explicitly) making the theatre simultaneously more 'public' and more spectacular, more continuous with the sensationalism of mediated mass culture generally.

Along with the dramas of enactment, we encounter figuration as the other mode whereby sensation is shaped and projected. Sensationalism, claims Cvetkovich, 'makes events emotionally vivid by representing in tangible and specific terms social and historical structures that would otherwise remain abstract'. Through figuration, then, 'the sensational force of melodramatic narrative organizes affective life',[18] with the body itself as the central focus. Given the examples of these abstractions that are made subject to sensational figuration – terms like 'nation', 'people', 'mass' – we can see that there is inevitably a politics of sensational representation. These sensational bodies are readily available for ideological uses, and indeed this follows from the logic of sensational figuration itself. Thus Streeby points out that popular sensationalism developed as the idiom of working-class cultures, in which context it was also a 'racializing, gendering, and sexualizing discourse on the body', one that 'risks obscuring the constructedness of bodies and reifying "differences" of race, gender, and sexuality'.[19] And the tendency to naturalize affect could be said to have the effect of presenting it as a matter of spontaneity, chance, the uncontrollable exigencies of embodiment, beyond rational control or social understanding, hence a potent resource for mystification. Critique thus seems implicit, almost demanded, by this culture of sensation; and doubtless it is Adorno who furnishes us with this in its most extreme and eloquent form, denouncing sensation as a cult of the new when there no longer really is anything new, and arguing that, from its original sense, 'sensation' has become 'the arouser of masses, the destructive intoxicant, shock as a consumer commodity'. In subverting judgement, it becomes 'an agent of cataclysmic degeneration'. All this culminated in Fascism, 'the absolute sensation';[20] and we are reminded that Goebbels was said to have boasted that at least the Nazis weren't boring …

On the first aspect of all this, the critics are certainly right to point to the way sensationalism does indeed remind us of the power of the two great essentializing, naturalizing discourses of modern times, those of race and sex. In its focus on the body, sensationalism confronts us with the way bodies present themselves as sexed and coloured, and this is hardly an unimportant fact about them. The body figured, in text or image, hence no longer an abstraction, cannot avoid this specificity. We are thus reminded of the power of sensation in possessing not just a presentational but a rhetorical aspect, in that when embedded in narrative, the power of persuasion can be superimposed on the immediacy of figuration. And certainly it is right to say that sensation works through *immediacy*; it does not, of itself, encourage a detached, analytical or philosophical stance. Immersion *in* experience is what is encouraged; it entails reaction, response, a registering of the sensation that may also be a recoil *from* it, or a further embeddedness *in* it. The sensational does not encourage *reading*, if that entails textual interpretation, treating the world as text, as a set of signifiers that need decoding, signs or markers of the social. That *can* come, but is not intrinsically *there*, in the sensational as experienced. The 'language of sensation' is the language of the extraordinary, of fate and chance, a language that points to real enough aspects of the modern world even if it may itself have consequences that have troubled its critics, just as its critics may, conversely, find it difficult to escape it, may indeed even succumb to it, or use it. Although he presents commodity fetishism as 'a process of sensationalising objects' that thereby mystifies and misunderstands the source of their power, Cvetkovich argues persuasively that Marx also deploys this language, draws on its own power.[21]

Really, much of the criticism only amounts to saying that sensational experience is indeed sensational *experience*, not analysis; and surely the latter *can* follow – it is not necessarily blocked off by the former. Emotional intensity is a powerful force, but precisely because it cannot carry its own reading with it, its *effect* can never be predetermined. The sensational body may indeed come sexed, gendered, coloured or whatever, but whether – or to what extent – these features come as culturally standardized or are matters of controversy within (or beyond) the culture is not prejudged merely by pointing to this as a phenomenal 'truth' of sensational experience itself; nor, therefore, can we know how any given individual will react in such situations. We can surely say, anyway, that the impact of sensationalism is not necessarily that of a mechanical, automatic imposition; sensation is *engagement*, involvement, the unpredictable drama of the reception that can also be a transformation. And it can as well stimulate ideas as foreclose them, it can explode meanings as well as reproduce established ones. In the context of the novel, its problematic relation to questions of interpretation has already been shown. Overall, it can be sense-making as well as sense-taking.

In short, to argue that sensational figuration necessarily dictates any specific ideological use to which it can be put is to misunderstand such figuration. Immediacy of impact inherently refers to specific bodies, specific affects, at particular times; in itself this does not entail any automatic codification of that experience. To suggest that it does is *itself* to fall for the undoubted potency of sensationalism, in an extreme form, rather than analysing it; and to allow possible ideological uses of sensationalism to shape our understanding of the dynamics of experience and representation that makes the 'sensational moment' possible is to risk remaining trapped within the sensational circuit itself. And finally, dare one suggest that lying behind all this is that combination of rationalist distrust of the body and intellectual distrust of popular culture that has made it so difficult to develop an adequate theoretical framework for the analysis of the culture of modernity, modernity *as* culture …

Anyway, it is clear that by the late nineteenth century, the culture of sensation was indeed producing a 'discourse of sensation', both at the level of newspaper commentary and in emergent social theory; and we can see the beginnings of what Singer, writing in the context of film studies, calls the 'modernity thesis', the discussion of how 'the unprecedented sensationalism of popular amusement' was related to 'the new sensory environment of urban modernity'.[22] Singer suggests that three categories of stimuli are most likely to be found stressful: namely those that are unexpected; those that are uncontrollable, or difficult to control; and those that are relatively ill-defined, experienced as confusing or chaotic. He adds that it is likely that the experience of modern life multiplies all of these.[23] Certainly this was *perceived* to be the case, and the perception could in turn both increase the sense of stress and the readiness to characterize problems and responses in these terms, hence the simultaneous emergence of a 'discourse of stress' that has accompanied modernity throughout.[24] These 'stress indicators' are also, of course, features of sensation and sensationalism, suggesting the possibility that 'sensationalism' could both be part of the problem, indeed could carry a particularly virulent form of it, *and* could be part of the response. This overlaps with another tension running through these debates, between the portrayal of everyday life as deadening, impoverished, on the one hand, or as over-stimulated, full of incident, on the other, since *both* could be seen as productive of stress, or as responses to it. 'Stress', after all – like 'sensation' – is a term that is poised uneasily between subjective and objective, feeling and external stimulus.

If we ask about the link between this external sensory environment and the amusements or entertainments that are in some sense a response to this, we can locate three main emphases or hypotheses. One, the most straightforward, presents an essential continuity. On this model, suggests Singer, 'the modern individual somehow internalized the tempos, shocks, and upheavals of the outside environment, and this generated a taste for hyperkinetic amusements';[25] hence, the intensification of modern entertainment simply reflects – or further intensifies – the sensory intensification of modern life. Miriam Hansen writes of the appeal of the variety format of entertainment, providing 'a short-term but incessant sensorial stimulation', mobilizing the viewer's attention through a 'discontinuous series of attractions, shocks and surprises', commenting that this was seen as a 'specifically modern form of subjectivity'.[26] A *Scientific American* editorial from 1905 claimed: 'The guiding principle of the inventors of these acts is to give our nerves a shock more intense than any hitherto experienced.'[27] A new era of entertainment was hence increasingly defined by 'immediate, gripping sensation' with 'concentrations of visual and kinaesthetic sensation' defining the modern era of 'manufactured stimulus'.[28]

The second hypothesis postulates a more complex relationship here. Singer summarizes this in terms of a response to a kind of sensory burnout: 'excessive sensory stimulus eventually exhausted and incapacitated the sensory apparatus'.[29]

For Simmel, this deadened sensation led to a blasé or jaded attitude: 'An incapacity thus emerges to react to new sensations with the appropriate energy … The essence of the blasé attitude consists in the blunting of discrimination.'[30] Hence sensationalism becomes a cure for exhausted sensation, as it were. Freud's theory of the consciousness shield, and the Elias idea of body armour, as the means by which the subject is protected from excessive stimulus, become relevant here; for both authors, failure of the 'shield' results in sensations of flight and trauma.[31] This would imply that the sensorium *needs* to be blunted, in which case it is difficult to see why entertainments should be sought that have precisely the opposite result, unless we adopt the theory (of Benjamin, among others) that there can be an insulating, prophylactic effect in being exposed to stimuli in a more measured, controlled way, through entertainment.

This can slide into a third approach, the 'compensation' model. Here, it is not so much a matter of jaded attitudes, as of a jaded world. For Siegfried Kracauer, writing in the 1920s and 1930s, sensationalism was a response to our alienated, impoverished experience of the world, a compensation response. Singer adds that this hypothesis presumably loops back into the blasé attitude/sensory exhaustion hypothesis: sensational amusement is just one more ingredient contributing to the 'inflationary curve of strong sensation'.[32] And the result is that 'The compensatory thrills of popular amusements reproduced the very register of hyperstimulus that vitiated modern experience to begin with'.[33] The upshot is, as Leo Charney puts it, that we see 'the increased appetite for mobile kinetic sensation' packaged as 'a respite from those sensations'.[34] Indeed, a 'craving for sensation' can be seen variously as a reflection of the frenetic pace of modern life, a kind of addiction to it; as a symptom of burnout; or as a means of compensation, of escape – nor is it clear how we could begin to distinguish between these, symptomatically or empirically. In short, we have a series of circulating hypotheses – all overlapping, empirically confusing, and in varying degrees plausible – that rather mirror the circuits of sensation themselves. And it is to this idea of a 'circuit of sensation' that we now turn.

The circuit of sensation

We have seen that the sensational flashes across all three registers – the characters in the text (or event), the reader of the text (spectator of the event), and the mass appeal of the text (the event as spectacle) – as if aspiring to an immediacy that will fuse them all into one experience, affect as effect. Like an electric current that requires two poles to leap between – an analogy that would have made immediate sense to nineteenth-century readers – 'sensation' plays between the great constitutive binary distinctions of modern Western culture, both threatening their separation while keeping them precariously apart. In effect, we have a circuit, a linking process, involving sensation as mediator between body and media, and body, media, and other bodies, in turn implicating the binaries of individual/social, concrete/abstract, public/private, distance/presence and mind/matter. Through figuration and enactment, sensation transmits and displaces the affective power of the body in and through mediated form, as moments in this circuit.

We can begin by observing that when used as terms to capture and shape experiences of embodiment and feeling, on the one hand, and the shocks and drama of media-inflected events, on the other, 'sensation' and 'sensationalism' convey a certain ethos, a certain way of living in, and relating to, the world of modernity. Thus Cvetkovich points to how 'sensational moments' get represented as 'the product of chance occurrences, uncanny repetitions, and fated events'; these 'sensational events' – sensational both in their extraordinary nature and their bodily responses – are described in 'the rhetoric of fate and chance'. This melodrama, these hints of control of the body by 'other forces', this passivity in the face of the impact of the contingency of experience, produces a world in which involuntary bodily sensation 'becomes a symptom of the self's subjection to the shock of chance or surprise events, and underwrites the process by which a sensational or melodramatic narrative can be constructed'.[35]

Drawing on both aspects of 'sensation', as feeling and as event, Charney draws our attention to a further point, namely that momentary sensations become startling as contrasts to the 'undifferentiated drift of everyday experience'.[36] This explicit contrast between the 'ordinary' and the 'sensational' is worth further consideration, along with a sense of the plurality of 'sensation': since any sensation is 'of the moment', it will give way to others, always against the background of this taken for granted 'ordinariness', the fact of 'background' itself. There is something discrete, disjunctive, about sensation, a sense in which it requires multiplicity, discontinuity; this is in the very nature of its impact. Nadia Seremetakis spells this out further: 'The sensory structure of everyday life is experienced as naturalized, almost cosmic time over against which eruptive, "sensational events" such as elections, performances, accidents, disasters, are profiled', adding that 'the narrativity of the sensational event is itself made possible by a relation of foreground and background.' Expanding this, she argues: 'The polarity between the sensational and the mundane is also the dichotomy between the sensational and the sensory in which the latter is left unmarked, unvoiced and unattended to, as a banal element of the everyday.'[37] What is pointed to here is really a *process*, that whereby the 'undifferentiated', which is precisely that which 'makes no difference', emerges as something distinct, something that *does* make a difference, in that it emerges as both product and condition of the sensational itself. Both come into being *together*. Hence the emergence of sensation out of the sensory, and of the 'sensational' out of either sensation or the sensory, is a process of foregrounding, of figuration as concentration, the very process by which sensation is constituted as such.

The terms fate and chance, and these notions of sensation and the sensational, can now be shown to be in some ways connected. Let us begin with fate and chance. While often conjoined, in these discussions, they are, on the face of it, opposites: 'fate' implies a determinism that is absent from 'chance'. Yet, at both a popular and a scientific level, the connection is there, if we map on a surface/depth distinction. What 'appears' as chance may actually reveal the deeper workings of fate … (Some conjunction of this kind is also implicit in our notion of the uncanny.) The world of experience, then, is the world of the unpredictable, of chance, central features both of sensation and of the sensational. But in the background is this 'deeper logic', whether coded as fate or scientific causation; and here, these notions can be seen to sit readily enough within the popular dissemination of the nineteenth-century scientific revolutions that gave us the laws of thermodynamics and the accompanying, underlying ontology of energy. Thus, comparing this emergent ontology of the later part of this period with that of the Enlightenment materialism of a century before, Rabinbach claims that 'the result is a material world far more random, arbitrary, and ephemeral. Only energy is constant and protean.'[38] 'Energy' constitutes the underlying backdrop; particular transformations, pulses, of energy will be experienced as 'sensation'. An important implication of all this for the notion of 'sensation' is spelt out by Gustav Fechner, one of the most influential psychologists of the time. In claiming the discovery of a 'stimulus threshold' whereby a certain *intensity* of energy, as stimulus, is needed before a sensation can be experienced, he both confirms the discontinuity of 'sensation' against its background and points to a kind of defence against it: 'The fact that each stimulus must first reach a certain limit before it arouses a sensation assures to mankind a state undisturbed to a certain degree by external stimulation.'[39] At the same time it ensures the constant potential, in an unstable era of rapid change and media penetration, for precisely such sensational stimulation …

We can now spell out the 'process ontology' of this 'circuit of sensation' in more detail. It is force, energy, *Kraft*, that constitutes the raw material of the universe; and a central feature of energy is that it is protean, ever-changing in form, these changes in form both masking and revealing the underlying process of circulation. These changes, in turn, involve jumps, discontinuities, which in the worlds of both culture and human physiology can be mapped as 'sensations'. Entities, and boundaries between them, become problematical, relative: this is an ontology of relations and processes rather than objects, so 'boundaries' necessarily become contingent, unclear. Exemplifying this, Pykett points out that the debate over the sensation novel was a debate over how and where to draw boundaries, given that the novel itself was about 'the unfixing and transgression of boundaries'.[40] With William Carpenter, an influential psychologist of the time, we find what is, in effect, a formulation of a version of the circuit of sensation: 'so does a Sensation, an Instinctive Tendency, an Emotion, an Idea, or a Volition, which attains an intensity adequate to "close" the circuit, liberate the Nerve-force with which a certain part of the Brain ... is always charged.'[41] These circuits run through, and across, orthodox distinctions between literature, mass media, psychology and science, and the subjects of these discourses: nature, society, the economy, the body, the person. All are reconstituted in this language of currents, flows and blockages. As Rabinbach puts it: 'Interpreted through the dynamic language of *Kraft*, the body appeared as a field of forces, energies, and labour power.'[42] Something of this is captured by Ernst Mach, the 'sensationalist' philosopher of science and critic of conventional notions of 'self' and 'ego' as separate entities: 'When I speak of my own sensations, these sensations do not exist spatially in my head, but rather my "head" shares with them the same spatial field.'[43] For Mach, the ego is chimerical, and the individual is really constituted by 'currents of sensation'.[44]

Notions of body and mind, subject and object, become destabilized, seen in relational terms; Christoph Asendorf suggests that the subject cannot close itself off, instead becoming 'a surface on which the movements of others are written'. The body thereby becomes 'noncorporeal, immaterial, arbitrarily subject to being charged with tensions'.[45] He thereby reinforces Rabinbach's contention that this ontology is a kind of 'transcendental materialism' (or, perhaps, 'materialist idealism').[46] This would be a 'materialism' of flows, fields, forces – and, one might add, images, which in their simultaneous vividness and 'immateriality', their instability as between subject and object, and their ability to circulate, cause endless difficulties across a range of discourses and experiences from spiritualism to newspaper sensationalism.[47] There is a widespread concern with 'influences' here, with the 'permeability and suggestibility' of mind and body, with 'materialized and dematerialized contact', and psychoanalysis itself could be portrayed as a language of transmission and translation in which the boundaries between psychic and somatic are necessarily insecure.[48] It is hardly surprising, then, that these processes could encompass sexuality, most widely interpreted in terms that emphasized the physical aspects. For the early sexologist, Krafft-Ebing, interruptions to the 'network of electrical circuits distributing finite amounts of energy', notably masturbation, would produce aberrant sexual behaviour, such as homosexuality.[49]

On further examination, this ontology of sensational circuits is by no means free of problems, and has in turn posed problems for its interpreters. We can use Jonathan Crary's influential reinterpretation of the changing nature of vision and attention in modernity to delve further into this. He points to 'dynamogeny', a term in vogue in the 1880s, meaning 'excitation', whereby 'sensation' was now seen in terms of force, movement, motor behaviour, often bypassing consciousness; and on the face of it, his claims that the transformation of the nineteenth-century awareness of sensation led to 'the disintegration of an indisputable distinction between interior and exterior' which in turn became 'a condition for the emergence of spectacular modernizing culture and for a dramatic expansion of the possibilities of aesthetic experience'[50] seems entirely consistent with what has been presented so far. He argues that modernity, and in particular the modernization of vision, collapses the old space of representation: sensations and stimuli now have no clear reference to a spatial location, so the distinction between internal and external becomes blurred.[51] Crucial here is that the revolution in mid-century psychology and physics appeared to have made sensation measurable, thus making human experience quantifiable. Fechner, who set about rationalizing sensation through the measurement of external stimulus thereby furthered an 'obliteration of the qualitative in sensation', a process crucial to modernization. This rendered Goethe's distinction between internal sensation (inner light, inner vision) and the external world obsolete,[52] along with the 'sensationalist' psychology of the eighteenth century, which characteristically implied a pronounced inner/outer distinction. By the late nineteenth century, 'sensation' was being experimentally produced and measured in laboratories, so 'an older model of sensation as something *belonging* to a subject became irrelevant'.[53]

There is much to be said for this, but it is important to notice that the argument is located firmly in terms of developments in science, which in turn is seen in its role as central to the rationalizing imperatives of the project of modernity; it does not really consider the wider cultural context. Even in terms of science, it is interesting to compare Crary's account with the significantly different emphasis offered by Emile Meyerson, one of the most influential philosophers of science of the period under discussion. Writing in the first decade of the twentieth century, Meyerson argues that scientific mechanism necessarily loses, and cannot reconstitute, our sense of the 'quality' of sensations. We cannot know the *manner* whereby movement is transformed into the experience of sensation, although the two ends of the process, cause and effect, can be known, even measured.[54] You can look inside a nerve for as long as you like, but you will never find a sensation. Hence, what we have here is 'a relation which we do not succeed in rendering logical'; it can be described as 'irrational', indicating a 'limit' we can never pass beyond, never understand.[55] Significantly, this extended discussion of sensation occurs in a chapter entitled 'The Irrational' (Chapter IX). How intriguing, then, that at the heart of the science of sensation itself we find a correlate to the 'irrationalism' that is often said to accompany sensation in its everyday, media-related use ...

And it is not just Meyerson. Crary himself implicitly acknowledges that luminaries like William James, from within psychology, and Bergson and Whitehead, from philosophy of science, argued that 'sensation' cannot ultimately be separated from a relationship with memory, will, desire and other aspects of experience, including 'inner' experience.[56] And Rabinbach, also writing of the impact of science, but within the broader cultural context of the experience of modernity, argues that defence against excess sensation 'gives birth to a radically *interiorized* subject, whose personality is shielded from all stimuli by the tomblike heaviness of late nineteenth-century bourgeois décor'.[57] Not only does the 'interior subject' not disappear, then; it is reinforced.

To some extent, it is clear that these conflicting interpretations can be explained by differences of intellectual context and focus; but there is more to it than that. The problems arise from features of the 'circuit of sensation' itself. Take Crary's claim that sensation had ceased to designate an element of the process whereby representation occurs: 'Rather, it is part of a sequence of events in which the end point is not an inner state, such as knowledge or cognition or perception; instead, sensation is that which culminates in movement', whether voluntary or involuntary.[58] But we have already seen, from Meyerson, that 'movement', as that which precipitates or results from sensation, does not have any simple relationship with it. Rather, there is a *discontinuity* here, a discontinuity that makes both sensation *and* representation possible. There is an intractable *gap* here, central to the very experience of sensation: precisely the gap, the distinction, between 'inside' and 'outside' that, as we have seen above, both permits the flow of sensation and is challenged by it. 'Sensation' is the impossible point of transition, the point of *intensity*, where 'inner' and 'outer' are constituted, and where background becomes foreground, the body becomes aware of itself and its continuity with what is outside, beyond. And this, then, is also the point or 'place' of representation, where 'inner' becomes constructed as the 'inner theatre' of representation, where ideas, images and feelings disport themselves, and 'sensations' become felt and figured. The emphasis on change, on movement, indeed reflects a profound shift from eighteenth-century materialism, but we do not, cannot, move totally away from the universe of David Hartley's *Observations on Man* (1749, still being reprinted in 1810), in which sensations feature as 'internal feelings of the mind' resulting from impressions of external objects on the body, and ideas are 'internal representations' of sensations.[59]

Along with this, we are of course reminded of the 'imaginary' nature of this inner theatre, constructed as it is of images in a spectral space that cannot, indeed – and here, in a sense, we rejoin Crary – have any clear or 'real' spatial location, being rather a result of this very construction of 'inner' and 'outer' whereby self and mind are posited in relation to body through the very discontinuities of the circuit of sensation. And just as sensation faces both ways, so do images, problematically related both to world and to mind. The 'sensational images' discussed by Henning in relation to *fin-de-siècle* newspapers thus represent this very conjunction of sensation and representation, that sense in which they both require and subvert the inner/outer distinction that serves to define them in their relation of mutual exclusion and dependence.

We can now return to the distinctive implications of all this for our sense of body and self. Henning points to an emergent understanding of sensation in terms of nerves and electrical currents,[60] so that 'the person' is a locus of currents of energy, translated into the language of nerves; indeed, the two are often joined, as 'nervous energy'. Writing of how readily news of approaching bad weather, or even distant earthquakes, produces rapid effects among 'the nervous', Proust points graphically to how this becomes embedded in a community: 'This is a measure of the links that bind the nervous, from the farthest points of the globe, in a solidarity they often would prefer to be less intimate.'[61] There is a hint, here, of a certain exclusiveness about this community; 'nerves' seem to play something of the role of 'sensibility' a century before, as a marker of quality. It is the refined who are most likely to manifest 'nerves'. The leading historian of nerves in science and culture, George Rousseau, indeed argues for a strong continuity from the eighteenth century, over which period 'the nervous system became the battlefield on which civilization and its discontents would be played out'.[62] Nor should the link with status obscure – and it may indeed be compatible with – the more general emphasis on how nerves accompany the stresses and strains of modernity, the 'modernity thesis'. Writing in 1891, Bahr refers to these 'new people', who 'live now only through the experience of nerves; they only react on the basis of nerves'.[63] As the raw material of the circuit of sensation, these nerves both register sensation and transmit it. The protective 'body armour' referred to previously thus turns out to be porous, often alarmingly so. Asendorf can thus assert: 'The invisible electrical currents are the metaphor of the life of the nerves: the body becomes a force field, a contingent intersection of effects determined elsewhere.'[64]

We can here rejoin neurasthenia, from a different angle. With energy, after all – with the discovery of the second law of thermodynamics – came entropy, the dissipation of energy, taken to entail the inevitability of decline, of exhaustion. In the language of the body, this meant 'the endemic disorder of fatigue',[65] the body's resistance to unlimited progress and productivity; and in the transformable language of body and mind, the psychosomatic, it meant neurasthenia[66] and hysteria. Here, 'the aesthetic sensitivity to nerve stimuli is transformed into a symptom of illness'.[67] The neurasthenic needs protection against the sensations and shocks of modernity. Above all, it reflected a weakness of *will* ('aboulia'), which in turn testified to an inadequately strong ego, an inability to bind and direct energy towards clear goals. Hence the ego had to coordinate conflicting impulses or sensations, whether from physiology or society, and Rabinbach suggests that 'fatigue was perceived as *both* a physical and moral disorder – a sign of weakness and the absence of will'.[68] Neurasthenia, then, reveals a blockage in the circuit of sensation, yet is also a manifestation of it, and indeed its cure requires a different kind of blockage, a form of rationing, carried out by a precarious ego that must somehow dominate the flow, impose its own (masculine) order, rescue the self from its passivity in the face of the engulfment of sensation. That this tension can actually be productive is clear from the case of Proust. His novel has, after all, been described as the story of a 'nervous Narrator',[69] who has to overcome neurasthenia by writing his way through it, without ever really escaping it. Michael Finn presents Proust as desperate to escape the trap of everyday talk – the apparent authenticity that is really just endless copying from others – through recourse to a more basic, quasi-corporeal 'mimetic language of the body' which must then be reproduced in metaphor by the language of art. Yet what results is a 'hysteria of imitation', a constant self-quotation, whereby the repetitive copying of everyday language is replaced by an equally repetitive copying of sensation, fundamental to his style.[70]

Sensational technologies

We can now return to the 'shocks of modernity' to put more emphasis on technological dimensions that open up new channels for the circuit of sensation. Walter Benjamin, in the 1930s, presents film as a medium of shocks, emerging to meet 'a new and urgent need for stimuli'.[71] 'The camera gave the moment a posthumous shock', states Benjamin, claiming that it is now film that can give us the sensation of 'plunging' into the crowd as into a 'reservoir of electric energy'.[72] This emphasis is not, of course, unique to Benjamin; a link between film, sensation and the shock experience runs through film theory of the 1920s and 1930s, particularly in Soviet montage theory and its major figure – both as filmmaker and theorist – Sergei Eisenstein, in turn a major influence on the film theory of Deleuze.[73] Discussing Eisenstein, Deleuze in effect identifies a circuit of sensation, 'A Circuit which includes simultaneously the author, the film and the viewer', adding: 'A complete circuit thus includes the sensory shock which raises us from the images to conscious thought, then the thinking in figures which takes us back to the images and gives us an affective thought again.' It is, he adds, as if cinema itself is saying 'you can't escape the shock which arouses the thinker in you',[74] and, as with Benjamin, this engagement with cinema, this reflective capacity stimulated by shock, can be critical, just as it is also influenced by the dynamics of figuration that escape conscious awareness. All this, however, develops out of a context of technological innovations that go far back into the previous century, and which are worth exploring.

'The sensation of the General Strike', Beatrice Webb noted in her diary in 1926, 'centres around the headphones of the wireless set', so that people 'gathered in rapt attention' to listen.[75] What is intriguing is a slight awkwardness about the use of 'sensation' here, as though the word is itself seeking to highlight its ambiguity and plurality, its ability to refer to various dimensions simultaneously: to the sensation, the feeling of experiencing events, events that seem sensational in themselves and that are further sensationalized by their mediated status, and the accompanying, rather unsettling, diffusion of the sense of the presence of others. Certainly the relation between the great nineteenth-century innovations in communications technology and the forms taken by these dimensions of the circuit of sensation may well suggest another perspective on the latter, not indeed unconnected with this incorporation of 'others' in the circuits themselves.

Spreading through the Western world from around mid-century, the telegraph seemed to carry radical implications both for the familiar and scientific problem of action at a distance and for the relation between mind and body. Bridging vast distances in a way that seemed to separate out and parcel up the components of consciousness, minus their normal embodied status, the telegraph simultaneously seemed to involve a radical materialization of mind. If, on the one hand, 'the electronic circuitry of the telegraph made possible the instantaneous exchange of messages in the complete absence of physical bodies', as Jeffrey Sconce claims, it is nonetheless true, as he observes elsewhere, that late-nineteenth-century medical science postulated 'a direct and most literal homology between the telegraphic network and the central nervous system'.[76] A clue to the tension here can be grasped in this description, by a commentator in 1852, of 'nervous energy' as 'an intermediate agent by which mind acts on matter, and which is itself neither mind nor matter'.[77] This suggests that this mysterious 'stuff' of communication, which can exist as 'mind' at both ends of the communication process, the encoding and the decoding of the message, exists in between in some almost, but not quite, material state: strange, different, but not radically discontinuous. By late century, the innovations of electromagnetism and thermodynamics had suggested that 'matter may be conceived as a configuration of energy alignments', as Stephen Kern puts it;[78] and the auditory taps of the telegraph, the dots and dashes of the Morse code, are manifestations, transformations of energy that can bridge distances because they are, ultimately, phenomena that partake of the very circuits of energy that were by then seen as the basic sources and mechanics of the universe and its processes. These taps, dots and dashes could also be seen both to signify, and to embody, those discontinuities in the flow, that ability to leap across gaps, that was central to the understanding of electromagnetism as the basis of the 'nervous energy' of the universe – a universe that could conceivably include the souls of the dead, continuing to exist as electric impulses …

Here it seems appropriate to introduce the ether, a concept that reached the height of its influence in the nineteenth century, only being finally laid to rest in science itself by Einstein's special theory of relativity in 1905, although it would long linger on in popular consciousness. Its appeal is not hard to see: the ether was a medium that allowed light, electricity and magnetism to work at a distance. For the greatest theoretical physicist of the century, James Clerk Maxwell, the ether was a 'wonderful medium', sensitive to any 'vibrations' that occur in it.[79] It appealed to the apparently commonsensical view that 'something' could not pass through 'nothing': there had to be another 'something', a medium. Hence Henry Adams, a commentator on the physics of the time, writing in 1909, called the ether an 'undifferentiated substance supporting matter and mind alike'.[80]

Popularly, it could seem interchangeable with 'air', hence the idea of a medium as not just the intermediate form, format or channel for transmission, but the whole environment, the 'pervading or enveloping substance'[81] within which an organism – and even perhaps a culture – lived (and died). Another favourite figure for this was the ocean, so that a message set loose on 'the open sea of the electromagnetic spectrum' became 'a small boat tossed about on the waves of this etheric ocean', in Sconce's words.[82] Human communication itself comes to involve those vibrations in the ether whereby initial sensations can be transmitted – not always with predictable results, as will be readily apparent.

All this opens a window on to what can seem the more bizarre aspects of the late-nineteenth-century cultural imaginary – in particular, the relative ease with which resolutely materialist science could coexist with spiritualist séances and related phenomena, such as telepathy, a term coined by Myers in 1882 to open up the possibility of direct mind-to-mind communication for scientific investigation. While it has been usual to emphasize the 'spirit' in spiritualism, to sharpen the contrast with science, this has always been to some extent misleading, and more recent scholarship has pointed to the continuities, emphasizing the tactile and the auditory as much as the visual, which has the effect of reinserting spiritualism into the world of everyday material practices. 'Talking with the dead through raps and knocks, after all, was only slightly more miraculous than talking with the living yet absent through dots and dashes …', Sconce suggests,[83] and indeed some spirits did seem to embrace Morse code as their means of communication readily enough. Nor were other technological innovations immune to these possibilities. The phonograph, for example, with its ability to separate voice from body and give an apparently independent existence to the former, contributed to this sense that 'messages' could be ubiquitous, always potentially present, whether detected or undetected.[84] Laurence Rickels points to the intriguing phenomenon of recorded voices of dead children; in an era of high childhood mortality, the custom of recording the voice of the child, a recording that would all too often turn out, before long, to be a voice from beyond the grave, contributed to the cult and the culture of mortuary ritual and the craving to communicate with the dead.[85]

The major presence of women in Victorian spiritualism, whether as mediums or as the primary audience, has often been noted.[86] It has also been convincingly argued that if it was women who constituted the primary sensational subjects of sensationalist fiction, so too the greater sensitivity and receptivity of the female body, its status as relatively 'other' to masculine rationalism and its orientation to control, made it a more likely receptacle for messages from the 'other side'. Building on this more broadly, Steven Connor outlines the 'mimicry of materialist language and modes of thought' present in the séance, emphasizing the 'sensationalism' that produces the 'sensory intensification' so central to the experience.[87] He quotes the medium Elizabeth d'Esperance on how the passivity of the situation, the loss of physical power by the participants, enabled normally inaudible sounds to become audible, and how 'a movement of any of the sitters sent a vibration through every nerve; a sudden exclamation caused a sensation of terror'; thoughts 'made themselves felt almost as though they were material objects'.[88] Well into the twentieth century the séance continued to draw on media technologies to associate the voice with a range of acoustic and kinetic sensations.

'There's something coming through from somewhere; but it isn't Poole': Sensations of communication

In order to emphasize the aural dimension, and moving to a later technology, let us take Rudyard Kipling's little story, 'Wireless', as a basis for further exploration.[89] It was first published in 1902, at the very beginning of the radio age, when the 'wireless' was still experimental, mainly used for communication between ships at sea, and between sea and land.

The key moment in the story comes as a conjunction of two events. Mr Cashell, a wireless experimenter, has set up advanced equipment in the back room of a chemist's shop, in order to send and receive messages to Poole, along the south coast. At the same time, the unfortunate Mr Shaynor, ostensibly on duty in the front part of the shop, and who has taken a drugged drink for relief from the symptoms of the tuberculosis that is clearly fated to kill him, has gone into a disturbed trance, and is beginning to write down lines from a Keats poem. Mr Cashell suddenly asks for quiet, announcing: 'There's something coming through from somewhere; but it isn't Poole.' The narrator, seated by Mr Shaynor, replies: 'There is something coming through here, too.'[90] In the first case, it turns out to be a couple of warships in the Channel, attempting forlornly to communicate with each other, but with defective receivers, so it is actually only Cashell who can understand what is going on. In the second case, it turns out to be John Keats who is communicating with, or through, Shaynor, Keats as he struggles to write a poem; this time, it is only the other third party, the narrator, who happens to be familiar with the Keats poem, who can make (disturbing) sense of it. And on to these two triangles, we can superimpose a third, with the reader as the third party, trying to make sense of these two events and the relation between them, since clearly links are being implied, whether metaphorical or literal or 'somewhere' that isn't clearly either, helping to transmit a sense of the uncanny. Indeed, Cashell's comment, towards the end, reinforces this, when he refers to the fragmented messages from the ships: 'Have you ever seen a spiritualistic séance? It reminds me of that sometimes – odds and ends of messages coming out of nowhere – a word here and there – no good at all.'[91]

Superimposed, these all give us a picture of a universe of messages passing ethereally, from whom and to whom we do not know, yet always *there*. And then, the uncanny sense is intensified, as we ourselves come to fill in some of the gaps, and pick up some of the clues, that lead up to the possession scenario, a process of reading and reflection in which increased knowledge actually *enhances* the uncanny effect. We thus pick up – but only later, and perhaps gradually – the sense in which Shaynor might in some sense *be* Keats, the hint of possession as repetition. Gillian Beer puts it well, suggesting that as readers we 'take for granted moving freely back and forth through time, yet are disconcerted when it occurs as event within the fiction. Evocations and prolepses are melded into the early part of the narrative, but so dispersed that they are at first inaudible …' Hence, 'We see it all, too late. We may pick up the mental vibrations early but they delay functioning as intertextuality. Keats is absent.'[92] At some point, perhaps suddenly, we *do* work it out: Shaynor, trained as a chemist, taking drugs, suffering from consumption, is in love with Fanny Brand, and takes a walk around St Agnes Church; Keats, trained as a chemist, taking drugs, suffering from consumption, is in love with Fanny Brawne, and is writing the poem 'The Eve of St Agnes'. And we have learnt that Shaynor has never even heard of the poem …

The effect is to *intensify* the paradox of the 'rational' explanation offered by the narrator as an amateur but 'scientific' essay in emergency sense-making, for this becomes all the more *im*plausible as the details that might seem to make it plausible are filled in. The explanation involves 'induction', a concept which maps into the story itself, with its electrical connotations. 'Induction' is the process by which electromagnetic properties are transferred, without physical contact, from one circuit or body to another; but it is also the principle of 'like causes, like effects' in scientific explanation, the idea that the accumulation of identical circumstances would produce identical outcomes. In this case, applied to the Keats/Shaynor scenario, the piling up of 'coincidences', and the impossibility of the resulting 'explanation', has the effect of throwing us back onto the impossibility of possession by a long-dead poet – and our oscillation here constitutes the heart of the uncanny. In effect, this testifies to our own *involvement* in the story, our role in the third triangle, which in turn means that we are likely to collapse at times into the equivalent in each of the first two, particularly the first. Just as the narrator finds his subjectivity fractured, so do we. The impact on him of what appeared to be happening to Shaynor was dramatic: in a 'rainbow-tinted whirl … my own soul most dispassionately considered my own soul as that fought with an over-mastering fear', and as his attempt at rational explanation kicked in, he found himself 'whispering encouragement, evidently to my other self', even while 'the other half of my soul refused to be comforted', cowering in some corner.[93]

In effect, the third party here plays the part of what is called the 'coherer'. This is the electrical component used to detect radio waves, which cause the particles inside the mechanism to 'cohere', thereby changing the current through the circuit. The 'magic', the 'manifestations', are due to the coherer, explains Cashell: this is what reveals 'the Powers – whatever the Powers may be', working through space and distance.[94] The coherer makes the radio circuit work, makes some sort of communication possible. Whether the coherer necessarily brings 'coherence' is, as we have seen, another matter …[95]

Moving on to the 1920s, with the cultural impact of modernism, we do indeed encounter 'the emergence of a subjectivity mediated through the mass-produced sounds and disembodied voices of gramophone, telephone, radio and talkies'.[96] In a short story by Virginia Woolf, 'Kew Gardens' (1919), we encounter voices before we can hear what is being said, or who is uttering the words, and sounds which pass out of earshot before conversations are over. Discussing this story – and other works of hers, notably *The Waves* – Melba Cuddy-Keane finds that time as progression, as in an unfolding conversation, is subordinated to 'relations among disparate points in space', and if there is any sense of a whole it certainly is '*not* unified round a center'. We seem again to be in the presence of the disconnected simultaneities of the airwaves. In this decentred, dispersed world of experience, we find 'disparate sounds – human, natural and mechanical – broadly diffused from different points in space and in the nonhierarchical mixing of voices and noises'.[97] Jane Lewty, in turn, suggests that James Joyce's *Finnegans Wake* is full of the language of the airwaves, messages from anyone going anywhere or nowhere, 'loftly marconimasts from Clifden' sending signals picked up by 'Nova Scotia's listing sisterwands', and disembodied voices shouting demands that others 'get off my air'.[98] In such hands, the novel itself is transformed into – or revealed as – not so much the unified product of a coherent self (a 'coherer'), but a space of diffusion, of networks, of multiple voices on different frequencies, broadcasting to someone, anyone, in the void.

Since the 1940s, it has doubtless been the gradual impact of communication and information theory that has tended to provide the language to clothe our experience here. DNA becomes a code of genetic information, neural synapses become switchboards, nerves become telephone lines, the brain becomes an 'information processor'. John Durham Peters suggests that this frequently seems to reverse the characteristic direction of nineteenth-century imagery, when the technological figured the organic;[99] and he adds that information also 'shares semiotic space with subatomic physics, coming in bits, flashes, bursts, and impulses'.[100] If the figures slip and slide and reverse themselves, this in turn points to the underlying continuity, the presence of a deep structure working through these substitutions and oscillations. For Sconce, all this suggests the extent to which 'the public imagination of a given historical moment considers these flows of electricity, consciousness, and information to be homologous, interchangeable, and transmutable', with 'electricity mediating the transfer and substitution of consciousness and information between the body and a host of electronic media technologies'.[101]

There have, of course, been significant shifts along the way. If we return to Beatrice Webb, glued to her wireless set to receive the latest news, we can point out that the momentous events came at the time of transition from 'wireless' to 'radio', or more accurately, from the point-to-point form of early wireless transmission, as in the Kipling story, to the centre-periphery form taken by radio (and television) 'broadcasting' as it became dominant from the 1920s.[102] Nevertheless, the continuities are marked: the disembodied voices, the effect of 'liveness' as a feature of the medium, and the fact that the radio signal has always been inherently *public* just as the context of its reception has been in varying degrees *private*. Peters suggests that 'Organizing radio's connection to the bodies of the communicants was a chief prerequisite of its naturalization into everyday life',[103] and this formulation, which can include a political dimension without being reducible to it, seems apt, as we can indeed see from the Beatrice Webb example. Bodies, voices, 'media objects', linked through oddly disembodied yet material networks: these constitute the raw material of the circuits of sensation, and the very possibility of that other rather odd manifestation or emanation – the social – in the mass media age. Nor are the boundaries at all clear here: the limits, if any, as to who can constitute the community of communicants. It is not only the dead, but assorted aliens and others who can potentially appear on this scene.[104] All this, in turn, gives the flavour, the forms and potential of the controversies, the fashions, the moral panics and enthusiasms that periodically flash across and illuminate the circuits, for good or ill.

Indeed, 'sensation' can come to stand in for the 'enthusiasm' that so troubled eighteenth-century commentators on the 'common people' and what they saw as their strange, irrational, potentially disturbing and uncontrollable ways. Stefan Jonsson reminds us that, in a later generation, the early sociologists and social psychologists of the decades around the beginning of the twentieth century defined the masses in similar ways to scientists defining physical mass: both postulated the existence of an 'undifferentiated matter' which, under appropriate circumstances, could be converted into energy. The outcome could be positive – the further development of 'civilization' – or negative, the irruptions of disorder, riot and revolution.[105] Recently, there has been a revival of interest in these 'mass psychology' approaches. Nevertheless, these more recent theorists, seeking to update and transform this model, have tended to use terms that clearly show these origins. For Serge Moscovici, for example, society is 'made up of the passions that flow through our lives', and these constitute the 'primal links' between us,[106] while for Teresa Brennan, a theory of the social as the 'transmission of affect' promises a way beyond the rigid dichotomy of 'biology' and 'society'.[107]

Let us conclude by returning to the idea of radio as a 'live' medium. In an interestingly ambiguous way, Peters claims that 'liveness' in radio was 'the effort to break the connection between death and distance'.[108] In the context, this seems to mean that life can be present across distances, *authentically* present, not a simulation; but it could also be read as the claim that death could come *closer* – as indeed it did, for the Victorians, for Kipling and for many since. The dead, apparently, cannot be excluded from the community of communication so easily. Just as 'live' radio may turn out to be pre-recorded, not 'live' at all, so the dead may simulate life and communicate 'live'. Peters also notices that 'live' can also mean 'containing unexpended energy',[109] transmitting power, as in a live shell or cartridge; and we can add that a 'live wire', as a person, can be a dynamic presence, just as a 'live' wire provides both power – and shocks; life – and death. In these sensational circuits, death represents the ultimate impossibility of its own exclusion, the limit of the circuit that is inseparable from its creative dynamism, the shock that empowers, and the shock that kills …

4

The Aesthetics of Sensation

Since sensation has been widely viewed as the basic subject matter of art, a consideration of whether it can ultimately be insulated in this role from the influence of popular and media sensationalism is critical for evaluating the possibility and coherence of an autonomous aesthetics, just as it constitutes a test for the potential of any 'cultural aesthetics' that aspires to transcend these self-imposed limits.

From Pater to Deleuze

By the late nineteenth century, the implications of scientific sensationalism for aesthetics were being widely debated. For both Seurat and Nietzsche, argues Crary, 'meaning in art was not about representation but a relation of forces', and with Cézanne, too, we find 'not a logic of contemplative distance … but rather an account of a nervous system interfacing with a continually transforming external environment'.[1] Cézanne himself wrote of 'becoming more clear-sighted in front of nature' but added: 'with me the realization of my sensation is always very difficult. I cannot attain the intensity that is unfolded before my senses.'[2] For the influential Walter Pater, the aesthetic critic should regard works of art and nature alike as 'powers or forces producing pleasurable sensations, each of a more or less peculiar and unique kind'.[3] For Pater, we should submit *only* to the laws of our nature, this 'magic web woven through and through us, like that magnetic system of which modern science speaks, penetrating us with a network, subtler than our subtlest nerves, yet bearing in it the subtlest forces of the world'.[4] Our physical life is a 'perpetual motion' of these 'elementary forces' that range beyond us, all around us, leaving us 'broadcast, driven' by them. Considered subjectively, however, these objects and forces seem to break up into unstable, inconstant, flickering impressions, sensations of 'colour, odour, texture' which 'burn and are extinguished with our consciousness of them'. Each moment is 'gone while we try to apprehend it' in this 'strange, perpetual weaving and unweaving of ourselves'[5] that situates both the challenge to art, and its potential – and here we move towards the more controversial aspects of Pater's perspective, with its own significance for future developments.

These moments of intense apprehension of experience in the flow of necessity, these bursts of energy in the networks of sensation, are 'pulses' or 'pulsations', moments of 'concurrence' between forces that immediately part; these are the moments that 'burn' in our apprehension of them, the moments to seek out, breaking with habits and 'facile orthodoxy', so that we can 'be present always at the focus where the greatest number of vital forces unite in their purest energy'. And so to Pater's most famous formulation: 'To burn always with this hard, gem-like flame, to maintain this ecstasy, is success in life.' It is great passions that manifest these pulsations, give us this ecstasy; in particular, the 'poetic passion … the love of art for its own sake' is what can give 'nothing but the highest quality to your moments as they pass, and simply for those moments' sake'.[6]

We can pause here, to note, in all this, the emphasis on instability, transience, the sense in which the moment is gone even in the 'apprehending' of it. Not only this, but the fate of the passing impression or sensation seems to be that of the apprehending self, too, woven and unwoven in each fleeting moment. The sensation only exists in its passing, just as it only exists in the apprehension whereby the transient self, too, has its being. Awareness of sensation depends on changing sensations, the friction of difference, just as the moment of pleasure in turn dissipates and fragments into flux. This pleasure in the very passing of the sensation, then, seems to involve a reflexive dimension, a fusion: the sensation is apprehended in that very transience that is *also* the transience of the act by which it is experienced as such. Hence, suggests Jonathan Loesberg, Pater is led 'to posit a self-validating aesthetic perception, in its own contradictory reflexiveness'. The abstraction of difference, embedded in the concreteness of sensation as experienced, permits the Paterian moment of aesthetic fulfilment: 'Here then is a sensation of flux that can be held onto, dwelt on, intensified without its own flux being denied.' Thus, 'we have arrived here at an essential sensation of self-dissolution that embodies the form of sensation as friction or contrast'. We have a 'founding sensation of a reflexive awareness of self-dissolution'.[7] Taking this further, we can suggest that in this 'founding sensation' we encounter two differences mapped on to one another: between a sensation emerging and passing away, experienced *in* this passing, and between the 'weaving and unweaving' of the self, in parallel, the self-dissolution that *is* this very experience of the sensation. And we can suggest that it is in the *intensity* of this fusion, this homology of process, a process embodying the very paradox of reflexivity, that the pleasure lies, as simultaneous fusion and release.

This emphasis on sensation itself, along with its distinctiveness on each occasion, carried on into modernism, but the latent hedonism here, so central to Paterian aestheticism and its impact on Victorian culture, was widely repudiated in the succeeding generation.[8] For the modernists, Shklovsky, in his 1917 manifesto, claimed that 'art exists that one may recover the sensation of life; it exists to make one feel things'. Hence the purpose of art is 'to impart the sensation of things as they are perceived and not as they are known'.[9] Underlying all this is a contrast between 'sensation', as the core of the aesthetic experience, and the alleged 'undifferentiated drift' of the everyday experience of life,[10] the world of tradition, cliché and banality. And we have already seen that a necessary corollary of this contrast is that since popular and media sensationalism is constituted by, and draws on, this very same dichotomy, the result is a serious challenge for aesthetic theorists who wish to defend the integrity and superiority of the arts, or even the very possibility of their separateness. This is a challenge that Deleuze, above all, proves only too willing to try to meet. Since his work provides a more extended and ambitious case for a 'pure' aesthetics of sensation than any other, it is worth detailed analysis.

The work of art, proclaims Deleuze, is 'a bloc of sensations, that is to say, a compound of percepts and affects'. He adds: 'The work of art is a being of sensation and nothing else: it exists in itself.' It is not subordinate to anything outside itself, either to human purposes or aspirations or to canons of representation in relation to the world beyond it. Nor is this affected by the material of art: 'Whether through words, colors, sounds, or stone, art is the language of sensations', he claims, adding: 'Art undoes the triple organization of perceptions, affections and opinions in order to substitute a monument composed of percepts, affects, and blocs of sensations …'[11] This series of distinctions makes it clear that what is being proposed here is not a psychology: the sensation may involve feelings or perceptions, but is clearly not reducible to them, indeed is constituted as autonomous from them; and we encounter the introduction of 'opinions' as something that art defines itself against, implying that in this respect, at least, we are still recognizably in the tradition of modernism.

As for the term 'monument', used in the passage above, and which might give the wrong impression, Deleuze explains that a monument 'does not commemorate or celebrate anything that happened but confides to the ear of the future the persistent sensations that embody the event: the constantly renewed suffering of men and women …'.[12] The term 'event' introduces a concern with time, process and movement, which are indeed central to the Deleuzian conception. At the same time, the reference to 'human suffering' suggests that in painting itself, for example, the ideal may not be abstraction – central to Greenbergian modernism – but something that remains closer to human concerns, something that accepts the challenge of figuration or the figurative even in transforming it. From this angle, it seems hardly surprising that Deleuze's choice of artist for close engagement, vital for the development of his theory of sensation, is Francis Bacon.

Apart from the inherent interest and ambition of his own account, and his evident determination to separate 'sensation' in art from 'sensationalism' in the wider culture – which enables us to ask about the plausibility of such a programme – there are two other reasons why Deleuze is particularly significant here. Firstly, his own work grows out of an immersion in that late nineteenth/early twentieth century universe of energy, nerves and force, that fusion of science, philosophy and culture crucial to the articulation of the 'circuit of sensation' discussed previously. Bergson's philosophy of process – discussed by Deleuze – grows out of this; if it is Bergson, in *Matter and Memory*, who claimed that 'our present is the very materiality of our existence, that is to say, a system of sensations and movements and nothing else',[13] it could as easily have been Deleuze. And John Rajchman points to the 'nerve-science' of the era of early cinema and its influence on the Deleuzian 'neuroaesthetic'.[14] Secondly, his critique of 'recognition' as the basis of everyday 'commonsense' and habit, along with his emphasis on the now and the new in experience, is part of a critique of the concept of representation itself, as used in art and philosophy, along with the concept of narrative. For Deleuze, these compromise the integrity of art by subordinating it to an 'outside' that cannot, anyway, perform the function intended for it. And if Kant's 'representational turn' involves a critique of metaphysics, it seems appropriate that Deleuze, in turning away from Kant, and almost single-handedly recreating a metaphysics for the late twentieth century, should turn back to Kant's two great metaphysical predecessors of the preceding century for further inspiration, Spinoza and Leibniz, particularly the former, whose materialism could be taken as an appropriate corollary of the science of process, energy and sensation.

This in turn reminds us that, with the possible exception of Badiou, Deleuze is the only one of the leading *maîtres à penser* to have emerged in France during and since the 1950s who did not have his roots in language-based analyses or in semiologies that implicitly or explicitly privilege language. Instead, language is returned to the world, the world of organism, process and energy, absorbed into thought considered as an attribute of body, Spinoza's 'thinking substance'. This relocates 'sensation' from being the product of a mysterious subject grasping or reflecting an inscrutable object to a position as the central component or compound of experience, as the nervous system in *immediate* relation with the world of forces and energies that it participates in. And art, as the language of sensation, is that aspect of thinking that works *on* and *in* sensation; again, no thought/world dichotomy is invoked here. As Daniel Smith puts it, to say that 'the aim of art is not to represent the world, but to present a sensation … is to say that every sensation, every work of art, is *singular*, and that the conditions of sensation are at the same time the conditions of the production of the *new*'.[15]

This, then, is a metaphysics of process, in which becoming, movement and virtuality replace identity, representation and fixity. Spinoza's determinism gives way here to an emphasis on flux, diversity and multiplicity, with individuality as an emergent perspective, a 'point of view' on our one world, a world that is thereby, nonetheless, uniquely different for each such perspective on it. This individualization involves not identity but performance, not thought as representation but the sign as a fusion of sensation and thought whereby individualization is simultaneously experienced and projected, produced *in* the world as a dramatization *of* it. And if this world of process and becoming is one in which 'events are the reality of the virtual',[16] then indeed the real must encompass the virtual as much as the actual. Hence this summary, by James Williams: 'The only things that can be considered to be real are both actual and virtual, made up of relations of ideas, intensities and actual things; these are individuals and signs, where signs prompt the evolution of individuals.'[17] And, overall, Dana Polan suggests that the aim is 'to go beyond the surface fixities of a culture and find those forces, those energies, those sensations that specific sociohistorical inscriptions have blocked and reified into social etiquettes and stultifying patterns of representation'.[18]

In the beginning, though, is intensity. Deleuze tells us that sensation has 'only an intensive reality'.[19] Sensations emerge out of, and express, intensities; in this sense, it is intensities that put the sensational into sensation, the element of novelty and challenge, the rawness of experience *as* experience, the experience of becoming as such. Hence intensity implies a contrast to the 'extensive', as the objective, the measurable, the world of ordinary perception. As Claire Colebrook puts it: 'Intensities are not just qualities – such as redness – they are the becoming of qualities: say, the burning and wavering infra-red light that we eventually see *as* red.' Later, Colebrook in effect elaborates aspects of this example, suggesting that sensation is not just 'seeing colour' as a sense-datum, but occurs when 'this seeing gives us the thought or image of that virtual difference that allows colour to be given, not just *as given to us* ... but as anonymous *affect*'. So we 'see' the colours of the art-work as 'there to be seen, as visual, as powers of the sensible'.[20]

This intensity of sensation, acting in and as the virtual, thus operates beneath and prior to any subject–object dichotomy; as Deleuze himself puts it: 'I *become* in the sensation and something *happens* through this sensation ...'[21] In sensation, the intensity of virtual difference is realized in becoming as event, more fundamental than any secondary differentiation into subject and object. And it is this relation, or encounter, that constitutes the reality of the sign, rather than the latter existing through representation of the object. In Flaxman's words, then: 'The space-time of cognition, of the image-sensations that affect us, we call a sign ...'[22] Seeing the implications of linking these themes of intensity, difference and the sign, Smith explains that 'The sign constitutes the limit-object of sensibility, an intensive product of differential relations: it is intensity, and not the a priori forms of space and time, that constitutes the condition of real, and not only possible, experience'.[23] Intensity *is* difference, the virtual condition of experience as actual, realized in and through sensation. Through the intensity of sensation, the virtual becomes embodied in the actual, and individual identity shifts.

Deleuze's language itself – a language of terms like resonance, vibration, envelopment, unfolding and infolding – testifies to a certain quality of unboundedness, of overflowing, in the phenomenon described, refracted as it is through metaphors that are also figurations, figuring forth, or embodying, the power of language as part of the very process it ostensibly describes. There is, after all, *movement* here, process, the 'becoming' of sensation that is also a becoming-aware. Developing a Deleuzian programme, Massumi points to the way sensation presents a 'directly disjunctive self-coinciding', in that 'It is always doubled by the feeling of having a feeling. It is self-referential.'[24] It is rather like a resonance, an echo, which remains self-continuous while occupying a complex unfolding in time. It is this resonance that indeed constitutes the intensity of sensation, and thereby also constitutes the sensation as event and experience. And this is also the process of individuation, of self-constitution, entailing as it does the aspect of performance, of dramatization. It is only thus – rather than through the impossible separation of representation – that an individual can both express, partake of this whole *and* be distinctive, a particular perspective *on* it. Hence Deleuze claims that 'intensity is individuating' and 'all individuality is intensive', and concludes: 'The intensive field of individuation determines the relations that it expresses to be incarnated in spatio-temporal dynamisms (dramatisations)'.[25]

There, in outline, we have the Deleuzian aesthetic, albeit in what are as yet rather abstract terms. It is probably film studies that has felt the impact of this perspective most strongly, partly no doubt because of the availability of Deleuze's film books in English since the late 1980s. Thus Steven Shaviro calls for a foregrounding of 'visceral, affective responses to film', describing the cinematic apparatus as 'a new mode of embodiment'.[26] Barbara Kennedy reminds us that the cinematic gaze is 'never purely visual, but also tactile, sensory, material and embodied', presenting the cinematic encounter as 'an "event", as a processual engagement of duration and movement, articulated through webs of sensation across landscapes and panoramas of space, bodies and time', whereby 'the affective is formulated through colour, sound, movement, force, intensity …', and perception is reconstructed through the 'synaesthetics of sensation'.[27] Nonetheless, Deleuze's single most extensive development of his aesthetic perspective, and his theory of sensation, comes in his close engagement with the painting of Francis Bacon, and it is this that will now be explored.

Bacon and Deleuze

Approaching Bacon, one can feel both fascination and repulsion, as if the paintings both induce shock and defend against it: the viewing process 'becomes an oscillating dialogue of intrusion and expulsion across continually adjusting permeable boundaries, a foray into psychic dislocation', as Robert Newman puts it.[28] This can lead us into a central tension running through the art of Bacon – and what makes him of particular interest is that this tension refers, in concentrated form, to a central strand in the aesthetics of modern representation and figuration generally, that is to say of any art or cultural product that aspires to refer to a world that in some sense lies beyond it. This is a tension between presence and representation, representation as a 're-presence', a doubling. That there is a forceful aspiration to presence in Bacon's work seems clear enough. In his own reading, Michel Leiris claims that Bacon conveys no message to distract us, nor any other form of distancing. In any painting of his, there are 'incandescent parts, seething with energy', against a contrasting, neutral background, and this 'marriage of hot and cold cannot fail to arouse attention and heighten the sensation of presence'.[29] Sensation *as* presence, one might say, and presence as sensation – the very being of presence *in* sensation, locking the experience in place. And the reference to energy is significant too, as though the force of presence is a force *in* the painting. For Deleuze, the task of painting is defined as 'the attempt to render visible forces that are not themselves visible', adding that 'if force is the condition of sensation, it is nonetheless not the force that is sensed, since the sensation "gives" something completely different from the forces that condition it'.[30]

At this point, Deleuze's use of the notion of 'figure' comes into play, for it is through figure that force can take visible form. Of Bacon, he claims that never since Michelangelo has anyone 'broken with figuration by elevating the Figure to such prominence'. The crucial contrast for Deleuze, then, is between the figurative, the representational, the symbolic, with its links to received meaning and convention, and figure as the direct presence of sensation (with 'figuration' as a term that can ambiguously encompass both). There is also a contrast with the retreat from figuration altogether, into abstraction: 'The Figure is the sensible form related to a sensation; it acts immediately upon the nervous system, which is of the flesh, whereas abstract form is addressed to the head, and acts through the intermediary of the brain …'.[31] This positive sense of figuration, in the production of figure, is also a process of *deformation* of figure-as-appearance, of figuration as a reproduced cliché of representation. Smith adds that Bacon's primary subject matter emerges as 'the body deformed by a plurality of forces'.[32] For Deleuze, 'sensation is the master of deformations, the agent of bodily deformations';[33] this is because sensation necessarily crosses between boundaries, levels, areas, just as it transgresses or questions subject–object distinctions. Kennedy adds that, if deformation is a kind of defiguration, a rendering of the subject depicted as 'less figurative', then, with Bacon, 'defiguration is used to achieve pure force and intensity, through the figural'.[34]

Two aspects of this are worth pursuing: the relation between deformation and violence, and the relation between deformation, appearance, and truth; and these are indeed connected. The suggestion of violence in Bacon's paintings is unmistakable. Bacon himself refers to his wish to 'unlock the valves of feeling and therefore return the onlooker to life more violently',[35] and suggests that the image, in his work, is 'an attempt to bring the figurative thing up onto the nervous system more violently and more poignantly'. This deformation of bodies *is* violence, but is a violence inseparable from deformation as a *painterly* strategy; thus Deleuze complains that merely figurative painting 'attains only the bogus violence of the represented or the signified; it expresses nothing of the violence of sensation – in other words, of the act of painting',[36] while it is the latter that is central to Bacon. This leads to the second aspect, for deformation is here a vehicle for truth; if mere appearance is vulnerable to commonsense appropriation, deformation seeks to go deeper. Bacon himself claims that 'if you want to convey fact and if you have to do it, then this can only ever be done through a form of distortion. You must distort, if you can, what is called appearance into image.' He links these points, by reflecting that the aim of the painter is always to 'reinvent the ways that appearance can be made, and be bought back into his nervous system more violently than what's been made before, because what's been made before has already become an absorbed solution'.[37]

Looking at the content of this 'deformation' takes us further. Even the most cursory glance at Bacon's paintings suggests that there is a strong emphasis on flesh – and indeed bone – so that 'presence' is thereby carried particularly strongly in this embodied form: presence-as-flesh. Newman draws our attention to the melting and spilling of bodies, the 'smudged close-ups of spasms and shrieks' whereby 'The outer shell, its solidity and continuity providing a familiar sign system ... implodes to interior ooze', and the 'amorphous, squirming remnants offer no explanations, yield no conclusions'.[38] At the same time, the lack of the more recognizably human details of individual bodily appearance can at times suggest not only a strong sense of indistinction, but a 'deformation' of the conventional boundary between human and animal. Deleuze's interpretation emphasizes the latter, concerned as he is that too much emphasis on 'flesh' risks a secular version of the doctrine of the incarnation, objectionable not primarily because it is religious but because of the recourse to meaning. 'Flesh is not sensation, though it is involved in revealing it', he argues; for 'what constitutes sensation is the becoming animal or plant ... Flesh is only the thermometer of a becoming.' Ultimately, then, 'the being of sensation is not the flesh but the compound of nonhuman forces of the cosmos, of man's nonhuman becomings ...'[39]

Here one can conjoin some suggestive thoughts of Bacon. Asking about how to catch 'the mystery of appearance within the mystery of the making', he replies that chance plays a significant role, enabling 'other shapes' to play a part in this process of deformation/reconstruction, adding that 'if the thing seems to come off at all, it comes off because of a kind of darkness which the otherness of the shape which isn't known ... conveys to it'.[40] In Deleuzian terms, one can say that the intensity of the virtual in sensation itself can be conveyed in no other way: as process, as becoming, it reveals the 'nonhuman' within – and beneath, beyond – the human, the force that 'animates' this process. (And 'nonhuman' is not 'inhuman', after all.) Nor indeed can this process really be captured in these static distinctions – human/nonhuman, organic/inorganic – which have only a relative meaning. In the virtual, they overlap, envelop each other. Hence we are, again, dramatically back in the late nineteenth-century circuit of sensation; we can envisage an 'inorganic life of things', reminiscent, Deleuze tells us, of Fechner's and Conan Doyle's 'splendid hypothesis of a nervous system of the earth'.[41]

But we are never far from this anyway, as another issue raised by this sensation/deformation nexus will show: namely, a powerful link to hysteria. Bacon's paintings frequently present us with an image of the body as visceral, yet oddly unbounded, undefined, as if flowing, shapeless, barely held together. *Reclining Woman* (1961) can serve as one example, among many. These particular images could be taken as near-perfect exemplifications of the 'body without organs', a concept ultimately derived from Artaud but one that Deleuze has made his own.[42] In effect, a clear contrast is drawn between the 'organism', as the mode of organization of organs, their subordination to specific functions, and the underlying dynamism of life itself: 'the organism is not life, it is what imprisons life'. So the 'body without organs' is not literally without organs; rather, its organs become indeterminate, interchangeable, displaced, no longer defined by their role in organization. This is important for our understanding of sensation. The latter results from the reaction between the life force of the body and the impact of an external force; this will affect a specific organ or organs, but is also displaced beyond, into another level or domain. Hence sensation 'takes an excessive and spasmodic appearance, exceeding the bounds of organic activity. It is immediately conveyed in the flesh through the nervous wave or vital emotion …', and this displacement, or series of displacements, constitutes 'the hysterical reality of the body', a process Deleuze himself presents quite explicitly as continuous with the nineteenth-century experience of the hysterical body.[43]

This hysteria can be linked to presence and the whole presence/representation dynamic. Indeed, one could ask – as Deleuze does himself – whether painting itself could be an articulation of this 'hysterical reality' of the body. If we return to 'classic' hysteria, one finds the displacement of symptoms, across the body, itself symptomatic of the simultaneous need to articulate meaning, the impossibility of articulating it, and the impossibility of not articulating it, in this register of the symbolic. Hysteria could thereby testify to the desperation to avoid representation and the impossibility of succeeding, making the connection to art all the more explicit. And it is a connection that Deleuze draws on directly, in arguing that 'there is a special relation between painting

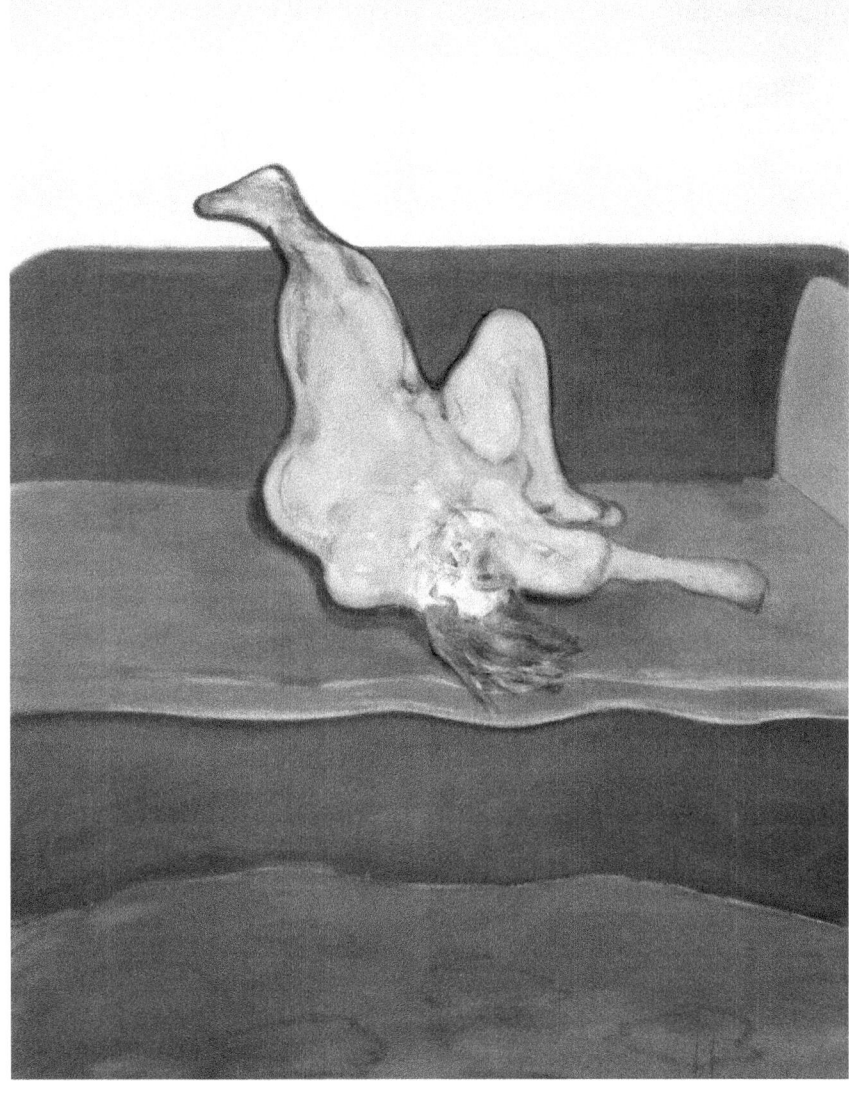

Francis Bacon, *Reclining Woman* (1961) London, Tate Gallery © The Estate of Francis Bacon. All rights reserved. DACS 2014

and hysteria', at least insofar as painting is based in sensation, and does not try to evade this by recourse to abstraction or the figurative. 'Painting directly attempts to release the presences beneath representation, beyond representation.' Hence: 'Everywhere there is a presence acting directly on the nervous system, which makes representation, whether in place or at a distance, impossible.' Thus we find presence, as we do insistently, in Bacon – and the hysteric.

'The hysteric is at the same time someone who imposes his or her presence, but also someone for whom things and beings are present, *too* present, and who attributes to everything and communicates to every being this excessive presence', so that in this excess we encounter 'the identity of an already-there and an always-delayed'.[44] Presence *insists*; it breaks through the conventions, the boundaries, of the representational economy; but this very insistence makes it excessive, carries its own overspill, displacement. It can never be present enough, and is always present too much; it calls on those very possibilities of representation that it tries to burst through, to destroy. And how could it be otherwise? Representation is re-presentation, an ostensible 'doubling' of presence that cannot reveal presence save as simulation. If representation is a kind of evasion of hysteria, an avoidance of its necessity, it nonetheless calls it into being through its very attempt to affirm presence through representing it, inscribing and inviting a counter-attack in the name of presence. Hence the significance of the figural or the figure, in Bacon, concentrating the aspiration to presence in its very intensity.

We find we have been led to a point which may not have been where Deleuze intended; instead of sensation entailing an end of representation, through presence, we find the possibility that the conflict between the two may be not so easily or conclusively resolved, or even ineradicable. Exploring this further takes us into the links between Deleuze's critique of representation and his critique of popular sensationalism, crucial for our understanding not only of Deleuze but of the challenges posed by sensation and sensationalism to aesthetics itself, going to the heart of its concerns.

Sensation without sensationalism?

What has become known as the 'screaming popes' series includes some of the most famous – and most discussed – of Bacon's paintings. They are known to have been derived from the Velázquez portrait *Pope Innocent X* (1650), and – in the case of the scream itself – to have been influenced by the famous image of the nurse shot on the Odessa steps in Eisenstein's film *Battleship Potemkin* (1925). As is often the case with Bacon, then, we are as aware of sources and influences as we may be puzzled by his own aims. It seems clear that the scream is not – or is not *intended* as – a howl of anguish at the human condition, or a protest at modern alienation;[45] Bacon himself contrasts his work here with the Edvard Munch *Scream* (1893), claiming that 'I'm just trying to make images as accurately off

Francis Bacon, *Study after Velázquez's Portrait of Pope Innocent X* (1953) Des Moines, Des Moines Art Center © The Estate of Francis Bacon. All rights reserved. DACS 2014

my nervous system as I can ... I'm not saying anything'. What he tells us, most directly, is that 'I wanted to paint the scream more than the horror'.[46]

The scream more than the horror: it may be that some visible horror or experience of horror produced the scream, or that the scream could induce horror, but it is the scream, as sensation-in-itself, that Bacon is trying to express in paint. One might say: a scream cleansed of what might make it either meaningful, biographically or politically, or 'sensational', as a media-inflected magnification of the drama or story lying behind it. What Luigi Ficacci writes of another Bacon work might be equally pertinent here: the painting shows us 'the lacerating expression of a cry, regardless of its nature or cause'. It is a cry 'reduced to its wild force, beyond the normal human need to identify and resolve the causes of malaise'.[47] So Bacon's scream exists beyond the human, beyond communication, connecting rather with the intuitive level of sensation itself. It could even be said that perhaps it is *we* who scream; Bacon's grotesque mouths remain open, caught in a strangled, interminable, eternal silence.

Moving towards Deleuze, one can say that the scream is not uncaused, but that the 'intensive forces' cannot themselves be captured in the scream. 'If we scream, it is always as victims of invisible and insensible forces that scramble every spectacle, and that even lie beyond pain and feeling.'[48] And if we think of our own confrontation with this scream, or the image of it, the scream in its relation to our sense of the other, in this context of ignorance of cause or context, how can we relate to it? Elsewhere, earlier in his work, Deleuze refers to the example of a terrified face – he is not explicitly referring to Bacon here, but might as well be – and suggests that its 'expressive value' lies in its revelation of a possible world, a terrifying world, the very sense of the 'possible' in and beyond the actual.[49] Williams glosses this as claiming: 'The other individual does not show or reveal an actual world to me. Instead, it shows a different relation of sensations, intensities and Ideas (the possible world is outside the frame and only expressed through the other's dramatisation of that world).'[50] In this sense, neither Bacon nor Deleuze show much interest in communication as such: relations between subjects become relations of envelopment, contraction, resonance, intensities, at a sub-conscious and sub-rational level, as possibilities actualized – dramatized – through the sensory.

The core of Deleuze's treatment of Bacon's scream paintings, however, takes us directly into his critique of the sensational, his determination to isolate 'sensation' from the pollution of the spectacular, the vulgarity of popular sensationalism. In the context of the scream/horror contrast, the dilemma or choice that faces Bacon, according to Deleuze, is most cogently summarized here, by Smith: '*either* he paints the horror (the 'sensational') and does not paint the scream, because he represents a horrible spectacle and introduces a story; *or* he paints the scream directly (the 'sensation') and does not paint the visible horror, because the scream is necessarily the capture of an invisible force.'

Hence, 'the violence of a horrible spectacle must be renounced in order to attain the violence of the sensation'.[51] This distinction certainly seems fundamental to Deleuzian aesthetics. Thus he refers to 'the action of forces upon the body, or sensation (the opposite of the sensational)'; and he suggests that Bacon has always tried to eliminate the sensational in his art.[52]

This returns us to the figurative and figure (or the figural), and the contrast between them. For Deleuze, the two aspects of the figurative are illustration and narrative, both of which trigger recognition, and both of which distract us from sensation, from the figure as constituted in the experience of the painting. As Andrew Brighton puts it, 'in a painting we should *experience* the sensation of a figured body rather than *recognise* the sensation of a depicted, figurative body'.[53] Rather similar language is used in Bacon's own reflections on his work. 'Illustration', for Bacon, means images that illustrate texts, and images that are secondary to appearances, merely imitating them. Thus he claims that he wants his art to be 'deeply suggestive or deeply unlocking of areas of sensation other than simple illustration of the object'. And 'story' plays a role equivalent to 'narrative', as in his observation that 'the moment the story is elaborated, the boredom sets in; the story talks louder than the paint'.[54] A notoriously self-critical artist, Bacon is known to have destroyed a considerable number of his own canvases, particularly when he felt them to be too close to narrative, illustration or sensationalism.

But are there nonetheless problems for Bacon here? As has been indicated, his own modernism, based as it is on 'figuration', in some sense of that term, clearly takes its distance from the abstraction that is for Clement Greenberg the purest form of modernism in painting. Not surprisingly, he encounters criticism from that quarter. Greenberg accuses him of cheapness, coarseness, the use of 'transparent devices', and adds: 'Bacon is the one example in our time of *inspired* safe taste – taste that's inspired in the way in which it searches out the most up-to-date of your "rehearsed responses"'.[55] In short: far from escaping the inauthenticities of sensationalism and cliché, Bacon merely reproduces them. Bacon himself seems to accept that in some degree this is inevitable, and that the resulting tension – not present in abstraction – is a powerful force in his art, as it may be indeed in *any* art that aspires to retain some connection with a human subject matter. Hence: 'I think that art is recording; I think it's reporting.' And, in a late interview, he explicitly 'confesses' that 'in spite of theoretically longing for the image to be made of irrational marks, inevitably illustration has to come into it'.[56]

Indeed, this is a painter who is most clearly subject to literary influences and inspirations, and who can hardly be said to avoid the figurative in practice. Both the figurative and the linear are significant in Bacon, and both conjure up again the issues of recognition, resemblance and representation. Expanding on one aspect of this, Brighton suggests that the linear 'works with the recognition of things rather than the optical sensation of the painterly'. One can say, then, that his work both stimulates *and* resists interpretation, involves *and* questions recognition. Of a 1971 painting, a triptych, Brighton writes that it disrupts our normal reflexes, making us conscious of them, in that it draws on and stimulates our awareness of the body: 'It calls forth acts of spontaneous recognition below the level of thought comparable to our spontaneous actions when encountering people in the street …' Bacon thereby 'sets up expectations of norms and fears of abnormalities'.[57] This does indeed engage us at a visceral level – sensation is crucially in play here – but this does not exclude words, meanings, interpretations, issues of representation; rather it exists in a tension with these that is part and parcel of the power of the work itself. Thus criticisms of Bacon – and his own self-critical strain – have a tendency to end up confirming the appeal or significance of his work, by reinforcing the suggestion that there may be something irreducible about the tension between presence and representation that is central to it.[58]

These points suggest the need to 'reconfigure' figuration, in that figure (the figural) does not need to be seen as existing in a sphere that is incompatible with representation; rather, that although there *is* indeed a tension between figure and the figurative, this is a tension that is in some sense *within* representation. Figure expresses the force of the other, the non-representational, threatening and fracturing representation even as it relies on it. This might be a way of understanding Brighton's claim that Bacon's paintings 'threaten nature speaking virulently through art … The instant horror, revulsion and fascination of these images attest that at some level we do experience them as real.' Thus, through these bodies of sensation, the horrors of nature are 'immanent within the ambiguity of fractured pictorial conventions'. He adds: 'The image incites a perceptual panic, a need to make sense, to conceptualise and to recognise …',[59] and it seems as though this is a version of the hysteria we have already encountered, confirming as it does the need to 'make sense' and the impossibility of doing so, the impetus to representation in the very craving for, and flight from, presence.

Here it can be pointed out that Deleuze himself seems to admit that representation is ultimately ineradicable, even if it is transfigured through art. While he defiantly asserts that 'no art and no sensation have ever been representational',[60] he also accepts that since fighting the figurative involves producing the figure, 'the pure presence of the figure is indeed the reconstitution of a representation, the recreation of a figuration' whereby we again encounter the 'hysteria' of painting. Once again, the very attempt to avoid representation seems to produce the hysteria Deleuze associates with the latter, this time as a feature of his own argument. Deleuze is even forced to acknowledge a type of analogy, whereby 'a sensible resemblance is produced',[61] but via sensation itself, rather than symbolically, via a code. As in Bacon's accounts, in his interviews, this resemblance is clearly distinct from the *initial* appearance of similarity, the arena of recognition; but if this is still *resemblance*, can this really occur without *some* implicit recourse to 'recognition'? Could one sensation be experienced *as* similar to another without implicitly drawing on established meanings even while transforming them, not being merely a mechanical application of them? And if the concept of 'figure' is to be of use, then it must exist in *some* relation to the (problematical) basis of representation in recognition, even if it also challenges this.

We are now in a position to move towards an assessment of the plausibility of a Deleuzian aesthetics of sensation. We can summarize Deleuze's position as follows. An aesthetics of sensation must take its distance from the banalities of everyday life. We live in a world of taken-for-granted, commonsense assumptions, which Kant's critical philosophy uncritically accepts as a 'harmony of the faculties'. This 'common sense' is a framework of recognition, permitting identification and continuity, and it is on this basis that codes of representation are based.[62] These become all the more elaborate and dangerous – dangerously persuasive, dangerously pervasive – in the era of mass media reproduction. In this context, 'sensationalism' is a mediated, intensified version of the clichés of everyday repetition, made startling and dramatic, apparently 'new', through this magic of the media. In order to avoid all this, 'we', as artists or audience, must return to the *intensity* of sensation itself, as experience; it is this that the artist transmits, or must endeavour to transmit.

We have already seen that there are grounds for questioning the plausibility of the first part of this, the underlying critique of representation and recognition, at least to the extent that this involves the possibility of eliminating these categories altogether. But, beyond this aspect, it is important to unpack the second part of the argument, and see that there is actually a dual critique mounted by Deleuze here: a critique of the sensational, and a critique of cliché. He himself tends to fuse them. Thus, writing of Bacon, he claims: 'The violence of sensation is opposed to the violence of the represented (the sensational, the cliché)'; and 'Sensation is the opposite of the facile and the ready-made, the cliché, but also of the "sensational"...'[63] The implication here is that the sensational, ostensibly in opposition to the everyday world of routine, repetition, and cliché, is actually part and parcel of that world: the sensational is dramatized, eye-catching cliché.

Up to a point, this is indeed a useful insight, but clearly the role of 'cliché' here needs further examination. If, for Deleuze, intensity and sensation are closely connected, it has to be said that there is also an intensity to his own engagement with cliché. Here, indeed, we seem to reach the panic-stricken, paranoid-hysterical core of this High Modernist aesthetic. All around, Deleuze is menaced by the threat, the perils, of cliché. It is endlessly, obsessively, denounced: Chapter 11 of the Bacon book consists of little else. 'We are besieged by photographs that are illustrations, by newspapers that are narrations, by cinema-images, by television-images. There are psychic clichés just as there are physical clichés – ready-made perceptions, memories, phantasms.'[64] Indeed, clichés have always already invaded the canvas: the artist has to go to extraordinary lengths to wipe them away, chase them off, expel them, using 'free marks' and chance to disrupt the ever-present risk of the figurative.[65] In this nightmare world, 'even the reactions against clichés are actually creating clichés ...'. Indeed so, one might respond; for in the context of this modernist tradition that Deleuze himself espouses, the attempt to escape cliché via shock – including the shock of 'sensation' – has itself become cliché, a tired repetition. Poor Deleuze: 'The fight against clichés is a terrible thing.'[66] All these horrors; it is enough to make one scream ... But that, too, would be a cliché ...

Considering this, one might firstly observe the characteristically modernist assimilation of the relatively undifferentiated, the ordinary, the everyday, to the world of cliché, banality and superficiality, so that the everyday is presented as always already stigmatized, as it were, with an implicit disparagement of the mundane, of the cyclical, relatively repetitive aspects of life. Thus Jacques Rancière can complain that Deleuze is 'too indebted to the modernist dramaturgy of the sublime break'.[67] And one can see how Deleuze is led to this. On the face of it, after all, there are real continuities between 'sensation' and 'sensationalism'; drawing as he does on the late nineteenth-century literature, where the physiological, the psychological and the media-related senses are closely linked, Deleuze seems aware of this himself. But clearly, this is a threat to his aspiration to found an unpolluted aesthetics. The way out, then, is to assimilate 'sensationalism' to the rejected world of cliché and everyday recognition.

The problem is that this rather desperate move runs up against the objection that sensationalism, too, seems to make the same move as Deleuzian sensation; it, too, defines itself at least partly *against* the everyday world of everyday continuity and ordinariness. To be sensational is to be extraordinary, vivid, intense, *different* ... Surely *both* these moves need to be questioned. We have seen that the very distinction between the 'everyday' and the 'sensation(al)' is contextual, relative; they are mutually constitutive. As for the sensational, one can of course agree with Deleuze that it is never as 'sensational' as it seems, since it draws to some extent on existing cultural resources, existing representational canons; but we have seen reason to believe this to be true of Deleuzian 'sensation' also. Can one really put the sensation into sensation without implicitly putting the sensational in as well? Isn't there an essential continuity here? In the cultural experience of the modern, 'sensation' occupies a precarious place between cliché and the everyday on the one hand, and the sensational, on the other; or, one could equally well say that it encompasses, slides into and across, *both* these zones. Tentative, provisional distinctions can be made; but there can be no sense in trying to make a strict distinction between 'sensation' and 'sensationalism'. Everything we have seen in this discussion suggests that they overlap, run into each other, subvert and replenish each other; ultimately, they inhabit each other.

Deleuze plays on the double meaning of *cliché* in French, as stereotyped thinking and as snapshot: both are 'born out of an instantaneous act that requires little effort and that results in a freezing of reality into a reified image', as Polan summarizes it. This is illuminating; one can indeed see connections here, reminding us of the essential continuity between the mediated culture of sensation and the immediacy of everyday sensation as such, just as it suggests the intensity of focus that can render *both* of them 'sensational'. It is all very well for Deleuze, as expounded here by Polan, to denounce 'the photographic cliché, in which the seeing goes too quickly past the photo to a represented world',[68] but this is the whole point and nature of the culture of sensation: the sensation works precisely *through* this speed, this assimilation, this instantaneity of the circuit of sensation as a feature of modern experience. It is entirely understandable – and may well be laudable – that the modern artist who is particularly aware of this, and sensitive to it, might want to differentiate his art from this dimension, give it some autonomy in order to explore the art of his art, and thus *not* have it reducible to the sensational moment of the circuit; but the artist can only do this against precisely this background, one that cannot ultimately be transcended or evaded, even if it can be transformed, transfigured. The artist is both *against* and *within* this culture, and that paradox suggests both the possibilities and the limitations of his task.

We can now consider the wider implications of this. After all, part of the hold of a 'culture of consumption' is precisely due to the fact that it is also a 'culture of sensation'; each helps to drive the other, and no High Modernist or elitist bemoaning of the fact, or yearning for 'true' sensation, makes one iota of difference, or contributes to our understanding of this intriguing phenomenon. The result, in Deleuze, is an aesthetic theory that gives a welcome centrality to themes of embodiment, intensity and sensation, but is ultimately narrow and flawed through presenting an inadequate theorization of the relation between sensation and representation, whether in the arts or popular culture, and through excluding whole swathes of cultural experience from its purview. And these exclusions and purifications even enter into the analysis of art itself, narrowly defined: much of it turns out to be corrupted by cliché, narrative, illustration, sensationalism … Thus an aesthetic justification for Art seems to have had the consequence that the category itself has shrunk alarmingly in its range of application. This outcome seems all the more disappointing in that, as shown in earlier sections, sensation can serve as a linkage between these apparently separate areas of 'high' and 'low' culture. In popular culture, sensation offers one of life's pleasures: the thrill, the novelty of excitement. 'Sensation' is a proof of life itself, an embodiment or dramatization of life. Such sensations can be pleasurable or painful, exciting or tiring; they are certainly intense, visceral, engaging. They may indeed be emotionally draining. And all this can be just as true of our engagement with art, whether as artists or as audience: 'sensation' cannot be used as the basis for a thorough demarcation of what can at best be separated by tentative, shifting boundaries, little more than differing emphases within a broad notion of the aesthetic.

Let us take, for another example, the issue of 'deformation', raised above. If it is true that, for artists, 'mere' appearance has to be transformed in being rendered as 'art', and in the case of Bacon, among others, it can be said to be thereby 'deformed' into art, is this not also true, in a sense, of the fate of appearance and everyday narrative in sensationalism? The mere appearance, the phenomenal 'truth', is 'deformed', through media techniques of abbreviation and exaggeration, into a 'sensational' truth, a truth of mediated experience, that can be as distinctive and provocative as any work of art. The point is not to argue that these are identical, but that they are sufficiently close, as variants of a pattern, to allow for an underlying continuity of cultural interpretation, rather than for this to be closed off by the uncritical reproduction of the hoary old dichotomy of 'art' and 'mass culture'. In their differing ways, both Poe and Bacon may be better guides to the tensions that occur *between* these, yet *within* this common problematic – particularly tensions between presence and representation – than Deleuze himself, valuable though his insights into the aesthetics of sensation undoubtedly are. Ironically, much of Deleuze's language of sensation in the context of art draws implicitly on these continuities, and the sense of 'sensation' as an experience that is prior to its own classification in evaluative terms, yet this insight is not developed. He is torn between giving us an analysis of sensation using a theoretical framework that would include both the narrower and the broader senses of the term, and remaining uncritically within one of these, thereby trapped into reproducing a limited and limiting, elitist model; and it is the latter that tends to win out.

Finally, let us remember and recover the radical cutting edge to modernism, often obscured by the concerns with methodological purity. Let us take another painter, Lily, struggling with her painting in *To the Lighthouse*. Virginia Woolf tells us: 'Phrases came. Visions came. Beautiful pictures. Beautiful phrases. But what she wished to get hold of was that very jar on the nerves, the thing itself before it has been made anything.'[69] Here, Woolf describes perfectly the challenge of the creative ideal, of capturing the very moment, the very 'feel', of sensation-in-itself. But how is this to be interpreted? Traditionally, there would be an emphasis on the quality of the sensation, its fusion of moral and aesthetic ideals, transformed into art. Not just any old sensation will do; there is an implicit hierarchy of experiences. On the face of it, modernism breaks decisively with this. The radicalism of modernism is the implication that experience simply *is* experience; there are no experiences that are *the* experiences that constitute the 'proper' subject matter for art or literature. In principle, *any* sensation is available to be transformed into art. This democratic insight, as it were, the potential universality of this experience of sensation, confirms the relativism of the distinction between the 'mundane' and the 'sensational'. Hence, again, the essential parallel here, whereby art and sensationalism both emerge from a background that they simultaneously constitute as such. The 'sensation' – whether as basis of art or sensationalism – simply *is* the mundane, but experienced as a challenge, with intensity and focus. And in either case, this experience then has to be 'worked up', into art or the media sensation. The fundamental aesthetic structure in place here is the same, whatever the other differences.

And there are differences, of course. If we return to the phrase 'intensity and focus', we know Deleuze tells us much about the former, but perhaps we also need to consider the latter. If we focus on focus, this idea of *awareness* as an aspect of sensation, then this could mark a significant difference of degree between art, as an immediately *reflective* grasp of sensation, a turn towards consciousness and self-consciousness *in* experience, and the 'sensational experience', in which the immersion in the immediacy of impact means that the aspect of reflective awareness is secondary, relatively undeveloped. The challenge for a cultural aesthetics is to theorize these two dimensions, or poles, of the experience of sensation – the relation between sensation as immersion/embodiment and as awareness/reflection – *without* allowing these to emerge as mutually exclusive, and identifying aesthetics with the concerns of one rather than the other. *Both* dimensions will be present, in varying ways, and to varying extents, in *both* art, conventionally defined, and popular culture. This challenge would, as we have implied, involve theorizing the figural in relation to the dynamic of presence and representation that runs through these two dimensions – a challenge that would be well worth meeting. Indeed, we can recall Pater here, for it could be that he comes close to meeting the challenge, even if he himself retains a characteristic primary allegiance to elite art. At the same time, his emphasis on the passing moment invites further consideration: we might, perhaps paradoxically, want to deepen this by trying to open up the possibility of a field or space of sensation. But we can best do this by moving on, into a brief consideration of a painter whose relentless abstraction seems to mark quite a contrast with Bacon.

The web of sensation

The early paintings of Bridget Riley provide some of the most arresting and eye-catching images of the 1960s. The patterned or broken black and white stripes, pyramids, circles and cones, producing sensations of shimmering or twisting movement, of lines shifting to and fro, provoked an inability to focus and a range of distortions, flickerings and dazzling effects in the visual field; indeed, some spectators complained of feeling dizzy, that the paintings made their eyes hurt.

By 1965, with these images reproduced on mugs, wallpaper, furnishings and clothes, even high fashion, Riley – a conventional modernist in such matters – was denouncing this 'explosion of commercialism' and 'hysterical sensationalism'.[70] In her study of Riley's art in the context of its time, Frances Follin writes that her pictures:

> … carried with them a multiplicity of meanings and associations that were so bound up with the concerns of the period that they produced a sensation of immediate recognition in their audience which was visually compelling then, and which has made them evocative of the period ever since.[71]

Bridget Riley, *Current* (1964) New York, Museum of Modern Art

It is easy to see how this can encompass the dimension of cultural investment and magnification that we refer to as 'sensationalism', just as this provides further evidence of the difficulty, even the impossibility, of any hard and fast excision of this cultural potential from an aesthetics of sensation wedded to the purity of art. Indeed, Riley's own reflections on her work can help us understand this.

Let us take another of these early paintings. It was initially to be called *Discharge*, 'with the idea of arrows, say, being discharged in your face as you looked at it', but – perhaps troubled by the evident hint of violence here – she settled on *Static*, in the sense of 'a field of static electricity', inducing 'visual prickles' from a 'sparkling texture'. The idea for the painting originated from a drive up a mountain on a hot day in which a vast expanse of shale was encountered at the summit, experienced as visually confusing: was this 'shimmering shale' near or far, flat or round? Getting out of the car intensified the sensation, and into her mind came images of 'a mass of tiny glittering units like a rain of arrows'.[72]

Such experiences, felt deeply enough, are the stuff of artistic creativity, but never in any predictable fashion. Always willing enough to use the language of 'sensation' to characterize her artistic preoccupations, Riley writes:

> ... if sensation alone is the yardstick, then the painting has to be a place that allows for the relatively independent workings of sensation. Although in the objective world sensations are always prompted by something or other, they are not necessarily bound to whatever may trigger them off. They have a life of their own, as every painter knows when he is working: they change, but not in any logical way ...

Bridget Riley, *Static 1* (1966) New York, Coll. Hannelore B. Schulhof

Once again, we encounter the idea of disjunctions and disconnections in these circuits of sensation, the way in which causes do not produce predictable effects. 'Disruption, friction, sudden ease and deceptively smooth passages all play an important part in the web of sensation', she claims.[73] There is, nonetheless, a sense of shared patterns or homologies underlying it all, patterns obscurely felt *and* recognized by the painter, since this is in some sense a transfigured product of her experience. The 'shimmering shale' on the mountain appears to bear no relation to the dots on the canvas, yet the sensations of the one, produced by the hazy movements of light and shadow, the dazzle of sunlight, on the shale, manifest in this obscurely patterned overall effect, is mapped into the patterned effects of the relation between the spots on the canvas, and thus in the sensations experienced by the painter and the spectator. One might add here that if, at a quick glance, one seems to see identical dots in straight lines in the painting, this is wrong on both counts: moving physically *in relation to* the picture, and *around in* the picture, brings out the sensation of waves and the differential impact of scale and level. Feeling, as sensation, operates as mediator between sight and the forces and energies of the world, just as the *way* this works seems to depend on these presupposed or virtual shared patterns, enabling us to refer to a 'web' of sensation, or a field that links painter, painting and spectator, just as it relates object, painting and painter. Memories of past sensations thus come to have some sort of 'correspondence' with those in the painting, but it is indirect; the 'shine' in a painting, for example, is not the 'original' shine (of hair, water or whatever), but something the painter produces on the surface of the canvas.[74]

In elaborating this idea of a web or field of sensation, we can begin by noting that the use of words like 'texture' indicates that we are in a sensory world, that perception is always *embodied*. Riley endorses Merleau-Ponty's claim that 'to look at an object is to inhabit it',[75] and observes that colour sensation involves not only shimmering and glittering but also dullness and brilliance, buoyancy, density and softness, all 'sensory relationships' that engage us through movement, orientation and response. 'For me', she writes, 'nature is not landscape, but the dynamism of visual forces', event rather than appearance, and her pictures convey 'the free play of visual forces' within a 'controlled structure'. These forces and energies cannot be *seen* by the eye; they have to be *felt*, sensed, as rhythm or movement – and these can really only be sensed in their passing. Repetition and rhythm are at the root of movement, and since there can be no movement without stasis, no change without a constant, this provides both the challenge to the painter, and the solution: 'If you can bring the two together in an image you have a dynamic, something that is not descriptive of movement but which gives the sensation of it.' Sensation, then, arises from the contrast, which may, and typically does, involve a pattern of *repeated* contrasts. In painting, '*contrast* is the basic relationship',[76] although it may take very subtle forms. For example, Riley suggests that the energy of colour is not released by direct opposition, rather by instability, 'a freely floating flux': a slight influence from a neighbouring colour sends the colour off-balance, releasing energy, and it is particularly along borders, edges, between colours and shapes, that this effect is most intense.[77]

This web, or field, is defined fundamentally through *depth*, 'the primary spatial dimension' in perception. This has two aspects: the space between the picture plane and the spectator, which is where the painting 'takes place'; and the 'interior space' of the painting, a layered, shallow depth.[78] This 'pictorial space' is 'made up of the contrasts and the different planes which colours adopt on the canvas', so that the paintings offer 'a space which invites and accommodates a certain group of sensations'. Space is 'grounded in colour organisation',[79] so that colour planes can take up different positions in space, advancing or receding, having different weights, and thereby bringing about a field of forces; indeed, recessing colours or pushing them forwards can produce the sense of rhythm. Riley distinguishes this sense of space both from traditional perspective and from the more modern fashion of presenting the painting as two-dimensional, describing both approaches as 'geometric'. And here, there is a significant disagreement with Greenberg's modernism. For him, the core of modern painting is the acceptance of the limitations of the medium: 'the flat surface, the shape of the support, the properties of the pigment'.[80] For Riley, the effect of this is to reduce picture-plane to physical surface, medium to means; the medium *as a whole* is the relationship between these means and the painter.[81] This reminds us of Op art's challenge to modernism 'in its insistence on the bodily character of perception and therefore of aesthetic appreciation', as Follin puts it.

Perhaps the most distinctive aspect of Riley's own 'fields of sensation' is the way they systematically disrupt the eye's ability to settle. As Follin suggests, 'there is no point at which the viewer can stand and perceive a static entity. The image is always both "here" and "there", sliding between points of focus.'[82] Riley confirms this: 'There is seldom a single focal point in my paintings',[83] although 'multi-focal' rather than 'unfocused' would be the more accurate term. So: 'What you focus on is *not* what you see. One looks *here* and colour is *there*.'[84] She adds that 'Focusing isn't just an optical activity, it is also a mental one'. The sensational field is the field of overall *awareness*, a sensory, not a purely visual dimension, a field across which sensations 'play', flickering and shimmering, disrupting and disturbing, a field of contrasts, tensions and nuances that produce the sensational effect through this very decentring, this inability to stop the flow, the movement, the evanescent effects. Light that dazzles, dissolves focus, like standing in a field of energy. What she claims of Mondrian could also be applied to her: 'the colour weights and planes … provoke relationships that concentrate or diffuse attention'. Riley inserts her paintings in the very diffusion of experience, in a field of scattering; the sensational becomes the concentration *of* and *in* the scattering, not its antithesis. And in positioning herself here, she reminds us that sensation 'is as much inside me as it is "out there" in the work',[85] and this would clearly be as true of the spectator. It is crucial, then, that we find *ourselves* located here, as part of the field.

This tells us not just about the *effects* of sensation, but also about its *construction*. We encounter here a series of situations that can be mapped on to each other: the original experience, the later sensation induced or experienced by the artist in painting, and the sensation produced in the viewer. Each involves a break, a discontinuity, between the physical energies of the world, and sight, in which it is feeling, sensation itself, with no determinate meaning – indeed, fundamentally with no 'meaning' at all – that mediates the gap, through sensing rhythm and movement, but can do so because it is already *implicitly* there, in the pattern of relations, just as sensation is there as outcome, as effect. What is distinctive in this particular interpretation is how sensation becomes a function of the *field*, not just a matter of startling or eye-catching shocks, even suggesting the possibility that that this might be the basis of sensation in its more obviously dramatic forms. If we break the 'field' down, retrospectively or analytically, into its 'scatterings', it can be seen also as a synthetic process: it can be built up, built towards, so that at some point a painting 'released a perceptual experience that flooded the whole', as Riley puts it, of her own activity in painting, or perhaps the field can be seen to 'accommodate the sensation it solicits'.[86]

Finally, though, we can see that questions of meaning are still present. If we look at a painting by Titian, with a mythological subject, Riley points out that there is 'a gap between the mythic illusion which one can "read" and the immediacy of the sensations one experiences …'; and this 'between' is a matter of relationships, rather than elements, signs or symbols, since it is here that Titian creates his 'intangible web' of sensations in the painting.[87] This gap, then, incorporates a horizontal or reflexive dimension, a reminder that sense-making may, in this context, be indissolubly linked to sensation-making but is not reducible to it. Hence meanings and memories come into play at all stages of these circuits of sensation, from the original experience, mediated through memories and meanings, personal and cultural, through to the problematic 'recognition' by the painter in the emergent work, to the attempts to 'make sense' of it, of *its* impact and *their* feelings, by spectators. Similarly, 'focusing' points both ways: towards sensation, and towards mind, through a relation to consciousness. All this entails that sensation, then, can be seen to grow out of an existing hinterland, or produce its own, through the very process by which it emerges *as* sensation; and this 'hinterland' is necessarily one of experiences always already impregnated with a cultural dimension.

In principle, then, it is hardly surprising if Riley's own work creates its own challenges of meaning and interpretation, being associated, for example, with crises of perception in the culture of the 1960s, including the hallucinatory effects of drug experimentation, along with the visual challenges of the spectacle of the city experienced through modern technology, such as the car windscreen at night.[88] Ultimately, the homology between sensation and its hinterland, its background of relative un-feeling, of experiential 'anaesthesia', and sensationalism and *its* hinterland, as the everyday, the ordinary, illustrates the difficulty of securing any hard and fast distinction between them. In Riley's case, this is further overlaid by the homology between the tension between diffusion and concentration in her work, and that in the modern world more generally – something which indeed she seems to notice, intriguingly commenting that the problem of focusing could be related to the loss of certainties, of central values, that characterize the modern age.[89] And this is an area where Riley's work points us forward to later chapters of this book, to the necessity, in particular, to explore the relations between conscious focusing and diffuse awareness and the constitution of the 'field of sensation' as a feature both of everyday experience and of art and media forms, such as, most notably, cinema, where these themes become particularly central.

5

The Distractions of the Modern

A spectacular adventure

Into the world of American newspapers in 1913, with their circulation wars and rampant sensationalism,[1] stepped an ambitious young journalist, Djuna Barnes, who would contribute short magazine articles on a variety of topics to several New York papers over the next six years, but became particularly associated with the magazine section of the *World*. One eye-catching piece, from November 1914, recounted 'My Adventures Being Rescued', in which she submitted herself to three different ways of being brought down by firemen from a high building. Swung on a rope a hundred feet above the pavement, she tells us: 'I dangled and sprawled against the horizon … A drowsy expectancy lay along Sixty-Eighth Street and touched the spectators with a sort of awesome wonder. I was a "movie", flashing transient pictures upon a receptive sky.'[2] Clearly this is not a journalist who is afraid of making a spectacle of herself;[3] nor does she miss the telling analogy with film spectacle, the appeal of which had become increasingly central to the popular consciousness of modernity over the preceding decade or so.

But it is an article she wrote a month or two earlier that is particularly worth lingering over, an article with a darker hue. Entitled 'How It Feels to be Forcibly Fed',[4] it can be read as a direct, sympathetic engagement with the politics of the suffragette movement and, in particular, a response to the forced feeding used by police and prison warders to break the resistance of protesting hunger strikers in prison in the UK. That this could also be about to happen in the US would have been brought home to her readers by reference to the possibility of it being inflicted on an agitator currently on hunger strike in a New York prison, and by articles in the news section alluding to current developments in suffrage politics ('Denver Man to Head Anti-Suffrage War', and 'Suffragists See Victory in Four Western States'). The article is written in her usual concise, pungent style, and is accompanied by photographic illustrations.

Typically she plunges straight in. 'Surely I have as much nerve as my English sisters?', she asks herself, as she is bound helplessly in a white sheet on a table by a doctor and accompanying warders, and goes past the point of no return: 'And then I knew my soul stood terrified before a little yard of red rubber tubing ... It was the most concentrated moment of my life.' Her throat burned from the effect of the cocaine and disinfectant mixture that had been sprayed into it, and the tube was inserted. She broke into a cold sweat; her heart plunged irregularly; a dull ache spread over her chest: 'It is utterly impossible to describe the anguish of it ... Unbidden visions of remote horrors danced madly through my mind ... Unsuspected nerves thrilled pain tidings that racked the area of my face and bosom.'[5] As she hovers on the verge of fainting, she enters a dissociated state: lights and windows seemed to sway; 'I, too, was detached and moved as the room moved', as if a 'physical mechanism', yet oddly separate from it. 'I saw in my hysteria a vision of a hundred women in grim prison hospitals, bound and shrouded on tables just like this ...', and she wondered whether, if she choked, the 'callous warders and the servile doctors' would carry on regardless, so that the 'shrouds' would truly become her winding sheets ... Then, suddenly, it was over. 'I had shared the greatest experience of the bravest of my sex. The torture and outrage of it burned in my mind; a dull, shapeless, wordless anger arose to my lips, but I only smiled.'[6]

So what are we to make of all this? Barnes herself writes: 'For me it was an experiment. It was only tragic in my imagination. But it offered sensations sufficiently poignant to compel comprehension of certain of the day's phenomena.' In her effort to understand what the suffragettes were going through, she could only share their experiences vicariously. If it was bad for her, and she was 'playacting', she reflects, 'how they who actually suffered the ordeal in its acutest horror must have flamed at the violation of the sanctuaries of their spirits'.[7] Yet to describe the sensations she experienced as 'poignant' seems to underplay the real anguish conveyed by the intensity of her own account: the pain was real enough; this dimension of her experience was 'real', even if in other, important, ways its context was different (she had *chosen* to go through the ordeal), and this could well have affected how she felt. In effect, through physical sensation, emotion, imagination and reason, she is putting herself in the place of the other, without pretending that she can *be* the other. And here, the 'playacting' can be given positive significance, reminding us that the term 'spectacle', as it enters modern life in the eighteenth century, has always had links with the theatre and theatricality. In his account of the history of spectacle, Luc Boltanski has no difficulty in linking theatricality to more general uses of spectacle as 'visual entertainment', but adds that this can have a broadly political dimension too. He identifies the separation of spectator from spectacle as the central principle, with a corollary separation of contemplation from action; and this in turn is embedded in a public sphere in which action on behalf of 'causes' can become possible, and subject to debate. He observes: 'Nothing promotes the formation of a cause more than the spectacle of suffering … it is through the cause that the public sphere and a politics of pity are connected to each other.'[8]

So far, then, we can see that the fact that Barnes makes a spectacle of herself, actively involving herself in the spectacular sensationalism of modern journalism, does not necessarily preclude her from displaying, through that very means, a sympathetic engagement with the suffering endured by those who are pilloried for their promotion of a controversial cause. Nor would it necessarily preclude public response. But we can go further – for it is apparent that the suffragette movements themselves, the marches, demonstrations and agitation that were at their peak in both the UK and the US in the decade preceding the First World War, presented themselves as 'spectacle' in both relevant senses of the term: as spectacular media events, and as theatrical in style and technique. Indeed, suffragism could claim to be the first modern movement to actively seek out, incorporate, and design itself for, the age of mass media publicity.[9] It is itself, of course, a successor to what was already an evolving history of organized demonstrations in the modern period, such demonstrations involving an expressive attitude never wholly reducible to the avowedly rational aims, as indeed is implicit in the word 'demonstration' itself – both an ostensibly rational elucidation or proof, and an exhibition, a 'show'.[10] But the suffragettes take this further. Susan Glenn suggests that 'As women on both sides of the footlights were making spectacles of themselves in public, being political and being theatrical became mutually reinforcing aspects of a new style of femininity'. As women emerged more and more onto the 'public stage', we increasingly encounter what Glenn calls 'a modern urban transatlantic culture of spectacle' in which 'A new generation of female performers fed public taste for sensation as they acted out and stimulated modern desires and fantasies'.[11] And all this could be said to culminate in the massive suffragette street parades of 1911–13, in which well-publicized and well-organized banner-carrying legions of smartly dressed women would march to make their point. As Glenn puts it: 'The purpose of the suffrage parades was to transform the perceived threat of women's political power into a visual spectacle of moral heroism and beauty'.[12] And within a decade or two, such mass movements and parades will have become a staple of the cinematic 'mass spectacle', Walter

Benjamin observing that 'mass movements ... are a form of human behaviour especially suited to the camera'.[13]

While this does, of course, engender controversy, it might be worth exploring the new sense of the 'public sphere' opened up here. In an interesting discussion, James and Stephanie Donald remind us of a late, little-known essay of Kant, 'The Contest of Faculties'.[14] Intrigued by the enthusiasm generated by the French Revolution, Kant notes how this is necessarily generated *at a distance*, depending on the sensational, dramatic quality of press and travellers' reports: 'the historical event has been translated into a *spectacle* or *drama* through the work of representation', as the Donalds put it, adding that 'Because the Revolution is presented to this public of spectators as a dramatic spectacle, they form an opinion of it on the basis of what is primarily an *aesthetic* judgement'.[15] Hence judgement itself has to respond to this new, mediated, cultural configuration; it cannot be conceived in dryly discursive terms, a debate between gentlemen in the coffee-house. If history, as historical events, becomes spectacle, then reception as 'spectacular participation' entails a notion of judgement that opens up – and crosses – conventional boundaries between the individual and the collective, between reason, feeling and imagination, whatever problems this may pose. Kant's own emphasis here is on *aspiration*: what is good about enthusiasm is not is not so much a matter of content, of agreement with any specific aim or goal; rather it is a recognition of communal aspiration and involvement, a sense of potential, pointing beyond the necessary particularity of individual self-interest. This is a response to content transfigured by form and feeling, a response that can indeed be appropriately coded as 'aesthetic' in the broad sense, pointing as it does to the presence of the ideal as potential in the real, an aspiration *in* the present that points beyond, transcending the limitations of conventional everyday boundaries.

We can move circuitously back towards Barnes by taking up this theme of 'boundary crossing' in relation to the public sphere. In her book on early modern cinema, Miriam Hansen writes of new forms of leisure, such as the Coney Island amusement park complex – another topic Barnes wrote about – and cinema itself, that 'the mark of their modernity, was that they encouraged the mingling of classes and genders'.[16] And this could, indeed, be profoundly troubling about them. This 'mixing' was a feature both of the content of spectacle, and of its public reception. In this mass spectacle of public voyeurism and participation, cinema emerged as both a key signifier of modernity and the place where its central features are presented, represented, and articulated, particularly through the sensationalism that could already be seen as central to its appeal. Hansen indeed refers elsewhere to 'This reflexive dimension of cinema, its dimension of *publicness*', and suggests this was recognized early on, by both defenders and critics.[17] As an example, Hansen discusses the 1897 film *The Corbett-Fitzsimmons Fight*, where women made up 60 per cent of the viewers, whereas live fights were attended exclusively by men; she observes that this film afforded women 'the forbidden sight of male bodies in seminudity, engaged in intimate and intense physical action',[18] still strongly taboo in everyday life, thus opening up new spectatorial positions for women in a public sphere that was already evolving rapidly beyond Victorian gender segregation. And by August 1914, when Barnes herself wrote an article on this theme – 'My Sisters and I at a New York Prizefight' – it had become possible for women to attend. Indeed, Barnes indicates that this had become fashionable, taking a degree of distance from it with her characteristically laconic observation that 'As the worst part of death is not the dead but those that mourn, so it is not the boxer that is horrifying but the crowd that knows no mercy and seeks but sensation'.[19]

Clearly there is a hint here that the 'sensational' aspects of this new public sphere could be problematical. In her thoughtful discussion of Barnes, Barbara Green points to the link between the suffrage protests and 'a larger frame of sensationalizing representations of female exhibitionism'. Elaborating this, she characterizes the Barnes piece as an instance of 'spectacular confession', a term used to 'indicate the ways in which feminist confessional gestures that display the female body for radical purposes are entangled with … a structure of representation that positions the female body as silent, passive, spectacular'.[20] From this point of view, Lisa Tickner is surely too optimistic in claiming that, in 'making a spectacle' of themselves, these women 'also produced and controlled it … Their bodies were organized collectively and invested politically and therefore resistant to any simple voyeuristic appropriation.' Indeed, she herself observed earlier that there was a potentially sado-masochistic aspect to suffrage posters displaying women being forcibly fed, posters which were 'intended to heighten a sense of outrage at women's suffering, but which might equally invite a covert pleasure in its spectacle'.[21] Glenn argues that there is a risk in all this that 'performative activism becomes a kind of fashion statement when women are asked to speak with the body'.[22]

In effect, Barnes is performing a 'masquerade' of femininity, both exhibiting and subverting conventional feminine passivity, and doing so, indeed, through a spectacle of the body as the violated object of the gaze, a body that becomes spectacle through crossing into the public sphere of representation. So this body carries a reflexive complexity at several levels, making 'reading' it all the more problematical and controversial. For Green, the element of masquerade subverts the radical potential of the article, which serves as a critique of activism rather than as supportive of it,[23] but it is difficult to see why this interpretation should have priority over the other possibilities implicit here. Green's argument is that masquerade subverts the 'over-identification' that characterizes women's 'normal' relation to the image, but simultaneously short-circuits the ability to move from spectator to activist; but this seems to assume that any 'gap' opened up here for 'reflection' must necessarily compromise any activist potential, and makes it difficult to account for the fact that such articles and images clearly *did* mobilize significant numbers of women.

It is surely important to remind ourselves of the context of all this. Barnes is writing on the cusp of a revolution, or several such: in one, running into the 1920s, the status of women will have been radically transformed; in another, film is in the process of displacing the varieties of theatre as the major form of popular entertainment. Both processes simultaneously open up new opportunities and arenas for sensationalism, along with possibilities for new forms of gender identity and representation for women, just as they also open up new avenues for gender exploitation; and, by the 1930s, the latter may indeed have become more prominent. We can see this in the increasing predominance of the 'chorus girl'. Well established earlier in the century, revues like the Ziegfeld *Follies*, the 'Tiller Girls', and, later, the Busby Berkeley musicals of the 1930s, promoted the spectacle of mass feminine beauty. In these revues 'this modernist fantasy of the girls revolved around the themes of sexual spectacle, commodities, male connoisseurship, and managed efficiency', as Glenn puts it, and the elaborate choreography emphasized 'impersonality, control, and repetition'.[24] New themes have come to the fore here, around ideas of the 'mass' – mass production, mass media, mass entertainment – that necessitate further analysis of sensation and spectacle; but, for the moment, one can at least observe that it is misleading to read this back into Barnes, as if there is some 'essential' relation between gender and spectacle that makes the relation inherently exploitative and mystifying.[25]

But, finally, one might point to another problem, central to the reception of the Barnes article. In an issue of the newspaper that was inevitably foregrounding news of the developing German offensive in Europe, when news was making itself 'sensational' without needing much help from the industry, would the article jostle successfully for attention? Is there a trap here – a tension between the reliability of witness, and the need to attract attention? And this would be a problem whether or not one conceded that news could at times be inherently newsworthy, intrinsically 'sensational'. If Barnes wrote of what she refers to as the most 'concentrated' moment of her life, it does not follow that the reader will have a similarly 'concentrated' experience, will feel similarly moved or agitated, although this is perfectly possible; it may be that the reader's response will be more 'distracted', skimming quickly through yet another moderately interesting story, in a newspaper full of them, over the morning cornflakes and coffee …

Paying attention

As every child in school knows, both paying attention and not paying attention involve costs, in boredom, discomfort, guilt and pain, and 'attention' can be both the coin one pays in and the demanding god one thereby attempts to propitiate. At the same time, there can be pleasure, too, on both sides of what is characteristically experienced as a cyclical swing from one to the other. This is, indeed, central to the whole culture of sensation and spectacle, clearly revealing important aspects of the disciplinary dynamic of modernity; and just as the concept of 'attention' has itself come to prominence as a topic in psychology and cultural theory since the nineteenth century, so has its salience in the experience of everyday life. Thus William James can claim that 'the faculty of voluntarily bringing back a wandering attention, over and over again, is the very root of judgment, character and will'.[26] There is already a hint of trouble here, in the suggestion that the attention can 'wander', but its importance is also emphasized. It provides focus, concentration, clarity: 'attention writes space, traces in it lines and triangles', as a later thinker, Lyotard, puts it.[27]

There can, of course, be differences of emphasis as to the causes and consequences of this process. In his impressively scholarly account of scientific and artistic developments, Jonathan Crary emphasizes the disciplinary aspects of modernity and the 'panoptic gaze', and the tensions here;[28] conversely, Jean Seaton argues that the long-standing concern with attention reveals 'an anxiety about the capacity of the media to reshape the inner subjective experience of the audience' that rather plays down the role of events themselves, the fact that 'news' can indeed be 'newsworthy'.[29] Problems of 'attention' are everywhere. Computer games are widely blamed for children's alleged inability to concentrate properly, just as television was in a previous generation, and film before that, and we have constructed the medical category of 'attention deficit disorder', accompanied by claims that rising numbers of children suffer from it.[30]

Quoting the assertion of the early twentieth-century psychologist Edward Titchener that 'the problem of attention is essentially a modern problem',[31] Crary seeks to substantiate this by arguing that attention becomes a problem 'only because of the *historical* obliteration of the possibility of thinking the idea of presence in perception; attention will be both a simulation of presence and a makeshift, pragmatic substitute in the face of its impossibility'. For Condillac, in the eighteenth century, this was not a problem – it was just taken for granted that sensory impact was immediate, that attention was simply a matter of 'the *force* of a sensation, an effect of an event external to the subject'.[32] But once 'paying attention' becomes a process, not a state, it unfolds in time, and is incompatible with the idea of immediacy of perception or consciousness; it thereby becomes a problem, not a taken-for-granted presupposition. This questions any identification between subject and experience, any positioning of consciousness as a fusion of experience *in* presence. Leo Charney suggests that we thereby recognize that 'presence cannot coincide with itself, that sensation and cognition are always already alienated' and that this 'opens up an empty space, an interval, that takes the place of a stable present'.[33] This link between subjectivity and time awareness is noted by late nineteenth-century psychologists, the suggestion that 'sensations linger in the perceptual apparatus, like after-images', as Tim Armstrong puts it. This gives us a sense of duration, while also suggesting that this makes time seem to be 'nothing but a kind of fatigue, the drag or noise which is built into the perceptual apparatus'.[34] This is what Charney calls 'drift', as 'the general condition of subjective experience in the form of presence',[35] inevitably a challenge to the imperative to pay attention. So if one condition for the emergence of attention as *itself* a focus of cultural attention and concern is this sense that experience does not automatically entail concentration and immediacy, then 'consciousness' in itself can come to seem an inadequate basis for self-knowledge.

The relation between consciousness and attention, raised here, can be explored further by drawing again on William James. Suggesting, in line with what has already been outlined, that 'My experience is what I agree to attend to', rather than 'the mere presence to the senses of an outward order', James develops the argument that as the mind is 'a theatre of simultaneous possibilities', so consciousness itself consists in 'the selection of some, and the suppression of the rest by the reinforcing and inhibiting agency of attention'.[36] Thus attention is the active power of consciousness, selecting from the possibilities opened up by our sensory engagement with the world. And the fact that this process is by no means straightforward, that it brings problems with it, is apparent from this extended formulation, an account of how attention can itself produce a 'curious state of inhibition' or reverie:

> The eyes are fixed on vacancy, the sounds of the world melt into confused unity, the attention becomes dispersed so that the whole body is felt, as it were, at once, and the foreground of consciousness is filled, if by anything, by a sort of solemn sense of surrender to the empty passing of time. In the dim background of our mind we know what we ought to be doing: getting up, dressing ourselves, answering the person who has spoken to us … But somehow we cannot start. Every moment we expect the spell to break, for we know no reason why it should continue. But it does continue, pulse after pulse, and we float with it.[37]

Truly, a state of drift, 'the lived sensation of empty moments', a 'floating inexactness', in Charney's words.[38] The attention itself, as our consciousness *of* something, can wax and wane; our ability to *focus*, a process of simultaneous concentration and exclusion, can itself become diffuse, unfocused.

One could say then that consciousness can become a problem from two directions. Firstly, it manifests focus and periphery. Its ability to focus, to 'foreground', refers to its relation, in varying degrees of presence and absence, with its objects, what it is consciousness *of*; its periphery, or hazy 'background', is the element of 'awareness' that accompanies this, a reflexive dimension, whereby one can be distanced from one's own consciousness of what one is doing (or saying), a kind of dissociation that is brought out vividly in James's account. But secondly – and not referred to by James at all – there is the problem posed for consciousness by its own hinterland, a distinction between its surface and its own inscrutable depth, increasingly available by James's time for theorization as the 'unconscious', and equally crucial to the relation between consciousness and sense of self (since these 'unconscious' dimensions are in some troublesome sense 'internal' to the self, even if they may *also* make reference to physiological factors, such as instincts or drives). And while Crary tends to imply that a focus on attention takes us away from a historically preceding focus on consciousness, it would surely be more accurate to say that we increasingly find two, relatively separate, traditions of cultural, philosophical and theoretical concern running alongside here, one of which – the study of attention – certainly becomes of more interest to empirical (empiricist) psychology than the other.

We can see this more clearly if we consider the term that would be opposed to 'consciousness' in these two patterns of thought. 'Unconscious' is only apparently a lack; actually, it designates difference: the unconscious is indeed 'full', an alternative rather than an absence. And although 'inattention' could have performed such a role for attention – and of course the word is used – it is 'distraction' that has become the most widely accepted 'other' term, precisely so as to capture this dualism, this apparent inadequacy or lack of attention that is also a *different* attention. (Hence another term can also occur, the one used by James: reverie.) If there is a certain parallel here, there is also a significant difference. It is always *the* unconscious, positioned as a structural contrast to a more-or-less homogeneous 'consciousness'; even when there is reference to 'unconscious processes' these are seen as occupying a reasonably definite, uniform 'site'. And, access barred by repression, this site is clearly 'elsewhere'. The situation is markedly different with regard to the attention/distraction pairing, however. These are both positioned within consciousness, or as aspects of it, with ill-defined boundaries between them, a relation between focus, periphery and contextual awareness that is itself fluid and diffuse, with the edge or periphery sliding into 'distraction'. And although when we consider the relation to the object (of attention), there may be a certain uniformity of the subject, as if concentrated into a self that directs the searchlight, dictates the focus, this other dimension is still there. Conversely, when the latter is emphasized, as 'distraction', we find a scattering effect, fragmenting attention *into* these distinct yet unfocused experiences in which the self, indeed, appears to lose itself. It is as though experience goes beyond any possible location in a subject.

Thus what we find here is not just new ways of making sense of the patterns of experience that have emerged in modern culture, but also the emergence of new paradigms, new ways of articulating the relationship between experience, consciousness and perception – paradigms which cannot easily coexist and which have differential impacts in different fields of inquiry. In the case of the attention/distraction pair, the possibility of 'dissociation' looms up, as we have seen, suggesting that the experience of distraction, of these new forms of consciousness 'distracted' into the objects of experience themselves, can appear to result not in the determination of consciousness by the unconscious, but in the fragmentation of consciousness into multiple subjects of experience. Paradoxically, the organizing directedness of mind, necessary for attention, can result in the collapse of that very intentionality.

It would clearly be useful to elaborate the hints given here as to how attention itself contributes to distraction, and Crary is helpful for this. The more it was investigated, he argues, the more 'attention was shown to contain within itself the conditions for its own undoing – attentiveness was in fact continuous with states of distraction, reverie, dissociation, and trance'. Distraction is, indeed, 'an *effect*, and in many cases a constituent element, of the many attempts to produce attentiveness in human subjects'.[39] Cézanne is credited with an intuitive understanding of this, of 'the creative discovery that looking at any one thing intently did *not* lead to a fuller and more inclusive grasp of its presence, its rich immediacy'. On the contrary, 'it led to its perceptual disintegration and loss, its breakdown as intelligible form'. One could say that just as there can be too little focus, so there can be too much. Distraction can result both from a 'diffuse attentiveness',[40] a kind of lateral drift into the periphery, and from a concentrated, centred attention, whereby the object of attention can wither, distend, fragment, finally dissipate, under the intensity of the gaze.

Another aspect is implicit here. Louis Sass notes the 'rigid and fixed stare' that 'bores through, breaks up, or withers its object', tracing the consequences of this in modernism in the arts – and in modern psychosis.[41] Indeed, this would imply that even if 'absorbed contemplation' of the art object is a defining feature of the reception of 'high art', it cannot serve to isolate it as a category, for it cannot exclude distraction; indeed, such a focused concentration on the object must in due course *produce* it. We have a cycle here, or an oscillation, not a relation of mutual exclusion. In short, if attention is supposed to be what prevents our perception from being overwhelmed by sensation, it is clearly most unreliable in this role. In the light of this, and moving from modernism to the experience of modernity itself, anticipating our further exploration of the latter, Charney suggests that 'Modernity's welter of stimulation made attention more crucial yet less feasible'.[42]

Getting distracted

To explore distraction further, and its possible status as both a stimulus to attention, and an unintended result of it, we can now begin to draw on a wider stream of European thought and culture, including discussion of a concept that is, indeed, often translated into English as 'distraction', namely *Zerstreuung*.

Seeking the '*a priori* conditions upon which the possibility of experience rests',[43] Kant argues that these lie in the categories that alone enable us to think the objects of experience, and which in turn must conform to the conditions of the 'unity of self-consciousness'. Without this necessary unity in the 'manifold of perceptions', it would follow that these perceptions 'would not then belong to any experience, consequently would be without an object, merely a blind play [*Zerstreuung*] of representations, less even than a dream'.[44] Here, Kant seems to be performing an idea experiment, postulating a limit scenario in which our capacity for a unified awareness of the world as we experience it is threatened by a tumult of incoherent fragments; yet there is also perhaps a hint, or an implication, that this could also – in part, at least – be a possible result of the very involvement of the subject in this process. If – anachronistically – we insert 'attention' as the face of this 'unity of self-consciousness' as it confronts, and focuses on, the 'objects of experience', then we can see that attention could *produce* this sense of a periphery or penumbra of the obscure, the fragmentary, the incoherent and the unintelligible. And as we have seen, concentration *itself* can dissolve its object. If attention produces a world of distraction, then, we see again that a world of distraction can produce attention, as both defence and coping strategy. And it is open to us to explore whether the experience of modernity itself can contribute to, reinforce, or even constitute, such a world, one where the oscillation of attention and distraction becomes of central importance.

Consulting the dictionary, we find that an old sense of distraction as 'deranged in mind' has died out by the eighteenth century, although leaving an intriguing residue in the idea of being 'absent-minded'. By then, its modern range of meanings seems to have become well established, around the nodes of 'being turned aside, diverted', and 'perplexity and confusion'. As a 'diversion', a distraction can also be a recreation or amusement. *Zerstreuung*, similarly, can range from distraction in its central meanings over to what one might be distracted by, namely entertainment; and, given its root in *Streuen*, it has connotations of scattering, dispersion. Consequently, distraction can be variously a contrast to attention, a supposed absence of it, and a different form of it, consciousness in a different mode. One is distracted by 'distractions', which involve both being distracted from something (supposedly more important), and finding other, positive qualities, as experiences or sites of experience, 'entertainments'. Consciousness in distracted mode involves a more diffuse focus, an awareness of context and 'flow', rather than boundaries. Distraction is relaxing, rather than challenging or bracing. There can be *degrees* of distraction, from a dreamy semi-conscious, possibly bored 'stupor' over to a more active engagement in the pleasures of the world. Distraction can indeed be boring, but also the cure for boredom. Always there is a hint of being disengaged even when being engaged, disengagement *in* engagement, a certain non-commitment; a hint of recording or observing – including recording or observing the self – rather than either participation or purposeful concentration. It is the basic orientation of the *flâneur* (although this can swing over into attention, when necessary).

Wandering in 1920s Paris, Louis Aragon found that, for him, *all* was distraction: 'Everything distracts me indefinably, except from my distraction itself.'[45] But if we consider this, we may find that getting distracted – like paying attention – is not necessarily so easy. If one is distracted, one needs to concentrate on whatever is distracting, or one is speedily distracted again. It seems as though either distraction must speedily recreate attention for itself, or it is doomed to fragment itself endlessly. Either way, it seems to drive towards self-destruction. But here, we can recall the other, related, meaning of distraction, as 'absent-mindedness'. This suggests a 'state of mind' that is not necessarily so fleeting, but is more settled; a different kind of attitude or orientation, perhaps, in contrast to the concentration of attention. In this sense, one can be 'distracted' without being distracted *by* anything in particular. One is 'absent-minded': not really, or strongly, 'present' to oneself; one's very consciousness, one's very sense of it *as* one's consciousness, becomes diffuse and unfocused (as we saw with William James). This can be readily linked to states of dissociation,[46] as if one's experiences are not really happening to, or in, 'one's self' (oneself). But this is also a state of heightened receptivity, in which one relaxes one's guard (one's guard relaxes, takes time out). And this is when distractions in the positive sense, as 'other' experiences, whether entertaining or relaxing – in short, 'diversions' – can seize their moment. Remaining in Paris, we can this time cite a passage from a guidebook of 1884, which tells us that 'no people in the world are so fond of amusements – or distractions, as they term them – as Parisians. Morning, noon and night, summer and winter, there is always something to be seen and a large part of the population seems absorbed in the pursuit of pleasure.'[47]

Distraction has a strong, but not exclusive, link to the visual, hence to the media. Thus the idea of the 'distracted gaze' emerges, as a feature of film and television spectatorship, with its potential for an 'aimless' switching of attention, always on the move … Distraction thus links us to the spectacle, which can be presented as a parade or panorama of enticements, of visual (and other sensory) delights, such that one can linger over individual items, but not for long; it is really the spectacle itself that 'distracts'. Thus we find that, as implied by the dictionary, the term 'distraction' can be unpacked to reveal a range of related meanings, linked by mutual implication, and together corresponding to dimensions of modern experience, testifying to a 'modernity' that is just as significant as the modernity of close, disciplined attention and rational action, to which they are, indeed, both a backdrop and a – frequently subversive – response.

While it has been usual to associate distraction with the visual mass media, it can be given wider application.[48] If we take the conventional realist novel, for example, we can see a sense in which the text seems to build in or imply the capacity – even perhaps the necessity – for distraction. In a classic George Eliot or Henry James novel, so much detail is provided that it becomes almost impossible to take it all in. Since it is not all essential to the plot, it is a distraction to read it, but you need to take it in, absorb the detail, because this builds the impression of the 'real world', the illusion of a kind of mimetic realism whereby imaginative truth maps the world of possible experience. The detail is distracting, and the reader can become distracted, inattentive – perhaps one's concentration lapses, one wanders off – yet one is, in a sense, actually being distracted *into* the real, in that the distraction helps to constitute the real as amorphous, detailed, overwhelmingly 'full' yet always incomplete, always sliding in and out of consciousness, always as much out of focus as in, a world of transitory and fragmentary impressions. Perhaps this distracted mode of apprehension is the appropriate way to grasp such a world. This seems to fit a point made by Virginia Woolf. In discussing her childhood, she refers to memories of characters who were 'filled out', in depth, but left 'finally incomplete', yet all the more 'real' for that (in contrast to characters who were indeed 'complete' but came to life essentially as caricatures).[49] In a sense one reconstructs here the whole transition in literature from naïve to reflexive realism, to the 'modernist moment' of streams of consciousness and fragmented narrative, in which the real is reborn through its own reproduction as dispersion – yet always in tension with any plot there may be. The plot is there as what one 'attends to' (the focus, but not necessarily the point, as it were …).

Here we can turn to Benjamin, whose significance is that he locates distraction and dispersion firmly in the culture and experience of modernity. But, in order to do this, it helps to follow him back in time, to the baroque. Arguing for the prominence of allegory in this period, he locates the 'figural centre' of allegory in a court, around which and in which 'a profusion of emblems' are grouped. He continues: 'This court is subject to the law of "dispersal" [*Zerstreuung*] and "collectedness". Things are assembled according to their significance; indifference to their existence allowed them to be dispersed again.'[50] Things are 'collected', according to some notion of meaning or purpose, but this is essentially external to the things in question: they always 'fall away' or 'disperse' from meaning, even as it is attached to them, as if exacting revenge for their reduction in status as mere means to human ends. The attention lavished on the objects of the collection is always self-defeating, bringing with it the sense of indifference to their very existence as they play and fragment into incoherence under the attentive gaze that dissolves their unity even as it evacuates them of meaning. This mutual recalcitrance of being and meaning is central to allegory, associated with the orientation of mourning and the theme of the transformation of all objects, all things, into ruin. In the context of the baroque, this melancholy is associated with the withdrawal of God, with allegory as the appropriate figure for grasping the dispersal of his impact, its receding echo in the ruination of things in a meaningless world.[51]

But already this cannot be wholly situated under the sign of melancholy. What, after all, is collected? The very dissolution of things, their liberation from an already constituted meaning, or 'place' in the scheme of things, is also a transfiguration that opens them up for further ventures of collecting, whether in the eclecticism of their uniqueness or the seriality of their repetition (as objects of a designated 'class'). After all, the collector is destined, in Benjamin's later work, to become one of those archetypal exemplary figures of modernity (along with the *flâneur*, the sandwichman, the gambler, the prostitute …). The negative moment opens up the positive one, in a process of repetition that is modern as much as baroque, or the modern *as* baroque. The moment of dispersion is also the moment of distraction, the opening towards it, making it possible, seducing us from the narrow path of attention and its accompanying self-discipline. And doesn't this reveal the dynamic of consumerism itself? The *flâneur* – the collector of looks and looking, but quickly bored, always moving on – and the collector – more tactile, more interested in the materiality and symbolic power of the objects[52] – could together be said to reveal its two faces, when acquisition always leads to its own emptiness, with 'consumed' objects evacuated of meaning and then treated with indifference to the point of being disposed of entirely – or being reborn as objects of desire for the collector. Writing of the latter, Benjamin explicitly draws a parallel with the baroque. The collector is appalled by the spectacle of the world's confusion: he 'takes up the struggle against dispersion [*Zerstreuung*]', and his 'passionate, distraught concern with this spectacle' shows that 'in every collector hides an allegorist'.[53] Yet all the allegorist finds is this endless slippage, displacement, the dream forever unfulfilled that is, nevertheless, the only dream worth having, connecting us, as it does, to the 'productive disorder' of the *mémoire involontaire*.[54]

Of these characteristic figures of the modern, Howard Eiland claims that they are at home in the world's scatter: 'They are touched and inspired by it. They spend themselves and expand themselves in being dispersed to the current of objects … Their struggle against dispersion succeeds only by dint of studious abandonment to it …'[55] Always there are distractions, and distractions from distractions, and the tension between these and the centripetal tendencies of purposive rationality could be said to reveal the core of this baroque dialectic of modernity: the sense that rational goal-directed action, action as project, whether in the individual life or as a cultural orientation, is ultimately as self-subverting as self-renewing. Here, the two strands of thought – the late nineteenth-century psychology of attention, drawn on in Crary's work, and Benjamin's cultural theory – can converge in an awareness that 'paying attention' raises questions of desire, feeling, of cultural meaning and cultural process, and is inseparable from the distraction and dispersion from which it springs and to which it returns.

Benjamin never loses his ambivalence about distraction: it can, after all, be a ready avenue for ideological mystification or manipulation, or mere habit. Nevertheless, the balance in his mature work is arguably towards the positive. In particular, the 'intoxication'[56] of distraction opens up new ways of perceiving and thinking, and an intensity of involvement with objects and experiences, thus recovering the surreal face of the world. In the arcade, writes Benjamin, objects reveal 'irregular combinations' and a world of 'secret affinities',[57] the world of Baudelaire's 'correspondences'.[58] The arcades, suggests Eiland, thereby become '*both* laboratory and atmosphere'.[59] In the light of this, we can suggest that dispersion is not 'mere' scattering, but a scattering around or beyond purpose, intention, or conscious meaning, a scattering capable of suggesting hitherto unsuspected 'affinities': links and patterns that can only be recognized, or can only present themselves, in this indirect, allusive way. What emerges here is a *terrain* – which can in principle be a contested terrain, over which battles of ideological influence can be fought – a place of possibilities and latencies, of reception, dream and creativity, of pleasures licit and illicit.

Benjamin's own work can be seen in this light: for Benjamin is not just the cultural theorist of distraction, he is the distracted subject *par excellence*. As early as the *Trauerspiel* book, we find him writing, of the approach he takes: 'Method is a digression. Representation as digression – such is the methodological nature of the treatise.' He adds, tellingly: 'The absence of an uninterruptedly purposeful structure is its primary characteristic.' So we cannot here treat digression – the textual equivalent of distraction – as sufficient in itself; it makes no sense without this relation to a 'purposeful structure' that is forever 'interrupted'. And if we note Benjamin's claim that in the 'treatise' the key element is the 'authoritative quotation',[60] which is both sign of intention *and* manifestation of digression, we have an uncannily apposite description, long in advance, of the culminating treatise of his life, the *Arcades Project*. 'Making sense', as an effort of will and theoretical project, is always there, flickeringly; but so is a *receptiveness*, an openness to the diversity of the fragments that carry their own authority as shafts of insight from an elusive (and allusive) elsewhere. And this receptiveness is, as we have seen, the latent *positive* content of distraction. Indeed, Benjamin goes so far as to suggest that 'The value of fragments of thought is all the greater the less direct their relationship to the underlying idea', rather as pieces of glass can glow in a mosaic independently of any overall impression, even though they also contribute to the latter.[61] And hence, more generally, the challenge to the modern artist is to explore forms that resist 'integration and closure', as Eiland puts it, revealing an 'articulation of dispersion, a dis-integrated form, a meaning in shock'.[62]

Distraction, shock and the experience of film

'Reception in distraction – the sort of reception which is increasingly noticeable in all areas of art and is a symptom of profound changes in apperception – finds in film its true training ground', argues Benjamin, explaining that 'Film, by virtue of its shock effects, is predisposed to this form of reception'.[63] Elsewhere he adds, even more strongly, that 'The values of distraction should be defined with regard to film, just as the values of catharsis are defined with regard to tragedy', and such distraction should also be conceived as 'physiological',[64] a term that can be taken to indicate the importance of sensory involvement and the realm of feeling in our engagement with film.

The ramifications of this are worth exploring. Benjamin writes that film's shock effect 'seeks to induce heightened attention'.[65] Film is distraction; yet it also enforces, or requires, attention. Of his own film experience, Steven Shaviro suggests that 'I am attentive to what happens on the screen only to the extent that I am continually distracted, and passively absorbed, by it. I no longer have the freedom to follow my own train of thought …'.[66] Our attention is captured, and responses are forced. From an earlier period, we have the critic Henri Wallon: 'If the cinema produces its effect, it does so because I identify myself with its images, because I more or less forget myself in what is being displayed on the screen. I am no longer in my own life, I am in the film …'[67]

One could say that there are different levels here: film is itself a distraction, but within this, it reveals the attention/distraction dynamic previously discussed. Perhaps film, *as* distraction, as entertainment, works *through* this dynamic. Thus Charney suggests that cinema 'was a distraction and contributed to distraction, yet it also, as a new technology of attention, tried to defeat distraction by marshalling concentration'.[68] Fluctuating attention was recognized as a problem by the industry, but it was also an opportunity, since it corresponded to the possibilities inherent in the medium as an entertainment unfolding in front of an audience over time. And we can recall its origins: until well into the 1920s, a film was generally put on as part of a variety show, one of a package of disparate thrills seeking to hold its audience.[69]

Pointing to the way that the resulting restructuring of attention into 'peaks and valleys' provided a 'regulated structure' for the fluctuating attention of audiences at shows, films and sports events, incorporating the element of drift, Charney argues that, in these cinematic techniques, 'the ephemeral moment became the engine of motion, the peak moment the spur for stimulation, the empty moment the site of spectatorship'.[70] One might suggest that if the 'peak' moment is the moment of shock, the 'sensational' moment, forcing itself onto our attention, then the 'empty' moment, the valley or trough, involves boredom, or a relaxing of attention, encourages the wandering 'distracted' attention, whether as daydream or potentially critical awareness, and the 'ephemeral' moment incorporates the whole dynamic of distraction itself, its constantly protean nature, always 'moving on', hence aligned with the unfolding nature of the film itself. Film as distraction, then, involves this exposure to impressions which encompass you, even overwhelm you, without necessarily *engaging* you: the flow of impressions contradicts the gaze of concentration or contemplation, or reflexive thought. However, both of these *can* be engaged, at peak moments, and at times of relative emptiness or drift. One might also note the observation by Hugo Münsterberg, one of the first film theorists, that the peak moments affect our awareness of the rest of the film: 'Whatever is focused by our attention wins emphasis and irradiates meaning over the course of events'.[71]

There are problems here. If distraction works in film partly through *enforcing* attention, this no longer manifests the proactive self, focusing on the world to master it, but the reactive self, with attention as a defensive, protective formation, along the lines of Freud's idea of consciousness as a defence mechanism. But in the quotes from Benjamin, Shaviro and Wallon, we also encounter what is almost a reverse emphasis: that a symptom of this 'captivated' or 'distracted' gaze is that the subject is somehow absorbed *by* the screen, or the film. The subject's thoughts are replaced by shifting, sliding images, *as if* 'exercising the imagination', but actually replacing or displacing it, or positioning it as mere empty receptacle, an absence to be filled by the presence of visions from and of elsewhere. Thus Daniel Frampton tells us that he prefers to sit near the front in the cinema, 'allowing the film to pleasurably swamp my senses', hence becoming 'fully *involved*'; questions of critical interpretation and assessment can come later.[72] And here it is Benjamin's one-time friend Kracauer who can be more helpful in following up some of the implications of all this.[73]

At a film, argues Kracauer, 'the self as the mainspring of thoughts and decisions relinquishes its power of control'.[74] The resultant drifting and dreaming can take us in two, contrary, directions: outwards and inwards. Firstly, objects can beckon us, invite us to come nearer; the viewer 'drifts toward and into the objects'. In order to comprehend the 'being' of an object, the viewer 'meanders, dreamingly, through the maze of its multiple meanings and psychological correspondences', thereby exhibiting a distinctive 'sensibility'. Nor can the spectator exhaust the object he contemplates: 'There is no end to his wanderings.' But, intriguingly, he may be able to listen to a 'confused murmur' where 'Images begin to sound, and the sounds are again images', and this cinematic synaesthesia of Baudelairian correspondences, this 'murmur of existence', may be about as far as one can get. But this dreaming can also go in the other direction, as a result of psychological influences from the past. Film shots may produce 'a flight of associations' from the subject's 'agitated inner environment' – and back into it, one might add – for this movement 'leads the spectator away from the given image into subjective reveries'.[75] In practice, these two movements are often inseparable. 'Trance-like immersion' can yield to subjective daydreaming, and the spectator is found 'wavering between self-absorption and self-abandonment', together constituting a 'stream of consciousness' imprinted with bodily sensations.[76]

Nevertheless, the distinction here is significant. The first attitude is present-oriented, towards the outer world of experience, towards events and objects as they impinge on us and in us, address us; the second brings this world into the subject's past, interpreting it in the light of unconscious influences. In the first, we find an openness towards experience, with attention as, effectively, a subset of distraction, with its focusing power as orientation rather than domination or defence; in the second, attention engages consciousness, as the defensive anticipation of shock and the disturbances that can result from failure of the proactive power of mastery. The big difference is clearly that, in the latter, the shock defence must indeed involve consciousness, which neutralizes shock and enables attention to function in its capacity as deliberate focusing, whereas, in the former, attention *itself* has to ward off distraction, if necessary, since consciousness offers no defence against it, in that such distraction is always *there*, in the periphery, in the penumbra that surrounds attention as its unfocused field of play. One might say that shock as what 'distracts' or attracts us engages the attention/distraction constellation, whereas shock as what *forces* itself on our attention, shock as *power*, is shock as sensation, engaging the consciousness defence system – which is potentially productive, in extreme cases, of trauma.[77] Shock is direct attack; distraction is always seductive, indirect. Distraction poses problems for attention, not consciousness. In effect, then, these are two distinct modes of engagement with the circuit of sensation.

Further implications are worth exploring. Insofar as whatever is sensation or sensational is dealt with by the consciousness system, there are implications for the sense of time, and trauma – or art – may be the result; insofar as it disrupts attention, it threatens to produce dissociation, which emerges as the (potentially traumatic) extreme form of distraction. Indeed, a sense of 'temporal depth', of past as depth, is a feature of the former, whereas, in the latter, the past is 'elsewhere', on the same level, 'shallow' rather than deep. Hence we find a resulting dichotomy of feeling. On one model, where the past returns, and can bring feeling expressed in the present, the result can be a depth of experience inaccessible on the other model, but there is a cost: this past is relatively, and normally, inaccessible. On the other model, the feelings, the whole sensorium, can be engaged, but only in the present, *as* present, with no depth. And, in Benjamin's work, this is presented as the central bifurcation of the modern experience: the tragedy of the modern, but possibly, also, a resource for its critical redemption.

On the shock defence model, 'consciousness' works rather like a filing cabinet; in 'registering' an experience, it is filed away as information, but simultaneously disempowered, denuded of its emotional force and meaning. It is experience minus sensation, as it were, or sensation minus the sensational. For shock to be truly 'sensational', to really work as shock, it must either trigger something, some previous residue, in the unconscious, the conjunction of the two giving an emotional force, *or* it must break through the 'shock defence' altogether. None of this can be under anyone's conscious control, whether that of the subject of experience or of some external manipulator, who may be the advertiser or the modernist artist trying to shock; if any of this *appears* to succeed, it can only be because the 'shock' is really superficial, connecting with consciously registered experience. Conversely, the ultimate in sensation cannot occur once; it takes itself out of conventional time, and presents itself in the stasis of repetition. The 'outside', the invading event or force, stays 'inside', confounding the boundary, thereby partly incapacitating the inside and hence the subject's very ability to function as such. This is trauma.[78]

Here we can move on to Benjamin's suggestion of a distinctive 'mode of perception' involving an 'optical unconscious',[79] and attempt to relate it to the other model, that of distraction. Never really developed, the concept can be taken to designate those conditions under which the world of modern experience can be knowable, can be grasped as such, by the modern mediated subject, the subject of distraction. The notion is clearly influenced by Freud, but is equally clearly not intended to be reducible to the psychological unconscious, or an aspect of it. Its workings are not inscrutable, subject to repression, but are there on or in the surface, as the relation *between* distraction and attention, in the tension lying there, and in the unruly *inclusion* of one in the other. On this approach, 'projections', as symptoms of unconscious desires, workings of unconscious fantasy, are subsumed under, or replaced by, 'distractions', as sensory, primarily visual, experiences that result from this distinctive mode of the subject's engagement with the world of shock and sensation, just as the 'correspondences' or patterns thus revealed can give clues to the world as phantasmagoria and its relation to the commodity. We can say, then, that, like the psychological unconscious, the optical unconscious can be said to challenge received notions of space, time and process, but not, now, in terms of the hold of an obsessive, repetitive past, but rather in the name of modernist experimentalism, and the displacement of history into the jarring distractions of images and experiences resonating in an ever-shifting present.

All this can give a clue to the tension in Benjamin between highly critical observations on modernity, linked to the destruction of any in-depth experience of community and the past (*Erfahrung*), and a more positive evaluation, perceiving critical potential in distraction itself, or in the reflections it makes possible. We can now see that this tension is called for by modern experience itself. If we focus purely on the shock defence model – modernity as a barrage of stimuli we need to be protected from – it is easy to see how this could indeed produce what Susan Buck-Morss refers to as a modern 'anaesthetics', a numbing response to over-stimulation.[80] Not surprisingly, both stress and the modern discourse of stress have their sources here. Distraction enters this account merely as the presence of the phantasmagoria that result from this over-stimulation. In addition, we can point to the parallel with pain: too much sensation produces pain, and then insensibility, numbness.[81] Aesthetics, as the embodied response to the modern world, thus produces anaesthetics. Given the nineteenth-century invention of medical anaesthetics, we can say that 'anaesthetics' in the broadest sense is both defence against, and a result of, 'excess' feeling, sensation, shock – and, either, way, numbness results. 'Unfeeling' is as much a result of excess feeling as distraction is of excess attention.

Here, the difference from the other model is crucial. If consciousness is basically about defence, about force and reaction, distraction cannot be seen in such narrowly functional terms. As has been seen, it is not simply 'opposed' to attention, rather it incorporates it, serving as the 'default setting' of consciousness in its mode of more open engagement with the world, reacting to the world as montage, as shifting sands and signs, of potentially meaningful encounters. And the latter is more likely to open up space for reflection; indeed, the peaks, troughs and 'empty moments' seem to solicit this, just as the shifting balance of dream and sensation cannot guarantee its occurrence. And while theoretical reflection is always possible, Benjamin's critique of the pretensions to autonomy of aesthetics in the narrow sense draws rather more on the strategies of distraction themselves. An appropriate caption for a photograph of poverty, for example, would be one that jars, one that 'wrenches it from modish commerce',[82] an incongruous disjunction or form of montage that would jolt the viewer into feeling and thought. The following insightful passage continues this theme, reflecting in its form something of the frenetic, convulsive world it conjures up:

> Today the most real, mercantile gaze into the heart of things is the advertisement. It tears down the stage upon which contemplation moved, and all but hits us between the eyes with things as a car, growing to gigantic proportions, careens at us out of a film screen. And just as the film does not present furniture and facades in completed forms for critical inspection, their insistent, jerky nearness alone being sensational, the genuine advertisement hurls things at us with the tempo of a good film … and in the face of the huge images spread across the walls of houses, where toothpaste and cosmetics lie handy for giants, sentimentality is restored to health and liberated in American style, just as people whom nothing moves or touches any longer are taught to cry again by films.[83]

So, the place of the distanced contemplation that makes 'criticism' in the traditional sense possible, along with 'absorption' in the artwork, is now replaced with the shock of the sensational, hitting us, hurling things at us, presenting us with a stream of dynamic fragments, never the completed whole. Yet this partiality, this one-sided exaggeration, can stimulate thought, generate insights appropriate to a state of distraction, just as film encourages 'an evaluating attitude' in the audience, which becomes 'an examiner, but a distracted one'.[84] And this state produces *feeling*, the vicariously real involvement of the sentimental, the feeling appropriate to the distracted subject, an ability to cry. Thus, according to Michael Jennings, Benjamin champions the liberating potential of shock, and shows how the human capacity for feeling can be reshaped through these new mediated relationships to sensation, relationships that are necessarily uncomfortable, disruptive. Jennings concludes: 'We are granted, through shock, in a state of distraction brought on by the ubiquity and sameness of advertising, a privileged glance into "the heart of things", that is, into the conditions that structure and obscure our ability to understand our world.'[85] Through shock, consciousness and feeling, experience and culture, come together: it is the node, the key point of transmission, between sensation and sensationalism. And cinema could be characterized as a privileged arena for people in the mass to encounter the underlying conditions of their lives in mediated form, which in turn invites us to think further about the relation between 'representing' and 'reproducing' in a context of distraction.

The masses go to the movies

Clearly it is important to show how the various incarnations of the term 'mass' – 'the masses', mass movements, mass reproduction, mass culture – can be related, and thereby show that the dynamics of concentration and distraction run through and structure these somewhat diverse domains. We can recall that an 'organized' mass, such as a mass movement, always exceeds its own idea of itself: its conscious awareness of itself, its goals and strategies, are never sufficient to characterize it. One might say that the element of 'concentration' that is obviously present here cannot wholly contain the 'dispersion' that is inherent in the existence of the mass. 'It is thoroughly "massive" – hence, always potentially "uncontrollable" – even with respect to itself', as Jan Mieczkowski puts it.[86] One might say that the 'movement of the mass', or mass *as* movement, has priority over the 'mass movement', the latter being a contingent phase of concentration that can never replace the logic of dispersion, but can indeed be seen as an aspect of it, as is apparent when we move towards broader and less focused notions of mass and 'the masses'. In this sense, 'mass' *always* involves 'movement': endless criss-crossing dispersion and divergence, fluidity and drift, ever threatening to dissolve into its constituents but never quite doing so, the individual as always, *also*, one of the mass. As Samuel Weber suggests, the mass 'is a movement that is going nowhere, and yet it is never just marking time.'[87]

And when the masses go to the movies we find, according to Benjamin, that they seek distraction, rather than the concentration that art demands;[88] but we also find that 'the reactions of individuals, which together make up the massive reaction of the audience' are 'determined by the imminent concentration of reactions into a mass'.[89] We can try to bring these dimensions together as follows. The audience is concentrated into a mass, and its attention is also concentrated, mass-like, yet the latter works as a kind of proactive awareness: this is the mass concentrated *as* attention, through its individuals as audience, oriented to the screen yet *also* aware of each other. This is the 'distracted' audience, concentrated and concentrating in a context of distraction; again, we encounter the concentrated moment or aspect of distraction. The 'mass' reaction of the mass audience involves this self-responsiveness, its ongoing relation to individual others in their capacity as others reacting in a similar way, as part of the mass, their 'individuality' existing, in *this* context, as screen-mediated mutual awareness, as subjects of the spectacle. And turning to the film, the 'reception in distraction' of the audience does not involve concentrating on the art object as supposedly separate, in its 'integrity', as an autonomous whole; rather, it could be said to lose itself in the flickering, transient passage of images on the screen – film as this endless series of images, in varying degrees unconstrained by the real yet always addressing it, conveying it, however elliptically. In this sense, the 'experience of film' is always in excess of the content of any particular film, and this experience is likely to be coded as 'positive' by the audience, whether responding 'distractedly' for the first time, or habituated to it; the audience thereby responds both to the screen *and* the awareness of shared involvement.

Benjamin writes: 'Any person today can lay claim to being filmed.'[90] It is important to recall – aware as we are today of omnipresent surveillance – that this was intended as an assertion of a fundamentally democratic potential in film. However, it is important for another reason. The camera operates as a kind of transformer here. To say that we can all be both viewers and viewed implies a kind of fundamental subject–object reversibility, a certain homogeneity that crosses distinctions between reality, representation and reception. Some suggestions in Kracauer seem to reinforce this. Film, he writes, presents us with the 'flow of life'; perhaps it is 'life in its inexhaustibility which the cinema offers to masses in want of it'.[91] Thus 'flow of life' and 'stream of consciousness' map on to one another; both are 'inexhaustible'. Flow and stream are alike disjunctive, not aggregative; they suggest reality as endless montage, not totality – the modern world as dispersion, with no inherent principle of coherence or essence. Kracauer refers to the spectator, responding to isolation, feeling out of touch with 'that stream of things and events which, were it flowing through him, would render his existence more exciting and significant', and who is attracted to the cinema 'because it gives him the illusion of vicariously partaking of life in all its fullness'.⁹²

Benjamin makes the point with a slight but significant shift of emphasis. Implicitly reminding us of the dynamic of concentration and dispersion *within* this overall mode of distraction, he notes the way modern institutions can seem to close in on us, restricting us, remarking that film then comes along, assuring us of 'a vast and unsuspected field of action', exploding our 'prison-world' with its split-second dynamite so that 'now we can set off calmly on journeys of adventure among its far-flung debris'.⁹³ This makes it clearer that what we are being offered here is not best seen as a rather crude compensation thesis – imaginary escapism permitting us to live in an empty, alienating world – but a structural homology between an ever-changing world of objects and events, on one hand, and the world as it is taken up, experienced, by a subject: both worlds are in principle 'full', a plenitude, worlds in which possibilities and actualities – adventure and prison – run into one another, and run across the line that appears to separate them. It is a world *already* 'worked up', appropriated imaginatively in its very dispersion, a world in which world-as-dispersion and consciousness-as-distraction are two sides of the same coin. Film both reflects this and *participates* in it, reproduces it not just in its content but in its mode of operation, the practice of its own construction. Indeed, our whole experience of the world is now technology-inflected, inherently mediated. And the key instrument of this transformation and interpenetration of these worlds, in their relation to each other, is the camera. It is time to consider this innocuous piece of equipment further.

The assumption that the camera is an instrument of realism, that it can 'represent' reality, coexists uneasily with our awareness that the whole technology of the camera is based on the fragmentation and manipulation of reality through the very techniques of image production and reproduction themselves. Cinematography is not secondarily or contingently creative; it is creative at its core, in its very functioning. It operates with the possible as well as the actual, fantasy as much as reality, and it always has. Further, any sense of closure here, any termination of the inexhaustibility of the world, cannot but involve the element of fabrication that is central to the cinematographic art. Hence Benjamin's claim that 'The equipment-free aspect of reality has here become the height of artifice, and the vision of immediate reality the Blue Flower in the land of technology'. Pure, unmediated reality can survive only as the fantasy object of yearning, of unsatisfied desire: the 'Blue Flower' of German Romanticism.⁹⁴ Film can perfectly well *appear* to present unmediated reality – you do not, as a viewer, see the camera, or any other technological devices or 'stage props' – but this occurs only on the basis of 'the most intensive interpenetration of reality with equipment'.[95] In this sense the cinematographer resembles the surgeon more than the painter; and whereas the painter can produce a 'total image', the cinematographer's image is 'piecemeal', involving multiple fragments, available for combination and recombination. Hence montage becomes a fundamental technique of cinematic construction, just as the capacity for producing shock is central to its effect.

Film, in this way, is inherently arbitrary and dispersive: it works not with 'natural' entities or identities, respecting boundaries; it intervenes *in* the world, through cutting and combining. Its entities are images, received through the mode of distraction, as aspects of the dispersion of the world. We can indeed add that there is clearly only a precarious sense in which a film is a coherent whole; any 'closure' is just the artifice that papers over the artifice of the rest. A film is, first and foremost, a series of takes and shots, and a resulting series of cuts and joins, both series being in principle as indeterminate as life itself. If film is death by a thousand cuts, it is also life through the endless reproduction its own techniques imply. There is no 'original' here; the current fashion for the 'director's cut' – as if there could only ever be one, and as if it could magically resolve the issues of authenticity and coherence – merely serves to reflect and mask the irreducible contingency.

As for the nature of reproduction, in the case of film one can see a contrast with earlier art forms, where the creation of the work is separate from its distribution (if the latter is possible at all). A novel is written; the publication process then involves a separate process of production whereby a number of copies can be distributed. But with film, and other recording technologies, the ability to produce an original becomes inseparable from the ability to *re*produce it *and* to alter it. In film, argues Benjamin, technological reproducibility 'is not an 'externally imposed condition of its mass dissemination'; rather, it is 'based directly on the technology of their production'.[96] These technologies reveal a dramatic new transformative aspect or level of reality, whereby the recording of the world becomes inseparable from an insertion *into* it, and reproduction is always already transformation: the output becomes available for further dispersal or for various forms and techniques of recombination. This is reproduction, but not necessarily subject to any code of identity, any reign of the 'same'. Modern technologies of reproduction are also technologies of dispersion, as fragmentation or diffusion. Montage and simulation become significant both as method and as outcome.

The significance of *mass* reproduction can now be approached. In a passage where Benjamin refers to this, the translations give 'mass existence' and 'plurality of copies'.[97] Weber points to the German here: *massenweise*, something 'massive or mass-like', which is said to be substituted for a unique existence; and this reinforces the connection with 'mass' and 'masses' elsewhere in the text.[98] We can note here that when there was a degree of public access to art in the past this was on the basis of hierarchy and stratification; it was not through true 'dispersion', the mass *as* undifferentiated individuals, producing a different kind of participation,[99] whether or not concentrated as a 'mass movement'. Benjamin remarks that 'Mass reproduction is especially favored by the reproduction of the masses', adding that in marches, mass sporting events, etc., mass recording techniques imply that 'the masses can come face to face with themselves',[100] just as this is inseparable from the potential for transfiguration and distortion. Thus, increasingly, 'priority is given to presenting the politician before the recording equipment' rather than parliament, so we find a 'new form of selection – selection before an apparatus – from which the star and the dictators emerge as victors'.[101]

In coming 'face to face with themselves', then, it may be that one identifiable person can 'stand in' for the mass of others, through metonymic displacement, embedded in the multiplicity of photographic 'takes', the images and reproductions through which such a person exists as a fundamentally *mediated* being. Weber suggests that 'The cinematic cult of personality imparts the aura of individuality to a product which "takes place" in many places at once, in multiple here-and-nows, and which therefore cannot be said to have any "original" occurrence'.[102] For Benjamin, however, 'personality' could be said to replace aura:[103] mediated aura becomes vicarious identity, occupying the place of aura in its very disappearance, and personality emerges as the charisma of the individual, the illusory coherence, the glue that holds it all together through its powerful projection as image, masking the dispersion. Processes of concentration and figuration thereby produce stars and celebrities, and if we remember the theme of subject–object, audience–actor reversibility in film, we can see how stardom and celebrity become in turn available to and reproducible through the mass, both as fashion and through the very idea of personality and its implications – the idea that *anyone* can be a star.

Celebrity – the hollow core at the heart of stardom – indeed helps reveal the self-reproducing oscillation between concentration, on the one hand, and dispersal and distraction on the other, self as identity and as flux.[104] The problem is that the celebrity cannot simply emerge in some natural, 'unconstructed' form; we know celebrities are media creations, constructed out of *us*, the mass, in our mediated, dispersed mode, just as their reception by us occurs in similar piecemeal and media-inflected fashion. Their 'integrity' is always at issue, because so is their very identity. But this does not contradict their appeal as objects in dispersal, manically unified as 'larger than life', projections of ourselves, and revealing all the more clearly how to perform the 'identity' that holds us together. But it is never enough. Hence the fate of celebrities: we build them up and pull them down – just like objects in the baroque court. As we pay them too much attention, and decompose them, so they lose meaning. As we focus, we realize there's nothing *there*: the essence of (their) celebrity dissipates. (It was doubtless never sufficiently 'there' in the first place.) Celebrity is oddly powerless, precariously standing out from the shadowy mass, the 'public' that can extinguish it so quickly. As mediated, magnified gossip, celebrity is itself 'public', defying the private that is nonetheless endlessly recreated in order to furnish the 'secrets' that must then be exposed, the nightmares at the heart of these allegories of identity – secrets that are themselves endless displacements of the secret that cannot be exposed, the 'nothing there' at the core of it all. Thus, with the celebrity, biography takes the place of achievement, image subsumes action into melodrama, and vicarious identity merges substance into form. And when we see idealized figures collapse into their antitheses, this 'bad' celebrity reminds us that the monstrous and the fearsome can also figure the 'otherness' of the mass, the mass as a more bounded entity, defined *against* others, who thereby return 'inside' to disrupt and displace – no longer the mass as 'everyman', but as *us* against *them*.[105]

6

Cinematic Sensation: The Sublime and the Spectacle

John Martin was a nineteenth-century sensation. Arguably more people saw his pictures than those of any other artist, not only because his development of mezzotint and lithographic reproduction techniques disseminated smaller, often altered, versions of his huge canvases, but because this in turn contributed to his becoming a global phenomenon, supposedly even as far afield as China. At the end of his life, his great triptych of the *Last Judgement* (1849–53) toured the country, being exhibited at every urban centre of any size, and seen by several million people. Always more popular with the public than with the arts establishment, his reputation was in decline by the 1870s, and only recently has there been any real revival of interest within the art world itself.[1]

One of his early works, *Sadak in Search of the Waters of Oblivion* (1812), depicts a tiny figure in a mountainous landscape, dwarfed by towering crags, rugged high peaks and plunging waterfalls, very much in the tradition of the eighteenth-century sublime, albeit already on a grander scale. This engagement with the sublime remains central, but many of his later works convey a novel twist. Nature and culture blend: the works of human labour – great cities, vast buildings – become awe-inspiring and terrible, inhabited yet alien. We confront forces we have released but cannot control; our mastery of the world cannot avert the catastrophe we may even have helped bring about, the apocalyptic devastation that reduces us to abject helplessness, constituting the drama at the core of his work.[2] In *The Destruction of Sodom and Gomorrah* (1852), a fiery vortex both manifests and highlights the force of destructive power, with buildings, whole cities, collapsing into the abyss. And if, as Simon Morley suggests, the contemporary sublime is mostly about 'immanent transcendence … a transformative experience understood as occurring within the here and now',[3] then Martin's work prefigures this: the 'beyond' is all-too-present, the

John Martin, *The Destruction of Sodom and Gomorrah* (1852) Newcastle, Laing Art Gallery

sensation of cataclysmic ruination conveys its own sufficient sense of the sublime brought *closer* in its distance from us.[4]

Martin's canvases were widely drawn on as a visual language for the articulation of feeling, and he himself described the receding colonnades and vertiginous viewpoint of *Belshazzar's Feast* (1820) as 'a perspective of feeling';[5] a disturbance in sensory awareness is indeed central to what his art conveys, a sense of the imagery of experience at its limit. This is a clue to the controversies around his reputation. The bracing quality of the sublime, implying a degree of distance and detachment whereby the awesome and the terrifying can be properly interior responses, qualities of self rather than primarily of the senses, is here threatened by 'excessive' sensory involvement and an engagement of the self in the theatricality of the spectacle. As Julie Milne puts it, his work 'unsettles our sense of cultural value, blurring distinctions between the trite and the esteemed, the authentic and the artificial',[6] in effect questioning the notion of 'good taste' as already established in official aesthetics, and refusing any clear distinction between 'fine art' and popular culture. He implicitly suggested the impossibility of separating art from that wider nineteenth-century world of popular spectacle and entertainment, the panoramas, dioramas and other innovations of the visual technology of the time.[7]

However, the contemporary revival of interest reminds us that, in a sense, he never really went away, for his work has been a significant influence on that most original and potent of twentieth-century cultural forms: film. Right from the start, film directors, set designers and 'special effects' innovators were drawn to him. D. W. Griffith acknowledged the importance of *Belshazzar's Feast* as the model for the set for Babylon in his film of a century later, *Intolerance* (1916), and so on up to Ray Harryhausen, George Lucas and Peter Jackson; recent films like *The Day After Tomorrow* (2004) and *2012* (2009) feature panoramic landscapes undergoing cataclysmic destruction in a way that rivals – but hardly exceeds – the Martin originals. Yet of course it remains true that Martin's works are *paintings*, hanging on a wall, in frames. The differences, as well as the similarities, are significant. So now it is appropriate to pursue the sublime further, into the experience of film itself.

The cinematic sublime

From Benjamin's parallel between surgery and the cutting involved in making film, to the 'director's cut', we have found that 'cutting' appears to have both practical significance and a symbolic dimension, and we can now take this further. Cutting is the incision in the real that separates the image *from* the real, liberates it into meaning, while ensuring, through that very act, that it necessarily remains imbricated with the real. Kracauer's essay 'The Mass Ornament', on dance troupes like the Tiller Girls, argues that it is not really bodies that are the component parts of the display, but 'arms, thighs, and other segments', and there is an implicit violence in the language here, a visceral language of cutting, in the 'ripping open' and 'dissecting' of organic unities.[8] While not explicitly referring to the filmic practice of montage, it is difficult not to be reminded of the way sections of film are cut up, spliced together, and reassembled to form the 'composition'. Here, 'cutting' in film takes its place in a culture in which such violence – both symbolic and practical – can have other dimensions.[9]

For an intriguing further twist in the argument, we can turn to Derrida. Beginning a discussion of the notion of the sublime in Kant, he points out that *taille*, usually translated into English as 'size', has a near-obsolete second meaning in French: '*taille* marked the line of a cut … all the incisions which … delimit a contour, a form or a quantity …'.[10] To mark this, the translators of Derrida use the obsolete 'cise' instead of 'size', with its suggestion of cutting (incision).[11] The implication is that whereas cutting can involve shaping, the imposition of form, the sublime must lie beyond this: it 'exceeds cise and good measure, it is no longer proportioned according to man and his determinations', as Derrida puts it. Following Kant quite closely, he suggests that the idea of the sublime can only be aroused by 'the spectacle of a nature … which no limit can border, finish, or define in its cise',[12] implying a sense in which the sublime depends on the notion of the cut for its very possibility.[13]

If we draw the two dimensions of 'cise' together, we can say that the cut has the effect of making something manageable, 'to scale'. And the sublime has a necessary reference to scale. In this sense, the 'cinematic experience', positioning the spectator in relation to a large screen, already suggests that cinema may be potentially sublime in a way not possible for other media: a film reproduced on television, as a small object in a domestic space, loses much of any sublime effect it may have had. In the light of this, the relation between 'cinema', as experience, and 'film', as the screen and its content, needs further consideration.

It is within the relationship between the camera, the eye and the I – between technology and the embodied subject – that the sense of cinematic space is constructed, in turn enabling the flow of the film, the sense of movement in time, to unfold. Cinematic space extends behind the screen, as if the latter is a window or opening, just as it extends in front, towards and through the audience, thereby giving the breadth and depth fundamental to our experience of the film. For this to be possible, there has to be a fluctuating relationship, a tension, between the two-dimensional image and the three-dimensional depth and breadth that position us in a distance *from* the screen but also *in* the world of experience that the very gap opens up, a space of fissure. Thus Richard Maltby suggests that the 'curious status' of cinematic space, torn between these two dimensions, neither one nor the other, ensures that our attention to the screen is 'a play of looks *at*, *into*, and *through* the screen space; it fluctuates in its intensity, direction, and point of resolution'.[14] Cinematic space thereby becomes a place both familiar and strange, somewhere we inhabit, belong in, somewhere continuous with, but not reducible to, the space of everyday life. It is a zone where everyday life – including daydream and fantasy – can be experienced through the embodied imagination in the mode of distraction, in a relatively relaxed and experimental way. This incorporates distraction (involving attention, perception) and dispersion (identities as 'mass', as other), the latter hinted at in Claire Colebrook's formulation, following Deleuze, that 'What makes cinema *cinematic* is this liberation of the sequencing of images from any single observer',[15] implying a 'pluralism' of the 'cinematic subject', shifting within various viewpoints. And of course camera technique – close-ups, long shots, the use of telephoto and wide-angle lenses – affects this, giving a fluctuating awareness of proximity and distance, possible spatial disorientation, and 'atmosphere'. This experience, then, is as much one of simulation as representation, the experience of a mediated world.

In this context, we can return to cutting and framing, the shots and their conjunction as montage. With the photo, the traditional frame of a painting becomes 'edge', signifying an inherently arbitrary intervention into the 'real' that reminds us, in the violence of its gesture, in its cutting into and out of the world, of the insistent presence of that world, of the fact that what lies to the side of the photo, around it, remains 'there' even in its crudely enforced absence. So this 'framing' of the photo is always potentially dynamic, as if the 'motion picture' is already implicit (implicated) in the photo (just as it can always return to it: the film still as still photo). Film enforces this movement of the frame itself, using tracking shots, cuts and fades to incorporate an ever-active relation to the absence beyond, an 'absence beyond' that becomes the dynamic source of the cinematic experience, a constant or potential source of the shock that both Benjamin and Deleuze, in their different ways, see as inherent in film technique and its effect. If the photo appears to 'fix' the real, partly by being fixed to, or in, the real, film relativizes or reinvents the real. Implicit in this, as cinematic experience, is the way the 'time of watching' is incorporated into the image, expressing duration, and incorporating moving fields of perception. This 'time effect' is disjunctive – the spectator's sense of passing time, of duration, is not identical with time as it develops in the film, as diegesis, and hence contributes to the shock/distraction dynamic. As an approximation, then, we can say that the 'beyond' of cutting, framing, the cise – what it makes possible but does not in itself constitute – is this sense of the cinematic experience as it incorporates a transformed sense of space, time, and – perhaps the most fundamental innovation – movement itself. And this is an essential clue to the cinematic sublime.

Here we can begin to draw on the work of Deleuze. His suggestion that 'montage itself constantly adapts the transformations of movements in the material universe to the interval of movement in the eye of the camera'[16] both reveals the ambitious scope of his philosophy of film and – whatever these wider possibilities – certainly seems appropriate for thinking the relation between the mobile camera and the technology-inflected aspect of movement that has become so central to the modern experience of movement as such, both in its repetitive patterns and its unpredictable outcomes. Nor is the audience's own involvement with movement ever purely visual: it is always embodied, responsive. Movement is not just about film or the world being filmed; it also resonates in the subject, in mind and feeling. For Deleuze, it is this apparently independent power of movement communicated in film that is central to its role in the circuit of sensation: 'It is only when movement becomes automatic that the artistic essence of the image is realised: producing a shock to thought, communicating vibrations to the cortex, touching the nervous and cerebral system directly.'[17] Whether this indeed realizes the 'essence' of the image may need further consideration; for now it can at least be observed that this formulation – intriguingly reminiscent of earlier, nineteenth-century ones – seems to have some resonance in Kant's own thought. Claiming that the sublime involves 'a *movement* of the mind' rather than '*calm* contemplation',[18] Kant elaborates this by suggesting that there must initially be 'a vibration … a rapidly alternating repulsion from and attraction to one and the same object'.[19] Clearly this movement, this 'vibration', is physical as much as mental, 'vibration' being a characteristic figure for sensation and its effects, from as long ago as Hume.[20]

It is significant that while, for Kant, there is supposed to be a process here, from displeasure to pleasure – as the imagination's sense of its own inadequacy gives way to the realization that reason can transcend these limits – the specific use of 'vibration' here seems to imply an oscillation in which *both* are present, an oscillation that is perhaps irresolvable. In swinging between attraction and repulsion, feelings negative and positive, we seem to encounter the pattern, the dynamic, of excitement itself, and sensation as the embodiment of this. In this sense, the sublime *in* sensation is what forces us *beyond* sensation, without specifying anything about the 'beyond'; but that very fact might suggest to us that imaginative 'reflection' is inherent to it, reflection as the attempt to think and hence 'image' the reflexive gap itself, as it opens up in and beyond the subject, in the very attempt to grasp it. The very act of reflecting on itself has to be from a 'beyond' that it cannot simultaneously occupy, and that enforces *figuration*, an inevitable projection into – or incorporation of – 'nature': generally, nature as external, but in principle nature 'within' as well, hence figuring 'mental' processes as vibrations, nerves, shocks, using them as raw material for imaginative transformation. Deleuze, too, seems aware of the gap that opens up here, just as he is also aware of the possibility of figuration, suggesting that 'the shock is the very form of communication of movement in images'.[21] It is feeling or emotion that appears in this interstice or gap, *as* the experience of the gap, which is then filled by an image.[22] Indeed, 'the whole becomes the power of the outside which passes into the interstice'.[23] The 'cinematic subject' can thus be seen as positioned both *within* cinematic space yet *outside* the film, so that the outside is immanent in the very relation between the two, in the gaps or interstices of the subject and/or as the cuts or interstices of the film, the 'beyond' that is also 'inside'. And this 'beyond' suggests a sense in which the cinematic sublime is a central feature of the cinema experience, not just a facet of film and a reaction to its content.

If this involvement with movement is one defining attribute of the cinematic experience, then this in turn is refracted in cinematic space through a double tension. Movement can engage directly with the sense of depth, draw us in, and impact on us, in what can certainly include a physical reaction. But movement can also be transverse, across the screen, as if to emphasize the tension between two- and three-dimensional: movement as panoramic, like the view from a train window. And of course the camera can move between the two, slowly or rapidly, within the same shot, techniques which engage the audience at various levels of involvement and detachment, shock and defence. No more than in everyday life can 'movement' be seen as an integrated, linear process of uniform development, even though *ideologically* this emphasis on subsuming movement into a coherent narrative flow, an unfolding, organic 'whole' – subordinating movement *in* the film to movement *of* the film – serves as a powerful constituent of the more conservative film production strategies. But the second tension can be mapped on to this. If the depth perspective opens us more to the shocks of the cinematic experience, the breadth perspective encourages a more reflective, detached view, more sensitive to compositional features and the framework of interpretation. This is, after all, encapsulated in the film 'still': even if it portrays a moment of depth, it is portrayed as stasis, as breadth, encouraging this more reflective, analytical mode. In using the method of montage to suggest the idea of flow, of movement in time, then, the camera operates as a transformer in yet another sense. It is sensation, force, impact, shock; but it is also image, composition, meaning. And just as there is no way one dimension can be reduced to the other, so any approach to the cinematic sublime must encompass both.[24]

The filmic sublime

Here, as we turn towards a more explicit focus on the sublime in relation to film *content*, we can turn draw more directly on Kant, invoking a celebrated passage from the conclusion to the second *Critique*: 'Two things fill the mind with ever new and increasing admiration and reverence, the more often and more steadily one reflects on them: *the starry heavens above me and the moral law within me*.' I connect them immediately, Kant adds, with the 'consciousness of my existence', the first referring to 'the external world of sense' I occupy in a relation of 'unbounded magnitude with worlds upon worlds …', and the second beginning from 'my invisible self', presenting me with a world of 'true infinity', one not merely contingent but 'universal and necessary'.[25] He even uses the phrase 'sublimity of the object', apparently referring to both dimensions.[26] One can say that, for Kant, the unified subject cannot but complement the world as totality, both being revelations of the law of reason in its legislative self-sufficiency. If the more sustained discussion of the third *Critique* crucially couples this with a thesis about the limitations of the imagination in grasping the sublime, this coexists with an awareness of the oddly empowering form this limitation nonetheless takes, as has been suggested above. Deleuze offers a succinct summary: the imagination 'goes beyond its own limit itself', albeit negatively, 'by representing to itself the inaccessibility of the rational Idea, and by making this very inaccessibility something which is present in sensible nature'.[27] And if there are problems here – if there is a reflexive gap, a disjunction or discontinuity – then what we cannot attain is also within: problems with infinity and totality, mapped into the immensity, the limitlessness, of nature, will parallel those with person and self, mapped into the immensity, the depth, of mind. There can be no real closure here; the gaps, the interstices, of film do indeed map the gaps, the interstices in the Kantian system of the sublime – which are inseparably linked to its insights.

The sublime, then, surges up through the gaps, around the edges, as the disturbing presence of the beyond within the content, the images, of the film as it is in turn mapped into the cinematic experience of the spectator. Here, Kant's distinction between the mathematical sublime and the dynamical sublime, drawn on by Deleuze, can come into play. It is captured succinctly by Deleuze: 'The feeling of the sublime is experienced when faced with the formless or the deformed (immensity or power).'[28] The mathematical sublime is the 'absolutely great', incorporating the idea of boundless extension in space and time, endless horizons, the infinite in extent, seriality and repetition; ultimately, the threat it poses is that of dissolution into the infinite. The dynamical sublime is an 'object of fear', but considered from a position of safety, and it allows us to 'discover within ourselves a capacity for resistance';[29] hence it incorporates ideas of force, impact, power and the ultimate threat is that of annihilation by superior force.

One arena of comparison, to bring out this contrast, would be technology. In the dynamical sublime, automata seem potentially animate, a threat to the power of the human, hence disturbing for that reason; in the mathematical sublime, it is rather that the human, as animate, is threatened by the possibility of reduction to the status of automata, losing individuality and independence. The contrast is between the machine as organic, and the organic as machine. In the mathematical sublime, interaction between human and machine becomes repetitive, mechanical, geometrical. Deleuze draws examples of this from the classic French school (Abel Gance, Jean Epstein, Jean Renoir),[30] but we are also reminded of the dance troupes already alluded to. Thus Kracauer alludes to the dancers as 'no longer individual girls, but indissoluble girl clusters whose movements are demonstrations of mathematics', hence functional, interchangeable.[31] But one might instance, in particular, the scene from *Gold Diggers of 1933*, choreographed by Busby Berkeley, when the girls dance in the dark, photographed from above, so they themselves become invisible, and what we see are the vivid, changing patterns of the lights they carry. The lines and circles of these patterns could, in principle, be endlessly extended. This is also, of course, the realm that can produce the large-scale military and gymnastic displays put on by regimes like those in China and North Korea. All of these can figure the spectacle in its spatial extension and unboundedness, its suggestion of a combination of drama and immensity as carrier of the sublime in the age of the mass and media technology.

This can, in turn, remind us of the dual perception of the mass, positioning it relative to the two sublimes: as homogeneous, whether atomized, diffused or patterned repetitively to infinity; and as surging, unruly, unbounded, defying its own limits – in short, as 'monstrous'. Now, it is intriguing that Kant himself, in a brief reference to the monstrous, positions it in the *mathematical* sublime. He writes: 'An object is *monstrous* if by its magnitude it annihilates the end which its concept constitutes.'[32] In context, Kant has just observed that known objects, in their normal state, whether animals or artefacts, cannot be sublime; so the claim seems to be that the 'excess' of the monstrous, while it might be *suggested* by something huge in size, is fundamentally a matter of excess in relation to our *categories*. So if the monstrous object defies classification, defies 'cise', it must do so in a way that nevertheless involves the latter: it must be in some respect *deformed*. And here we can enter a caveat about the characterization of this (in Kant and Deleuze) in terms of 'formlessness'. Strictly speaking, form calls into play notions of size and shape, of foreground and background, and, in particular, of figure against background. To be totally 'without form' would be to disappear into background, into infinite undifferentiation. So the monstrous is indeed *de*-formed: it makes sense only as transgression of form, not lack of it, although that transgression can include *relative* lack, and a *process* of emergence of the de-formed out of the background, as the object with obscure boundaries. The monstrous can be sharply outlined, but also relatively shapeless, the clarity of the line always semi-dissolved, whether expanding or contracting, as endless movement, invading space. All this is the stuff of the monstrous, in Hollywood and popular culture generally: the Thing, the Blob, the creature from the infinite depths, or the pit, the beast from hell … And 'lurking' here, in the depths of the Western cultural tradition, is the body itself, as threat, as the danger of the undisciplined: the body as always excessive to itself, fat, grotesque, yet potentially *tempting*, as a route to self-expression, defying the slim body, the body beautiful.[33] How appropriate, then, that the monstrous should trouble the boundaries of Kant's own classification …

Could the Kantian sublime also be troubled by another category, that of the abject? While displeasure or pain is supposed to lead to pleasure, we have noted the uncertainty in Kant's formulation, the positive and negative appearing to 'vibrate' together, suggesting the possibility of irresolution. Trapped here, the subject could find the experience of the sublime inseparable from that of the abject. A stage in the emergence of the sublime is the abjection of the human subject before the grandeur or power of nature; but since the 'reason' that is thus projected into nature is itself in some sense either beyond the embodied self or mapped into it (as 'superego' perhaps), the potential for abjection remains present. If the subject can reach for the sublime, it can also be barred from it, abject in its inadequacy, the 'other' now embodying this alienated power. If in turn it becomes flooded by this other, its boundaries overwhelmed, it becomes truly abject. And where there is apparently irresolvable suffering, there is always the potential for the sentimental. Where the sublime purports to transcend time, the sentimental is embedded in it (nostalgia); and where the sublime attempts to maintain the integrity of the self by subjecting the body to the demands of reason, the sentimental subverts this distancing, this control, in the name of the body itself, wallowing in abject embodiment. The abject, hinted at in the sentimental, is perhaps the bathetic 'other face' of the sublime, subverting, even ridiculing, its pretensions.[34] For a dramatic example of the convergences that are possible here, we can instance the famous scene in *Uncle Tom's Cabin* where Eliza flees to freedom carrying her infant across the jagged ice of the frozen river. Noting that the scene has frequently been depicted in film and popular representation generally, Lauren Berlant suggests it makes the spectator 'merge awe at the woman's power in the face of the danger she endures for freedom, love, and family with the techno-aesthetic of an entertainment medium to reframe the real, to generate surplus pleasure and surplus pain at the spectacle of the sublime object of sentimentality'.[35]

When we incorporate this whole dimension of technology and mediated mass culture into the analysis, we can say that the sublime is the world experienced as 'special effects', combining the attributes of magnitude, immensity and power as a particularly dramatic and focused instance of spectacle, one that draws attention to the way technology itself – nature beyond nature, as prosthesis, instrumentality for its own self-transformation – can itself produce effects that are out of all proportion to itself, just as nature sublime is nature beyond all proportion. Special effects, suggests Sean Cubitt, enable us to 'marvel at the capabilities of the medium itself, throwing before the audience the specificity of the medium as well as a terminal form of illusion that succeeds by exceeding the apparent limits of the medium'. Such effects must be 'cutting edge' if they are to be sensational and spectacular. In this way, appearing to transcend its own status as media technology in the intensity that results, the special effect nonetheless 'circumscribes its own sublimity, identifying the boundary of communication with the technical limits of mediation'.[36]

All this invites us to ask more precisely about the relation of the sensational to this spectacle of the sublime. We might say that the mathematical sublime is crucial for the spectacularization of sensation, and the dynamical sublime for the sensationalizing of spectacle. This suggests the fundamental convergence here, albeit a convergence in difference, in different registers or aspects of the real. As infinite dispersion or distraction, spectacle tends towards the sublime in its mathematical mode; as concentration, or enforcing concentration, the sublime tends towards the dynamical mode, a sensationalism that intensifies the power of spectacle.

In one way, as spectacle, special effects can be said to freeze time, not because the time of duration cannot be incorporated into spectacle, but because *grasping* spectacle as object, as a whole, takes it out of time, just as it is actually *experienced* by the subject in time. Expressing the tension of this sense of totality as incorporating the subject that reflects on it, the sublime presents challenges of belonging, of identification and of power, in the context of the reflexive gap that constitutes its very possibility. If, in general, the sublime is a refracted and rarefied projection of our sense of everyday experience as it presents itself to us as encompassing us, stretching beyond us in space and time, and at times impacting on us, as shock, in ways that can seem threatening, we can now see how cinema can be its appropriate vehicle. Cinema positions us in a space that incorporates a relation between us and a screen such that this congruent world, involving depth, sensory immersion and visual spectacle, acts as a perspective on the everyday world, a place from which this world appears as other in itself, as 'real' yet only as one world among possible others. Like fiction, cinema is a parallel mode of experiencing and appropriating life *as* real, constituting it as such, and in cinema this is made vivid and distinctive through the disjunctions and juxtapositions on a screen whose 'edge' functions as *absence* of frame, identifying the sense of depth and spectacle. This sharp edge, parallel to the very different 'edge' around our visual gaze, with its qualities as penumbra, similarly enforces the presence of the *outside*, the beyond, letting the outside in, permitting focus, while hinting at the way in which everyday experience itself tests the frame, beyond 'cise'.

Sensation and spectacle

Sensation has always been difficult to 'place'. The scientific language of sensation, a language of forces, causes and effects, of organism or electricity, suggests a firm location in nature; the language of nerves and 'nervousness', frequently overlapping with the former, suggests a psychology of mind; and the media sense of sensation, albeit still suggesting impacts and effects on mind and body, seems to locate it in culture. Part of the place occupied by sensation, though, is its claim to *reality*, however paradoxical this may now seem, with sensation, as part of media culture, frequently denounced for exaggeration and fakery. It exists in its effects: if it is seen or experienced as sensational, it *is* sensational. A sensation is what passes as a sensation, no more and no less. Although it is true that the *embodied* aspect of sensation can in principle be faked, the general point remains: if I feel a sensation, then that is conclusive, whether or not there is something 'there' a scientist would recognize. One could perhaps say, then, that we have reached a point where Baudrillard's language of simulation becomes appropriate.[37] Sensation addresses the aspect of sensory experience in the age of spectacle, experience as self-constituting, self-sufficient in its impact, whatever its source. Sensation in this sense is not sensation as culture *rather than* nature or mind; it is what *interrogates* these pigeonholes, questions the very classifications through which it has been appropriated. And spectacle corresponds to the mediated, representational aspects of experience, positioning subject and object, reproducing the gap, the distance, within which sensation can occur as the force or charge that flashes in the gap, both bridging it while yet maintaining it, *in* its distance. A suggestion by the painter Fernand Léger, writing in 1924, seems appropriate here: he presents 'the shock of the surprise effect' as 'the origin of the modern spectacle'.[38]

In this world, visual technology and its consequences, mass reproduction, and 'the masses', never encounter each other as abstractions because they are all alike constructed as and through material practices, continuities and disjunctions, shocks and flows. This is the world as plethora, with spectacle as its visual mode, the mode of its appearance. Spectacle is 'that which distracts', the totality of distractions, the totality *as* distraction, corresponding to infinite dispersion. In this sense, there is no grand 'spectacle of spectacles', only the endless disjunction of spectacles, calling for our attention, whether or to whatever extent they actually get it. 'To say that the world is conceived as a series of spectacles is to say that it is treated as something to be attended to', as Nicholas Abercrombie and Brian Longhurst put it.[39] When sensationalized, this does indeed become the spectacle to which we *have* to pay attention, spectacle concentrated. And if film draws all this together in a particularly vivid fashion, it is not of course unique.

Douglas Kellner suggests that 'the society and culture of spectacle is creating a new kind of information-entertainment society'.[40] This is by no means totally new: the eighteenth-century spectacle of sympathy,[41] revealing a vicarious interest in the plight of the other, coupled with the aspiration to relieve it, was balanced on an unstable terrain between a detached, scientific interest in learning about the nature of suffering, on the one hand, and the risk that a voyeuristic *pleasure* could be derived from the spectacle of the other's pain, on the other. And just as the nineteenth century saw the impact of the news media, the innovations of photography, and the diffusion of 'special effects' in the theatre, so the conjunction of these in the modern media spectacle reveals continuing overlap and convergence with the cultural experience of sensation, from its eighteenth century origins up to the later cult – and culture – of the 'sensational', to the point where they become difficult to disentangle. Nevertheless, the 'spectacular' in the sensational does add a distinctive emphasis, and this is worth exploring.

A spectacle could be defined as something that appears as display before a subject. 'Display' seems to come from the Anglo-French *despleier*, with an associated medical meaning of 'disperse'. To 'display' could then be taken to mean 'unfold-as-dispersal': a display is an unfolding that is not determined in its origin. That such display incorporates a visual dimension is brought out in Steve Neale's characterization of spectacle as exhibiting a concern 'to *display* the visibility of the visual'.[42] But it is not reducible to this. Describing panoramas and dioramas in late nineteenth-century Paris, Vanessa Schwartz suggests that what we find here is that 'to capture "life", a display had to reproduce it, not simply represent it. The display had to fit motion and the entire bodily experience of its viewers into the spectacle.' Spectacle should be sufficiently distracting to catch the attention, as a fully embodied power of focusing, and sufficiently startling, detailed or diverse to hold it – at least for a while. What was 'modern', then, was the idea that 'the everyday could be transformed into the spectacular and the sensational'.[43] Discussing the popular wax museum, which claimed to be a *journal plastique*, a 'living newspaper', she points to the 'intertextuality' here, the assumption of a public already familiar with newspaper stories. Rather than simply representing reality, the *Musée Grévin* was 'a representation of a representation of reality: it had the reality of a newspaper, which most people enjoyed as reality', showing that 'reproduction was inscribed in layers of representation'.[44] In turn, Tom Brown argues that in the film *Gone With the Wind*, the relationship of Scarlett O'Hara (Vivien Leigh) to the spectacle that surrounds her 'vivifies or "naturalizes" her relationship to her world'.[45] This confirms that display is not 'mere' display, as it were: it emphasizes figuration as 'realization', as a making-real that simultaneously constitutes it in a possible relationship with a viewer.

The element of theatricality that is apparent here can be further brought out by this definition of spectacle given by Thomas Richards, working within a broadly Marxist framework: 'a state of signification in which much of society becomes a theatre for the fictions it has created for its commodities'.[46] Objects 'come to life' *as* commodities through the spectacle, a vivid emplacement of our experience of the world as a world of commodities that is explored in Benjamin's own texts, and which is, in turn, vividly exhibited in the profuse illustrations in Susan Buck-Morss's book on Benjamin, including a concluding section, 'Afterimages'[47] – the whole point being that these are also *not* 'illustrations'; rather, they embody, 'realise', Benjamin's own descriptions, peopling the world of spectacle with the commodities that variously entice, seduce or repel us, in all their multiplicity. We might also note that its claim to be *noticed*, in its autonomy, emerging against its context, claiming our attention, reveals *excess* to be a central feature of spectacle. This excess can include various dimensions: there is excess of detail (the miniaturization of space), excess as expanse (space as horizon), and excess of movement (action as speed), just as these can be combined in excess as distortion, exaggeration.[48] Spectacle 'invested the quotidian with the panache of the extraordinary', as Richards puts it.[49]

Schwartz suggests that, increasingly, 'the cultural context for using the term reality was one in which life itself was framed – in which events were experienced as what could be represented'.[50] This brings to a head an intriguing tension running through all this: 'framing' is an active process, an intervention, involving 'cutting', as we have seen; yet, as spectacle, the world 'presents itself' to us, before us. 'We' seem to slide from active to passive here. This is not just the different positions of director, producer and artist, on the one hand, and audience, as spectator, on the other. How is it that the world can present itself both as *ready* for framing, but also as *already* framed? As has been hinted at, in Schwartz's account, we live in a culture in which we are used to the world being ever-available for photographic and filmic appropriation and reproduction, one that already *has been* represented and experienced in these terms, that addresses us in these terms. We can do this because, as display, this world of (and as) representation differs from itself, unfolds itself, by virtue of the irreducibly arbitrary aspect of the cutting that separates it in the very act of representing it, the interventionist approach of the camera that necessarily fragments and recombines even as it records and thereby reproduces the real in its difference, concentrated into spectacle, only ever precariously integrated. The spectacle is thus the world as it presents itself as, inseparably, artefact and artifice.

Thus positioned as 'artwork', spectacle implies a distinctive angle on the familiar problem of whether 'meaning' is a function of the artist's intention or the audience's interpretation, a dilemma rejected in Jacques Rancière's formulation: 'There is the distance between artist and spectator, but there is also the distance inherent in the performance itself, insofar as it subsists, as a spectacle, an autonomous thing, between the idea of the artist and the sensation or comprehension of the spectator.'[51] This seems appropriate, with a reservation over the term 'autonomy' here. The spectacle incorporates dispersal through the cutting that is central to its mode of presenting space and time, through movement and action, just as its own ever-threatened dispersal back into the nothingness of its own background is precariously kept at bay through the mechanisms of concentration spectacle itself pioneered – its 'technology' in the broadest sense, the means whereby it displays itself and thereby distracts its audience.

Let us push this further. Suppose that in some sense the whole world had become a spectacle. This is the thesis that is developed in its most cogent and influential form in Debord's *Society of the Spectacle* (1967). 'Everything that was directly lived has moved away into a representation', and since '… reality rises up within the spectacle, and the spectacle is real' we can no longer appeal to a reality outside or beyond it. Since our experience can only be expressed through the spectacle, it becomes alien to us: '… the spectator does not feel at home anywhere, because the spectacle is everywhere'.[52] What we contemplate in spectacle is life detached from truth, and what we experience is the suffering that is precisely this. Here is the concentrated core of an argument that is already highly concentrated:

> The origin of the spectacle is the loss of the unity of the world, and the gigantic expansion of the modern spectacle expresses the totality of this loss: the abstraction of all specific labor and the general abstraction of the entirety of production are perfectly translated in the spectacle, whose *mode of being concrete* is precisely abstraction. In the spectacle, one part of the world *represents itself* before the world and is superior to it. The spectacle is nothing more than the common language of this separation … The spectacle reunites the separate, but reunites it *as separate*.[53]

In its way, this is a vivid summation of a whole tradition of Western thought: the original fall from Eden, whether seen in Christian or Hegelian–Marxist terms; and Plato's picture of the resulting entrapment in a cave of shadows playing on the wall, a mystified reality. What is missing here is the usual hope of redemption or resolution, a vision of utopia as return to a transfigured origin. This is implicit in Debord, but notoriously what appears as the all-encompassing determinism of his analysis makes it difficult to leave any opening for it.[54] But let us dig deeper.

The mode of realization of spectacle, we are told, is through abstraction. The notion of 'abstraction' here is derived from the labour theory of value, whereby the individual forms of concrete labour lose their individual content or meaning through the transformation imposed by the logic of the market. Yet, we learn at the very beginning that modern life 'announces itself as an enormous accumulation of *spectacles*',[55] and the analysis frequently emphasizes the diversity and plurality here. How is the uniformity of 'abstraction' to be mapped onto this? The abstraction of the spectacle, *as* concrete, is manifested in its rendering of particulars as purely arbitrary, contingent, and interchangeable. The spectacle 'represents itself' as the endlessly empty sign, empty in the infinite possibility of its meaning, its content, available to be anything for anyone, and therefore nothing. Objects become random signifiers, unrelated to any real or particular need or purpose, and linked to consumers via the equally random working of fashions and trends, which in turn trigger *desire*; and since such desire is as transient as anything else, it moves quickly to new objects. Every product promises 'a dazzling shortcut to the promised land', but once brought home 'it reveals its essential poverty'. The object has lost the aura of the real, now existing only as a projection of the self, image of a desire that can never find satisfaction in it. Desire reads reality as appearance, seeking to possess it as image, and this dynamic of possessing and appearing reproduces the desiring subject as subject to fashion and to transient reputation, reproducing itself narcissistically through an ever-slipping, ever-inadequate self-image. Indeed, what Debord writes of commodities would seem to apply also to those who consume them: 'Every given commodity fights for itself, cannot acknowledge the others, and attempts to impose itself everywhere ...' Thus consumerism 'liberates unlimited artificiality, in the face of which living desire is disarmed'.[56] Looked at in this light, Debord's critique may remind us, however distantly, of an earlier critic of market society: Rousseau.[57]

The relation between abstract and concrete thus seems to imply a dispersion of 'Spectacle' into spectacles, in some tension with Debord's own drive to a concentrated, totalizing analysis; yet this tension is also present in the *content* of his argument, for he suggests that spectacle exists in two forms: concentrated and diffused. The former involves centralization and bureaucracy, and is ultimately liable to culminate in the figure of the dictator, intriguingly characterized as the 'absolute celebrity', whereas the latter involves the free play of the market, in which the consumer can nonetheless 'directly touch only a succession of fragments of this commodity happiness'.[58] Glossing the latter, Abercrombie and Longhurst suggest that spectacle is 'all around and fragmented, diffused throughout and infused into everyday life – just like the diffused audience',[59] and Kellner's case studies emphasize the 'plurality and heterogeneity of contending spectacles'.[60] Conversely, the concentration pole indicates the potential for the projection of 'mass identity' on to the 'mass celebrity', as a function of mass mobilization and its manipulation. Debord's later views, suggesting a certain convergence between these two forms,[61] could be developed to suggest that the 'absolute' celebrity may merely become the omnipresent mass-produced one, providing the potential for moments of fashion-driven identification that coexist readily enough, as moments of concentration, with their dissolution into new ones, all in an overall context of diffusion and distraction, sensation and spectacle, just as the power of the dictator is transformed into a competing field of tension between the concentrating impetus of bureaucratic surveillance and its own antithesis in rival institutions and individual strategies of counter-surveillance.

We can move towards a conclusion by recalling that the notion of spectacle in relation to dispersion or unfolding implies *process*. To consider the implications of this, let us take two examples, both continuing the political emphasis. From within the 2003 Gulf War, the reporter Sarah Boxer wrote that 'with the war rolling ahead on television, you the viewer are made a part of the invading army', and 'Meanwhile, just as the audience feels part of the army, the army becomes part of the audience. American troops on an aircraft carrier watch CNN to see how the war is playing and progressing. Soldiers are watching other soldiers on television.' Hence, she adds, there is 'general confusion as to who is acting and who is watching'. She asks: 'Are the television cameras witness to war, or are they part of the weaponry?'[62] Before commenting, let us take the second example, from the fall of Communism in the Eastern Bloc in 1989. Jean Seaton refers to the television images of cars streaming out of East Germany, with the authorities no longer making any effort to stop them: 'The sudden, shared vision of possibility altered people's lives, brought down a regime, and changed the world. It was composed out of a classic media process: a loop showing the audience its own behaviour.' She adds that such images foster 'allegiance through sentiment and identification'.[63]

One could say that the moment of spectacle itself, the moment of its appropriation *as* spectacle, undoubtedly does pose a clear distinction between the performance, or what is happening on the screen, and the audience, but when one sees this as a moment in a *process*, a rather different picture emerges. Then, the distinction between passive viewing and action becomes blurred: viewing has consequences. This can get lost if the term 'spectacle' is restricted to a narrow sense, as the moment of passive appropriation, one that positions subject and object in a relation to each other of timeless abstraction. If 'spectacle' is taken to include the moment of subject–object distance, but also to characterize the process as such, the unfolding that necessarily incorporates the moment of reflexive difference, we can make sense of these examples. If spectacle incorporates this irreducible reflexive element, we can see that, *pace* Boxer, it is not *necessarily* the case that the viewer is made 'part of the invading army': the war produced plenty of opposition, demonstrations and controversy; many recoiled from and felt alienated by the unfolding spectacle of events, and were not necessarily 'immobilised'. Then again, Seaton's 'sentiment and identification' can play strange games, inhabiting the reflexive gap in ways that are necessarily unpredictable. Indeed, rather than 'identification', it may be a sense of 'belonging with', of shared *participation*, that is crucial here – Kant's 'enthusiasm' again. A structural approach, incorporating feeling, reflexive awareness, and the possibility of judgement, can incorporate the possibility of critique as immanent rather than closing it off altogether or making it impossible to account for its occurrence. But in an age when the spectacle has become ever more sensational, problems still loom …

7

Sensational Affect

The 'affective turn' of the first decade or so of this century seems to have developed out of a growing interest in embodiment and sensory experience, across the humanities, cultural studies, cultural history and sociology, coupled with a reaction against the emphasis on discourse and language associated with the influence of French theory from structuralism through post-structuralism and deconstruction; and these, in turn, have gone hand in hand with the growing influence of another French theorist, albeit of a different stripe: Gilles Deleuze. Most recently – and controversially – this has been joined by developments in neuroscience and the trumpeted possibilities of 'neuroaesthetics'. While few might want to take this as far as William Connolly in claiming that 'Affect is part of biology, if anything is',[1] it is nonetheless true that the idea that affect connects us with currents and energies that circulate beyond and outside the human, as well as inside it, seems central to these recent discussions. As this suggests, then, 'affect' may turn out to be just as difficult a term as those it aspires to replace or bypass, notably 'feeling'; and since, on any reading, it overlaps substantially with the range and concerns of 'sensation' as presented here, it would clearly seem appropriate, and indeed important, to consider it.[2]

For Teresa Brennan, an affect is 'the physiological shift accompanying a judgment', yet seemingly unconnected with it, whereas feelings can be articulated through the appropriate words. 'Feelings are thoughtful, and affects are thoughtless.'[3] Indeed, affects without feelings are potentially troublesome; feelings convey information about whether a state is pleasurable or not, they convey a reactive awareness of events, whether internal or external, whereas affects do not do this. As Lawrence Grossberg puts it, 'An affect can never define, by itself, why things should matter'; it does not carry values and meanings with it. Yet it can be seen as having significance, even if not signification; it cannot be pinned down with labels, even if it seems to invite the attempt. It reveals how invigorated we feel, it shows our levels of energy or will. 'Affect is what gives "color", "tone", or "texture" to our experiences.' It conveys a sense of embodied well-being (or the reverse), through another vague but useful term, 'mood'. As directed outwards, it gets us a sense of 'what matters', and how much: 'Mattering maps define different forms, quantities and places of energy',[4] Grossberg concludes. Misha Kavka adds that 'affect "matters" in a double sense, because it links the material world to structures of feeling', and, in turn, 'we are always responding not just to a sensate object but to others' feelings lodged in it', bringing into play a necessarily social dimension.[5] We can say, then, that if I am 'moved' by your gift, this does not seem to require any specific emotion or feeling, or way of expressing it; it is more like a diffuse state, an overall positive attitude of mind and body, with no particular, necessary manifestation, yet highly specific to that situation, that relationship. 'Affect' underlies naming or expression, but is not yet either, nor can it be fully grasped by either. It is a prelude to meaning, and an excess beyond it: the energy that drives figuration. Margaret Wetherell concludes that whatever the 'neurobiological polyphony' involved in its production, it cannot be separated from thoughts, evaluations and social contexts.[6]

Affects seem to exist on the borderline between awareness and the conditions that produce or 'affect' that awareness. For Brennan, 'Affects are conscious as states discerned by feelings, but their production is involuntary and unconscious', perhaps involving a shift of mood, such as from calmness to irritation.[7] But this sense of affect as being on a borderline seems to be true more generally; when Kavka suggests that 'affect is to be found at the join',[8] this 'join' can clearly include not just conscious and unconscious (or non-conscious), but also mind and body, and contact between bodies. Hence again the frustration one might encounter in characterizing affect is complemented by its powerful figurative potential. It also follows that although affect cannot, perhaps, be seen as a form of cognition in itself, it seems to question the boundaries of the latter, hinting as it does at an implicitly relational view of the world, whereby its self-referential quality is linked to an embeddedness in relations beyond the self. Indeed, this suggests that the whole notion of 'cognition' needs to be broadened, to bring out its necessary involvement with sensory and affective experience.[9]

A flash of lightning

It is Brian Massumi's work that seems to have become most widely cited in this context, after that of Deleuze himself, whose influence is indeed quite overt in this statement of Massumi's aims, namely to show how 'movement, sensation, and qualities of experience couched in matter in its most literal sense (and sensing) might be culturally-theoretically thinkable'.[10] This interest in matter, process and affect, and their effects on both the context and content of experience, is well brought out in an example that Massumi takes from a brief allusion in Nietzsche, and develops in his own way: a sensational event from the natural world, a flash of lightning.

It is, argues Massumi, the event itself that counts: 'There is no subject before or behind it whose deed it would be. It is an autonomous doing.' *Before* the flash, there is, of course, an electrical field, of charged particles, a *potential* for the flash, but nothing pre-determined. The actual triggering of the charge is 'a movement immanent to the field of potential, by which it plays out the consequences of its own intensity'. The lightning strike does not, then, 'resemble, represent or reproduce' the charged field.[11] It is a culmination of it, playing it out, performing it. The flash exists through or as that dramatization, in this intensity that characterizes the field as a continuum that only now reaches its expressive potential, actualized in the flash that retrospectively resolves or determines the field, through the event itself. Drawing on this example, Wetherell suggests that intentions, too, are often partial, uncompleted; they are like 'the moments preceding lightning strikes when sophisticated still photography shows threads of electrical connection beginning to manifest with the tallest objects in the field, before the strike completes the connection'.[12] One could say that a cloud of barely formulated 'intentional possibilities' only condense *as* intention in the moment of realization, or become *the* intention only retrospectively, in a rationalizing back-formation.

In both cases, we can say that completion or culmination are not inherent outcomes; there is a sense in which they are in excess of the processes themselves, not resulting *from* them but dramatized revisions or expressions *of* them. Indeed, Massumi writes that 'expression' here involves an immediate or unmediated revelation of 'processual immanence'.[13] In open systems, in interactions between entities, other entities, and enfolding environments, 'effect' never follows mechanically or proportionally from 'cause'. Indeed, it is the event itself that constitutes 'cause' and 'effect' as such, in their mutual disjunction, just as the absence of the event, in all its intensity, ensures that potential causes are never 'realized' at all. We can indeed cite Deleuze himself in this context: he suggests that when there is communication between heterogeneous entities, 'Something "passes" between the borders, events explode, phenomena flash, like thunder and lightning …' and the system is thereby 'populated by subjects'.[14]

All this is presented as entirely continuous with what happens to *us*, observing the lightning flash. The shock of the flash, the ray of light and associated sound, impacts on us through various interlocking levels of embodied experience, whether physical, chemical or biological, such that each stratum 'has its own rules of content formation to feed its level-specific functioning, as well as unique forms of expression to transmit the generative impulse to other levels ...', along with 'gaps of systemic indeterminacy' between the strata.[15] Hence again we find the disproportion of cause and effect. The human body is thus an integral part of these flows and currents of energy, marked by disjunctive intensities at points of transition, and 'consciousness' only arrives on the scene relatively late in any particular instance of these processes. Brennan suggests that we do indeed need to recognize that 'the body and its actions have always been ahead of the slow calculations of reflective consciousness'.[16]

And here we encounter the 'missing half second', the temporal gap between physiological and specifically neurological evidence of brain activity and activity in the autonomic nervous system, and the actual moment of perception or feeling, the conscious *awareness* of the impact. The half second is not empty, then, but full, excessively so, and Massumi argues that, in consequence, 'Will and consciousness are *subtractive*. They are *limitative, derived functions*, that reduce a complexity too rich to be functionally expressed.' If, in this sense, 'the present is lost with the missing half second, passing too quickly to be conceived',[17] then what does get registered is crucially affected by the conjunction of this with the 'subtractive' effect of consciousness; it disregards singularity and uniqueness, instead manifesting responses of habit, which, at its most general, acts to contain potential and channel it in pre-constituted, recognized ways, classifying and routinizing it.

At the point of perception, then, with the lightning flash separated from its process, it is already subject to appropriation in language, to sense-making beyond sense; it becomes available for absorption into meaning and myth, for thinking by analogy. Thus, Zeus is 'like' lightning, takes over its properties and its effects; his thunderbolt 'expresses his anger'.[18] The lightning flash 'flows into rhetorical captivity'.[19] Perception is a conscious, surface phenomenon, vulnerable to ideological appropriation, while sensation or affect make the deeper connections through the process, the currents or flows that can only be represented by being stopped, stabilized, reflectively distorted and rendered static. Invoking Bergson, Massumi positions these moments of reflective stasis as 'stop-operations', appropriate only for occasions when 'things coincide with their own arrest',[20] but otherwise making movement and process appear derivative and secondary, and reducing nature to inertia, its dynamism erased.

In contrasting perception with sensation or affect, Massumi argues that sensation as such is inaccessible to systematic thinking,[21] and testifies to the sense in which there is more to a thing or process than there is in our perception of it: this 'extra' is the dimension of the potential, the virtual. What gets lost is the registering of the *intensity* of the flash of lightning, the flash *as* intensity, as manifestation of the virtual field. These claims are drawn together in this formulation by Gregory Seigworth: 'An affective path cannot be threaded through those places where representations or images of thought are predominant or hold sway ... Affect, then, cannot be converted into or delimited by the discursive, by images or representations, by consciousness or thought.'[22] Pointing up the connection with the virtual, Patricia Clough positions consciousness as 'a derived function in a virtual field' such that its actualization delimits the field; hence 'Affect and consciousness are in a virtual-actual circuit, which defines affect as potential and emergent'.[23] Thus we encounter the world as available for interpretation and representation, the actual world as a limitation or 'subtraction' from the underlying processes and relationships which can be seen as 'virtual', both excessive yet also intense. For Massumi, the virtual is 'a lived paradox where what are normally opposites coexist, coalesce and connect; where what cannot be experienced cannot but be felt – albeit reduced and contained'.[24] In short, suggests Wetherell, affect, as virtual, is 'always in the process of becoming, and the leading edge of the wave of any engagement with the world before human minds get to it'.[25]

A corollary is clearly that insofar as we *are* necessarily aware of them, conscious of them, 'feeling' and 'emotion' do not count as affect. Emotion both reveals, yet also captures and limits, the affect that makes it possible, fixing it with a label that marks it as subjective and personal, yet also conventional, 'owned' and recognized.[26] Beneath appearances, then, this effectively positions subjectivity, for Massumi, as a kind of 'no-place or waiting room' through which these affects pass, as 'autonomous lines of force'.[27] Hence we are presented with a fundamental contrast between a world of subject and object, captured as such in perception and representation, and manifested in emotion, thereby rendered static, as states of being; and a world of processes and forces, of virtualities becoming actual, of intensities that escape even as they are pinned down, a world where dualisms and distinctions give way to fluid relations, concentration and transposition, manifest in affect as what is felt *as* change, experience as the integrity of the ongoing and the novel, the singularity of duration.

Overall, this is an invigorating and challenging application of that fusion of Spinoza and Bergson that contributes to Deleuzian metaphysics and, in particular, has led us into Massumi's thesis of the 'autonomy of affect',[28] which now needs more consideration, and critical assessment.

The autonomy of affect

In image reception, our response to perception, Massumi distinguishes two levels (or systems): those of content or quality, and effect or intensity. The former pair fixes the content and form of the image in relation to conventional, intersubjective meanings, whereas the latter characterizes the strength and duration of the effect. Intensity as affect is embodied in purely autonomic reactions, most directly apparent in Galvanic skin response, whereas other autonomic responses, such as heartbeat and breathing, belong relatively more to the quality level. This may be because they are linked to our expectations, which in turn depend on consciously positioning ourselves in linear time, narrative continuity. Hence such alterations of heartbeat and breathing involve 'a reflux of consciousness into the autonomic depths, coterminous with a rise of the autonomic into consciousness'. Intensity is separate from this, to the side of it, a non-conscious 'autonomic remainder'; it cannot be assimilated to, or appropriated by, function, meaning or sequential narration. At the same time, there is a relationship between the content and intensity levels, in that an image with a more factual emphasis can dampen the intensity effect, whereas an image with an emotional emphasis can amplify it, as if compatible with intensity rather than interfering with it.[29] Affect, as intensity, may have links to the autonomic nervous system, then, but it is clear that it cannot be definitively located there. Indeed, it never loses this emergent sense of obscurity, defying any clear sense of place: it is already as though it cannot be *located* anywhere, as though it questions any notion of 'location' – as would perhaps be expected, given its 'virtuality'.

Elsewhere, however, Massumi offers further hints to clarify the relation between affect and the body's sensory and nervous systems. Affect is not located in exteroception (the five senses); it is associated first with interoception, the visceral, the enteric nervous system, centred on the intestines, independent of the nervous system of brain and spine, and responsible for releasing hormones. This, one might observe, also furnishes appropriate imagery in everyday language ('gut feelings'). Secondly, and more importantly, affect involves proprioception, which depends on organs such as the inner ear and the muscles (incorporating muscular memory), giving a sense of body rhythms, pulses of energy, movement and the overall state of the body (often recorded in moods and mood swings). Additionally, every exteroceptive perception incorporates proprioception of the state of the body, normally non-conscious.[30] This last dimension, giving a sense of embodiment as somehow unified, as both condition and result of ongoing movement and positioning in the world, as well as a diffuse – and somehow *internal* – sense of well being (or the converse), would seem to have potential for further exploration, although it is only indirectly developed in Massumi's own work.[31]

While affect, in its autonomy, is not to be equated with experience as such, all this implies that it does nevertheless mark experience, through intensity, just as it does through its capacity to move across contexts. 'Autonomy' does not mean 'isolation'. As Gregory Seigworth and Melissa Gregg put it, 'affect is found in those intensities that pass body to body',[32] and what Massumi refers to as affective 'atoms' are open, not closed, in that they are in touch with a whole universe of potential. Indeed, all this is redolent of Spinoza: affect is the whole world, looked at in a particular way. Affect is not owned; it is not subjective or individual, or, in a sense, really divisible, though it is expressed *in* and *through* particular events and situations. Hence, drawing this together: 'Impersonal affect is the connecting thread of experience. It is the invisible glue that holds the world together.' Affect connects *across* contexts, through the events whereby it evades capture *in* contexts. Actually existing things thereby live 'in and through that which escapes them', which immerses them in the autonomy of affect;[33] and this invisibility, this potential, refers us again to the virtual, for it is through the virtual that the autonomy of affect is constituted. Affect participates in the virtual up to the point of actualization, of emergence, that is also the event, simultaneously, of capture and of escape. In Wetherell's summary: 'If the quality track is mundanely predictable, tawdry, and stifling, then affect and its intensity keep a space open for life to erupt.'[34]

All this shows how characterizing affect entails a string of dichotomies. For a start, affect itself can be contrasted with feeling and emotion. We then encounter non-conscious and conscious, expression and representation, virtual and actual, immediacy and habit, sensation and perception, situation and context, and finally process and stasis. But it is too simple to equate affect with the first term in each pair. Indeed, since 'process' seems basic here, what we really find is not so much virtual versus actual as 'virtual-becoming-actual' (and also, 'situation-emerging-from-context'). Here, though, problems loom. After all, fixing affect in terms of these distinctions is still *fixing* it; and as we have seen, to capture it in this way is to lose it. To 'fix' affect – inherent in any attempt to 'think' it, even if we can avoid 'representing' it – is, at the very least, to distort it. It is an exercise in quality, in qualification, and loses the intensity in the pursuit of an understanding that can only be an external capture of it as its inner intensity escapes. Intensity becomes the unspeakable life of affect, giving a 'meaning' to our lives we can never actually grasp or articulate. The autonomy of affect seems to be brought at rather a high price: the price of its becoming ineffable. As we have seen, Massumi is forever at pains to tell us what affect is and forever precluded from doing so, forever alluding to it, elliptically, indirectly and metaphorically, while insisting on the necessity of its escape, preventing us from getting too close to it by refining it away with yet another qualification or distinction.

An essential component of the autonomy thesis, the distrust of representation, recognition, and of the linguistic and semiotic structures within which they are embedded – fundamental to the Deleuzian perspective, as we saw in an earlier chapter, in the discussion of Francis Bacon – becomes particularly crippling in Massumi. An intriguing example of the effects of this is given in a brief analysis of the act of reading itself. Arguing that every thought is accompanied by some physical sensation or other, of 'effort or agitation', such as knitting the brows or a quickening heartbeat, so that reading can never be purified of sensation, he adds that reading involves seeing through the individual letters and words, so that through the letters, 'we directly experience fleeting visionlike sensations, inklings of sound, faint brushes of movement'.[35] The effect of reading *as* affect thus involves rigorously excluding all content. Yet there is a palpable tension here that comes out in reading Massumi's own account. One initially reacts to the claim about the quickening heartbeat by assuming this is going to be precipitated by something in the *content* of what is being read; only subsequently does one realize that somehow this is supposed to happen *through* yet *despite* the content. One reads 'behind' or 'beneath' the letters; one does not read the letters at the level of *words* with meaning. So again, if this is an implication of the 'autonomy of affect' thesis, the whole thesis has to be thrown into question.[36]

In particular, the link apparent here between the autonomy thesis and an implausibly rigid model of representation, as mere habit and convention, necessarily distorting and conservative, with language itself embedded in this, would rule out Wetherell's suggestion that what is most likely is that there is a pattern of affect, 'loose and often post hoc, arising in the moment of categorisation', a pattern that arises as 'the registering of core affect combines with representational processing'[37] – a suggestion that seems highly plausible and cuts through the complexities. Following this up, and dropping this exiling of affect to a nebulous, impenetrable realm, one could argue that to make an affective statement, in the language of feeling, is to respond to a growing sense of pleasure or discomfort, or a change of mood, when this reaches some tipping point. It is a response to change – we become aware of feelings *as* they change, as the process forces itself sufficiently on our attention – that labels it, or 'captures' it, and thereby contributes to making it what it *is*, for us. In this sense, yes, it can be seen as 'virtual becoming actual', but in *registering* its becoming, we do not thereby betray it, or lose it; rather, we 'place' it differently, in a different 'register', that of language, another aspect of reality that has its own patterns, its own structure, its own integrity. This reflective grasp does indeed imply a moment of relative stasis, and a transformative reconstruction that, in making the feeling what it is for us, *also* registers, simultaneously, the gap of the reflective grasp itself. What we can say, then, is that it is not so much affect that is lost, as the *activity* of appropriating or representing it. What is at stake is not the distortion of some underlying but inscrutable truth, but a realization that the sense-making of ongoing experience has to meet the sense-inscription of language, and it is at this point of tension, of conjunction of incommensurables, that affect becomes partially constitutive of our experience of life.[38] The novelty, the charisma,[39] is in this disjunctive conjunction; it is not that experience is inherently novel, or language and its categories inherently conservative. Despite its inadequacies, then, we find that the 'autonomy of affect' thesis *does* point to something important: the mutual irreducibility of affect, of the circuits of sensation, and the arena of image, meaning and idea, caught and transmitted in the network of language.

To develop this argument, it is useful to bring in Deleuze at this point. He asks us to think of the affective encounter, or affect *as* encounter. This is the moment of 'sense', of what can *only* be sensed, as opposed to recognized. 'In recognition', he writes, 'the sensible is not at all that which can only be sensed, but that which bears directly upon the senses in an object which can be recalled, imagined or conceived.' Affect does not involve an object, 'placed' in the imagination, memory or thought: 'It is not a sensible being but the being *of* the sensible. It is not the given, but that by which the given is given.' From the point of view of recognition, it is indeed 'imperceptible' (*insensible*).[40] Leaving aside the critique of recognition for now, Claire Colebrook helpfully presents this in terms of language: sense is 'the virtual milieu through which we live and become. Sense is not reducible to the "meanings" of a language; sense is what allows a language to be meaningful.' Language is not owned by subjects and used to name or represent objects, or not until it helps to shape, articulate and produce itself as flow or process, 'stream of consciousness' perhaps, its power as affect '*moving towards* designating a world'.[41]

It is indeed important to be reminded that this encounter between a living language and the living world of which it is part may indeed have affective presuppositions as well as consequences, though this should not be confused with the *internal*, structural presuppositions of language, explored by semiological and other theories, let alone used to disparage the importance of this dimension. If affect as encounter requires that affect involve contact, impact between entities, and refers to the singularity of the effect, we can add that, in the modern world, this can crucially involve the impact of a book or film, of media transmission, as readily as a conversation. Such impact is never reducible to the content, but it does not exclude it, either. Meaning can have affective consequences, can be experienced, felt, even though an analysis at the level of meanings, of meaning as such, will never locate it – any more than such an analysis would be reducible to it. As for 'recognition', the extent to which this happens is internal to these encounters of language, bodies and worlds; it is not the exclusive preserve of language and its representational capacity. 'Recognition' need not preclude affect; we refer to a 'shock of recognition', after all, the singularity of the encounter having a dramatic effect. The affect is the impact-as-experienced, as felt, an active response *within* the passive – which may well involve recognition. But if affect, in Deleuze's 'sense', is not usefully conceived as the necessary *absence* of 'recognition', it is nonetheless true, and important, that it runs along a distinctive track. In effect, this has enabled us to reconstruct Massumi's distinction between two levels or tracks, 'content' and 'intensity', without the indefensible aspects of the autonomy thesis and the implausible and self-defeating critique of representation and recognition.

We can clarify this by pointing out that language *does* make a difference here, precisely because affect, in its impact, follows from the message – whether as form, content or context – as effect follows from cause, rather than as logical or imaginative connections in a chain or pattern of meanings. These latter connections, of course, have their own importance; but they are not connections in circuits of sensation. They cut across, at a tangent. Hence the appearance that signification is somehow secondary or irrelevant is not without foundation; from this latter point of view, meanings *are* secondary, in the sense that their status *as* meaningful is elided in the very triggering of the affects. This does not mean that 'effect follows cause' in some deterministic way – as argued earlier, the gap here, the sense in which effect (affect) is in excess of cause, is still crucial – but they are homogeneous in kind. If, for example, figuration in terms of electrical energy is seen as appropriate for one – as has often been the case – then it will be appropriate for the other, too. This is what tells us that we are situated in the circuits of sensation.

If 'affect', in the most undifferentiated sense, is severed completely from its translation into specific affects as they occur as feelings on particular occasions – and it is important to insist that it is indeed *translation* that is involved here, the work of culture, a shift of register that involves language in specifying feeling, rather than just 'expression' or 'manifestation' – then indeed there seems to be nowhere else to anchor it save by latching it decisively on to the neurons or other appropriate physiological entities postulated by contemporary neuroscience, on pain of it disappearing completely into the nebulous or the ethereal. Nor, as we have seen, is this move so very new: indeed the language and imagery of neurons and synapses goes well back into nineteenth-century science (and it is important to insist, again, that it is 'language' and 'imagery' that are involved here).[42]

The core of this would seem to be the claims made by some neuroscientists that when we observe an action, specialist 'mirror' neurons are activated, just as if we were about to carry out the action ourselves; the one is mapped onto the other. This is also said to apply in situations where we observe someone in pain, with the result that we can experience something of that same feeling. Put like this, the claim has a degree of plausibility, and is not particularly novel; examples that fit this have been discussed since Hume and eighteenth-century sensationalist psychology, even if the language of 'mirror neurons' is new. Furthermore, unless one is wedded to an extreme mind/body dualism, it is difficult to see how changes in feelings could fail to have some correlation with changes in the nervous system, and, more specifically, the brain. Taking it further, though, causes problems. Daniel Stern writes, of the mirror neuron activity just described, that it 'permits us to directly participate in another's actions, without having to imitate them. We experience the other as if we were executing the same action, or feeling the same emotion.'[43] Considered critically, this claim reduces questions of meaning to descriptions of brain function, allowing no place for the relative autonomy of language and thought and the cultural appropriation of natural processes as necessarily involving a transition into a different register or mode of nature, that of culture as nature's reflexive mode, its difference from itself. What the quote certainly *does* do is present us with a textbook case of the language of the circuit of sensation, where affects flow between and across populations in an unmediated, direct way, like contagion: boundaries dissolve, individuals blend into an undifferentiated mass, bobbing around in a sea of neurons, illuminated by flashes of lightning across the turbulence …

In summary, there does seem to be a sense in which affect is coextensive with the whole universe, *insofar as* this can be seen in terms of energy, of chains of connections and disjunctions, experiences of impact and shock. This much is in common to both Deleuze and Massumi, and is consistent with the arguments developed here around circuits of sensation and the way they have been experienced and theorized in the modern world. What Deleuze is concerned with, beyond this, is not so much the autonomy of affect, as its irreducibility to recognition, to appropriation as representation or categorization. While Massumi shares this emphasis, he ties it to the requirement that affect be autonomous in such a radical way that it becomes 'virtually' inaccessible, at the level of conscious experience, or – so as to ensure escape from the latter – swings over towards flirting with neuroscientific models that would indeed keep it resolutely distinct from actually experienced sensation, but at the cost of an uncritical scientism that rather gives up the ostensible aim of making the language of science 'culturally-theoretically thinkable'. In order to preserve the insights of this work, we need to drop the autonomy thesis, but we also need to abandon the critique of representation, common to both authors,[44] since, as has been seen, this mislocates the distinctiveness of affect and makes it impossible to think the processes whereby sensation and sensationalism can show the power of affect as it moves *through* and *across* image, representation and media, and the way in which our theories of affect are *themselves* embedded in historical processes.

Sensational subjects

While affect does of course relate to the nexus of issues around attention, distraction and shock defence, it really addresses a set of concerns at a tangent to this. Given that affect does in some sense 'get through', whatever its source, we can ask where it is located, *in* its effects, and what implications does it have for our sense of selfhood. How, indeed, does the self become such that it can be 'subject of sensation'? In considering the nature of affect and where it happens, it was suggested above that its occurrence below or prior to events that impact our senses and consciousness – related to its virtual aspects – should not be interpreted in a way that renders it inscrutable. Avoiding this seems to position the self as a channel, passage or switchboard where circuits of affect pass through and intersect, with implications for our sense of self-awareness and embodiment. But – as with its place in other discourses of modernity – it is difficult to avoid the figure of the self as an interior space, even though here the emphasis is on this space as the relatively passive subject of these sensational currents that have their being, origins and effects in ways that operate, at least partly, 'beneath' or 'beyond' the reflexive grasp, even though, as we have seen, this grasp, as a 'making sense', also figures them in the form in which they can present themselves to us. Hence this model of selfhood is difficult to reconcile with ideological emphases on a substantive, 'rational' self, one that 'owns' its experiences and is 'master' of its body.

The point about affect is that it happens *to* us, locates us in circuits that connect the body in its internal and external states, in its fragmented reality as body parts, and the bodies of others, yet it does so in a way that brings in to play some notion of a whole body response, a sense of embodied personhood at least in the minimal sense of a capacity for integrated orientation and for 'feeling' beyond individual senses and organs. At the same time, there is never a simple fit between this ever-unfolding state and its appropriation in language and thought, just as this appropriation also marks an intervention in this process that both introduces the possibility of a split between self and body yet also marks a continuation of the process itself. Hence Rei Terada, in her critique of 'auto-affection', as 'the mode of transparent self-reflexivity' that reveals the ideal of immediacy, of presence, in the tradition of Western thought, follows Derrida in postulating auto-affection as 'the self-differential encounter of experience itself',[45] beyond any possibility of seamless recuperation in a state of pure self-consciousness.

Expanding this, we can point to 'awareness' as a significant but difficult concept here. It is not necessarily a matter of being conscious of something, in the sense of a capacity to be articulate about it, describe it adequately; it may be more diffuse, contextual, responsive, more a matter of background than of foreground. At this point, some similarity with the 'distracted' self, encountered earlier in this book, becomes apparent. One can be 'aware' of something without it being at the forefront of attention. Perhaps it is an overall sense of 'belonging together', of parts or aspects being in some sense related to 'self' as a focus or perspective, something 'felt' but presupposed, rather than available for conscious registration. In terms of the body and its sensory organs, it is clearly proprioception that is most significant here. At the same time, something is 'felt' in the stronger sense, too, in the sense of 'impact', hence bringing intensity, or the *variation* in intensity, into the picture. Intensity can involve discontinuity, across thresholds, the boundaries that separate parts, entities and levels, while indicating relations between them, the fact that they are *in* relation. In sensation, the variation in intensity is felt, for Massumi, as self-relation, manifest in this 'feeling of having a feeling', hence '*the felt reality of relation*', giving one a sense of vitality, of being alive, in a 'continuous non-conscious self-perception'.[46]

In order to make further sense of this, Massumi invokes the concept of resonance,[47] a concept that plays a significant and stimulating part in his account, while not getting much explicit discussion – as indeed is the case with Deleuze, who is clearly, once again, the source of this. Sensation has a self-referential quality, hence can be described as 'a resonation, an interference pattern'. Taking the example of an echo, Massumi argues that its location is problematical – not *on* but *between* the walls – and that its complex patterning involves a kind of self-relation via self-replication, such that the bouncing back and forth of the sound multiplies its movement without cutting or fragmenting it, hence its 'complex self-continuity'. The reverberation of an echo can therefore be understood as a self-multiplication via superimposition. This 'complicating immediacy of self-relation' can be seen as intensity,[48] and is a clue not only to our awareness of self as relation but also to the way the impact of sensation works more generally, leading us to understand that classic dualisms, such as mind and body, passivity and activity, could be seen 'not as binary oppositions or contradictions, but as resonating levels', with affect as their 'point of emergence' from virtual coexistence to actuality, such levels being conceptualized as foci of self-organization, always precarious, but 'locked in resonance with each other' each recapitulating the same event in different ways.[49] If we now draw directly on Deleuze, we find that when two sensations confront each other and communicate, 'we are no longer in the domain of simple vibration, but that of resonance', and that even with simple sensation, the fact that it passes through different levels means that 'Vibration already produces resonance'.[50]

At its most general, then, resonance is a feature both of the impact of a sensation as it crosses levels or boundaries between systems, whereby it is registered in these different levels or systems, and of the intersection of sensations with each other, producing novel configurations. All this invites us to consider extending the range of application of the concept, however speculatively (and despite the likely disapproval of Massumi and Deleuze). If a cave or valley can resonate with the echo of a voice, the poet Shelley reminds us that there can also be 'fertile valleys, resonant with bliss'; and an old building can 'resonate' in ways literal and metaphorical (and is there a difference here?), with memories perhaps, the presence of the past in the present, conveying a sense of 'presence' that is encompassing, excessive, potentially uncanny.[51] And when the dictionary tells us that resonance is the 'sound produced by a body vibrating in sympathy with a neighbouring source of sound', then this is itself a definition that resonates with its own connections, its own history, the conjunction of 'vibration' and 'sympathy' recalling Hume and the eighteenth-century cultural imaginary when these terms played off one another to encapsulate not just the whole discourse of sensibility and sentiment but to communicate something of the structure of feeling itself.[52]

If 'affect is the zone of potential emotions', a 'primordial soup' of feelings,[53] then resonance is the sensory experience of this indeterminate domain, a domain which is as much an undifferentiated state of space and time as something that exists within it. Returning specifically to that level of experience that we call 'awareness', with its hint of the pre-conscious or not fully focused, where affect resonates, reverberates, as if simultaneously stretched and deepened, we can say that this is a powerful stimulus either to full reflexivity or to creative figuration, as we try to convey this experience of a perhaps disconcerting otherness within the same, or the 'becoming' in the given.[54] When sensations cross each other, or cross boundaries, the reverberation or resonance that transmits impact into intensity shows how a *relation* is established, a relation of the smallest possible difference, within the 'walls' – which, in this case, are partially constituted by this very impact, as an effect, just as consciousness *reinforces* this, 'actualizes' it, by the reflexive act itself, with its projection and distancing. Massumi's 'complex self-continuity' is at any rate not self-identity, but the 'echo' of these smallest differences may well resonate *as* continuity, as we experience a sense of the *diffusion* in intensity, the intensity in sensation that constitutes it *in* its uniqueness, as experience, as the becoming in stasis, the moment as process, Terada's 'experience of self-differentiality'.[55]

A sensational world

Affect corresponds to a truth of experience: that the world *does* impact on us, that there is energy and force in this, that it is apparently unpredictable, and cannot ultimately be subsumed under meaning, even though this disruptive power of affect can equally well be transmitted through media and the products of culture. Thus Anna Gibbs tells us that 'Contagion is everywhere in the contemporary world. It leaps from body to body, sweeping through mediatized populations at the speed of a bushfire.'[56] Affects swirl around, pushing us this way and that, ever capricious, yet all the more domineering in their manifestations, characteristically affecting us, initially, below the level of full conscious awareness. Contagious, transmissible, they leave us vulnerable both to the media and to reinforcement through interaction with others,[57] like disease epidemics or fashion. Indeed, 'fashion' and 'affect' can reinforce one another, in the similarities of their initiation, transmission, and dissipation. Both make possible, and strengthen, aesthetic and moral responses, even though ostensibly both are apparently autonomous, uninterested in such effects. Additionally, sensationalized affects can be appropriated as melodrama, embroiled in an unthinking politics of denunciation, again powerfully reinforced through the media. The very features of affect that apparently make it distinctive can also make it dangerous, and theorists who reinforce this sense of its autonomy can be part and parcel of it, unwittingly contributing to the problem rather than helping us understand it.

On the face of it, then, Fredric Jameson's much-quoted characterization of the postmodern in terms of a 'waning of affect' would be wide of the mark, overtaken by events: affect has not 'waned', it has attained plague-like proportions. But when he adds that feelings increasingly tend to be 'free floating and impersonal',[58] we can make sense of this as suggesting a transformation of affect that detaches it from the earlier, moral concerns of sensibility, giving it both a harder edge and a potential for multiple forms of signification, opening it up as both resource and channel for consumerism. Affect becomes diffuse, off the peg, personalized rather than personal, yet always available for intense display and self-assertion, and a contributor to the politics of trauma. In this sense, 'waning' can suggest a kind of desensitization to affect that, in turn, opens it up for reinforcement: sensational affect can all too easily be part and parcel of a melodrama of affect. And any theorization of this that merely has the effect of reinforcing it should at least consider the narrowness of its own premises – whether a rigid separation between affect, on the one hand, and feeling and emotion, on the other, for example, as suggested by some proponents of the 'affective turn', can really provide the basis for understanding, or merely reproduces the 'waning of affect', as reinterpreted, at a more abstract level.

When we think of these currents as 'impersonal' we are hinting at another problem – not just that individual persons can be 'picked on' in essentially random or capricious ways, but that such a 'de-personalizing' is also in a sense 'de-humanizing'. A significant slide occurs here: personal to impersonal gets mapped on to human to non-human, culture to nature and mind to body, along with a series of loaded corollaries, such as the alleged primacy of self-interest (coded now as biological, hence immutable). This is where the contemporary obsession with neuroscience, as the successor to fashionable sciences of earlier in the modern period, can be linked in, along with, more generally, the cultural prestige of reductionist psychological and biological approaches. All this becomes both explicable, in the light of these cultural developments, but also dangerous, uncritically normalizing what are actually *historical*, cultural and economic patterns of behaviour that 'resonate' powerfully through modern Western civilization. Hence another slide, perhaps most dangerous of all: from historical contingency to trans-historical universality and necessity. We thus witness an odd revival of *one* aspect of the Enlightenment legacy, amid the wreckage of so much of the rest: a new credibility attached to the search for 'laws of human nature', laws which can envisage the emergence of the posthuman along with the residue of the pre-human, blessed alike by the uncritical acceptance of contemporary techno-science, abstracted from its context.[59]

The collapse of the grand narratives of 'the social', along with associated notions of 'progress' and 'emancipation', together with a reduction of 'reason' to 'technological mastery', means we are seen increasingly as naked, unprotected, buffeted by the forces of chance or fate that show the Janus face of modernity as mastery, the 'mastery' that that promises us control but ends up controlling us – not through some malevolent design, but through the very unpredictability of its effects, effects which are, nonetheless, invariably socially differentiated in their impact. In short, the creativity inherent in sensational affect, and its capacity to transfigure experience in positive ways, remains trapped by that very autonomy, celebrated by some of its theorists, that also, in practice, leaves it bereft of any meaningful links with the cultural, emotional and intellectual currents that could realize this transformative potential in our lives.

8

The Melodrama of the Modern

The attack on the Twin Towers, and their subsequent collapse, constituted a sensational spectacle on a cosmic scale: this much, at least, was apparent from the start, as was the parallel with 'special effects' in Hollywood disaster movies.[1] In a discussion of Hollywood film, Linda Williams refers to a moment when villainy and innocence come into sharp focus in a 'sensation scene', which is 'felt as sensation' by the viewer, not just as detached information;[2] and this seems to fit the popular reaction here, the impact of the planes being mapped onto the impact on the spectator as the drama unfolded. It is likewise not difficult to see the justification for invoking the sublime, indeed the dynamical sublime, in its combination of the awesome, the spectacular, the terrible – in principle, fear-inducing, yet viewed from a position of relative safety. All this is appropriate enough, but perhaps the reference to villainy and innocence suggests a dimension that needs further consideration. After all, the events, then and subsequently, were characterized by an intensely *moral* language, indeed a language that imbued the responses of politicians and the media with vivid tones of outrage and denunciation: clearly we were confronted with a battle between Good and Evil. We have, indeed, become rather used to this, from Reagan's battle with the 'Evil Empire' through to Bush's obsession with an 'axis of evil'.

'Badness' is a falling away from goodness, paying tribute to it; it is not an alternative value, a serious rival, on the same level. It is not Manichaean.[3] For that, we have to call up evil, so that there can be a real contest, real war between two opposing principles, which can easily be personified. Evil conjures up the idea of the *absolutely* bad, immeasurably bad, bad beyond all comprehension – 'sublimely' bad, one might say. But as a rival value, evil presents problems: either, in following it, you follow it because it is 'not-good', in which case it again remains derivative of the latter, not a separate principle; or you follow it because it is a distinct, different value system, in which case it becomes 'good' for you and for others who follow it (just as the 'other' good becomes evil). But this is not just a problem for evil: it contaminates the good, too – it turns it against itself. Good has to recognize that something may masquerade as 'good' that is actually its opposite. The appearance of good, even doing good, may not be sufficient: the devil is infinitely cunning ... Hence, within the Christian tradition, God is needed to sort out the mess: the day of Judgement is the exercise of his omniscience; he alone can tell the difference with absolute confidence. In the absence of the immediate presence of God, the only certainties are that evil is a permanent possibility, as is the impossibility of being confident about identifying it, and, hence, rooting it out – just as it is, nonetheless, essential to try to do so.

From the point of view of the follower of the good, evil is always the ultimate transgression: it must retain its link to 'breaking the rules', since this is required if it is to be bad; yet it also goes beyond this, it is inherently excessive, since this 'excess' reveals the presence of these 'other' values that can never be allowed to emerge clearly as such, since they could then indeed emerge as a real *alternative*, rather than as signs of pure wickedness. Indeed, the fact that in practice evil must involve pure wickedness seems to be central to it, wickedness either as apparently unmotivated, or motivated by love of evil itself. Either way, evil becomes in some fundamental sense incomprehensible, beyond being explained (away), even though we can say more about its meaning and effects. What evil *signifies* is the attempted corruption or destruction of innocence; what it *does*, through this, is produce suffering. And this is a clue to two aspects of evil, as absolute value and as absolute deed, the other of rational morality and of rational self-control respectively, one as manifestation of the other. Evil as deed is evil as passion, excess of passion, desire unconstrained by morality, revealing a fusion of excess of mind, as imagination, and body, as drive, resulting in lust, the appetite for conquering the other through sexuality or death.[4]

If, in a post-Enlightenment world, reason is supposed to have taken over from God, it can be seen that the same structural tensions remain: reason, like God, can be given no non-circular justification for the universality and necessity of its diktats, just as 'universality' and 'necessity' are the whole point. The ever-present possibility of reason's unspeakable 'other side' is built into it, its grinning, malevolent caricature, as is its capacity for projection onto the other, its projection *as* other, carrying the evil it must disavow as its own condition of possibility, the other side of reason itself, in its universalizing pretensions, reason as Law.[5] And hence this again reinforces the fact that the evil other is always 'inside', if only because there can be no real 'outside' here, just as good must always battle evil and forever fail to vanquish it, condemned to misrecognize its own complicity in its production.[6] The relentless pursuit of evil can indeed contribute further to this production and reproduction of evil itself: those who seek evil will generally not only find it, but will, in attempting to vanquish it, end up perpetrating their own version of it ('witch hunts'). Motives are impenetrable, reinforcing the sense that the evildoer may be among us, unrecognizable, apparently normal, and that evil is as potentially ubiquitous as it is irredeemably other, so that even when 'exposed' it retains its unending ability to subvert, corrupt, and destroy.

Let us return to Kant, and situate all this more firmly in post-Enlightenment culture. In its awesome immensity and power, the sublime indicates the limits of imagination and understanding, while those very attributes point us towards the grandeur of reason in its autonomy, its legislative capacity to define the good in itself as the imperative to will what is necessarily good for all. 'Practical' reason, as autonomous, appeals to nothing beyond its own principles of reasoning. The essence of reason is that it lays down principles that are necessary, universal, and internally consistent, hence principles that ought to be held to by all, whatever their cultural circumstances or personal situations. Yet notoriously Kant's own version of this has proved highly indeterminate in its moral and political implications. More generally, this Enlightenment vision, intended to define the direction of human emancipation, always presented the problem that, in practice, no single self-sufficient programme ever carried conviction as the only such; there was always the potential for radically divergent ideologies, including those generated by reaction against aspects of the Enlightenment vision itself. The politics of progress has swung between totalitarian imposition and conflictual pluralism, between the politics of mass mobilization and concentration and mass-as-dispersion into competing individualisms, subject to the gales of fashion and the media construction of unacceptable otherness, any consensus on values to resolve the frequently incommensurable or incompatible goals being very hard to come by and always precarious. In effect, Kant may have been right that the sublime forces us towards confronting these ultimate questions, but over-optimistic about the possibilities of their rational resolution.[7]

With the revival of religious belief – or the likelihood that it never really went away – in the context of increasingly visible multicultural communities, this effect is intensified. In *After Virtue*, Alasdair MacIntyre vividly illustrates the consequences of the inherent undecidability of disputes between rival post-Enlightenment ideals and their implications for action. If a belief system leads to the conviction that abortion is wrong, then one cannot take the easy multicultural way out (you stick to your beliefs and I'll stick to mine), because, posed in these terms, the whole point is that if it *is* wrong, then it is wrong for everyone, universally.[8] Ultimate values are precisely that, *ultimate*: there is no higher court of appeal, no arbitration and conciliation service to provide some messy but vaguely agreeable compromise. And a corollary is that the ultimate values of others can come to appear not merely misguided or wrong, but mad or bad with it. This is because if the practical incompatibility of the outcomes of rival positions is taken as evidence of the incommensurability of their underlying assumptions, then this carries with it a necessary element of mutual incomprehension; and the combination of these attributes makes it all the more likely that conflict and mutual denunciation will intensify. In effect, we have returned to the distinction between 'bad' and 'evil', and the conditions under which there is most likely to be a slide from one to the other.

One might draw briefly here on another aspect of the modern project and its consequences. The endeavour to dominate and control the world (of nature and society), exploiting it in the name of ideologies of human secular progress, has itself contributed to our sense of paradoxical powerlessness in the face of the unpredictable aspects of that same world. In the world of disease, for example, the more we know the more we become aware of how much we don't know, and this generates fear, and indeed the attempts to extend knowledge can make matters worse (drug-resistant bugs flourishing in hospitals …). This can readily be combined with the previously mentioned capacity of the modern project for dynamic processes of exclusion and antagonism, involving the demonization of tendencies, groups and individuals defined and denounced as 'other' (the onset of AIDS in the 1980s providing a vivid example). We are thus simultaneously reminded of the promise of the modern project, and of its outcome, in the tension between control, concentration, and the spectacle of a distracted, dispersed, world, a tension readily available for dramatization in the pursuit of an ever-problematical closure, some overall 'meaning'. So, with the bad sensationalized into evil, pushed beyond its own limits, and the spectacle sensationalized into a whole cosmos, a moral drama of extremes, we find ourselves at the mercy of forces, of powers that can never be adequately explained, understood or controlled, and which are endlessly productive of suffering – forces which we are encouraged or tempted to experience and represent in the form of a battle between good and evil. Hence our sense of living in a distinctively modern form of the *theatrum mundi*, a stage across which post-sacred or multi-sacred conflicts can be played out. And we have a word for it, a word that has indeed been around for as long – and only as long – as the modern period. That word is:

Melodrama

'Vice and virtue make the destinies of the world: these are the two opposed spirits that fight over it', proclaimed Robespierre.[9] And if the politics of the French Revolution could be said both to manifest and to inaugurate the age of melodrama, this also suggests that the traditional perspective on melodrama, as a specific genre in the arts, particularly in the theatre, needs to be broadened out.

We can say that melodrama develops from the late eighteenth century as a distinctive form of theatrical entertainment, directed at a mass audience. It conjures up a world of powerful, mysterious forces, reinforcing this through an intense use of special effects, and through an obsession with moral polarity and moral absolutes; these stereotypical contrasts are more important than traditional novelistic virtues like 'development of character', here replaced by a portrayal of character as 'a theatre for the interplay of manichaeistic forces, the meeting place of opposites', as Peter Brooks puts it.[10] By the 1820s melodrama had become 'a source of heroic identification and an aesthetic model for the artist of modernity', claims Mary Gluck, adding that melodrama 'satisfied the newly awakened taste for public excitement and passionate spectacle that had originally been nourished by revolutionary events', also providing a language and an ideology to make sense of it all.[11] If, by the 1840s, it was going out of fashion in the theatre and among the avant-garde, it was spreading into, and influencing, other areas of culture, notably literature (very clearly so in the case of Dickens), and was spreading as a distinctive mode of mass media expression and popular consciousness. With W. T. Stead's 'Maiden Tribute of Modern Babylon' reports in the *Pall Mall Gazette* of 1885, a founding moment of modern media sensationalism, aptly summarized by Elaine Hadley as 'the melodramatic story of virtuous heroines sold into sexual slavery by the despotically mercenary drives of pimping villains', the potential for melodrama on the mediated public stage became fully manifest. Hadley adds that villains in melodrama 'embody all the ills of modernizing Victorian capitalism', but are always defeated, in the end.[12]

Melodrama never really goes away; it returns – endlessly – in the great twentieth-century cultural innovation, film. 'Melodrama is the fundamental mode of popular American moving pictures', a democratic form that 'seeks dramatic revelation of moral and emotional truths through a dialectic of pathos and action', argues Linda Williams. 'It is the foundation of the classical Hollywood movie.'[13] We know about Hollywood 'domestic melodrama' of the 1940s and 1950s,[14] but if her claim is to stand up, it clearly entails revealing melodrama in places where we are not conventionally taught to look for it.[15]

Williams unearths the fact that as late as the 1960s a whole series of what we tend to see as separate genres – including science fiction, the Western, crime – were being classified as sub-genres of melodrama in AFI film catalogues. In effect, melodrama has functioned as a 'basic mode of storytelling': exciting, sensational, moving.[16] Male action movies can be presented in these terms: the films of Ford, Coppola and Spielberg all combine realism, sentiment, spectacle and action to reveal virtue that is at least partially hidden and has to be manifest in moments that are 'climactic', in a drama that is simultaneously 'special effects' and emotional release. In the first Rambo film, the hero breaks down and cries in the arms of his former commander.[17] Such moments are easy to pass over – particularly, perhaps, for a male audience – but are crucial to the overall effect, in that they reveal how narrative thereby serves melodrama, rather than vice versa. Such moments *display* 'spectacles of pathos and action',[18] though one might say that they thereby position action *as* pathos, and, in the process, express or project such 'meaning' as a film is capable of, in its relation to its audience.[19] Stardom itself, the projection of the actors beyond their roles, can also be presented as a vehicle and instance of melodrama, with implications for our notions of personal identity, whether in film or everyday life.[20]

'Melodramatic moments' in a film are distractions – but they are the distractions that reveal what the film is most fundamentally *about*. Such moments *subsume* narrative, give it its 'point', beyond any point that exists purely as narrative end point. They bathe the film in meaning, but it is a 'meaning' that is as much a matter of feeling as of thought or sense. And this reveals the problem of purely *narrative* closure: the end, like the start, is in a sense arbitrary; the problem solved, the life ended, leave an infinity of 'loose ends', of the unresolved. The closure of melodrama is, in an ultimate sense, just as arbitrary, the meaning of the 'whole' just as forced, but the change in register, the emotional high, carrying layers of meaning *and* feeling, makes it potentially more effective. The 'whole' is indeed an *effect*, not an attribute of the film 'in itself'; it is an immanent product of the filmic relation to the viewing subject, the embodied subject whose own body, in its reaction, becomes the 'completion' of the film.

There is a moment near the end of *Schindler's List* (Spielberg, 1993), when Oskar Schindler, the war profiteer who has saved over a thousand Jews, breaks down, revealing his regret at not having saved more. Noticing this, Omer Bartov denounces the 'positively repulsive kitsch' of the concluding scenes, the 'emotional catharsis' with which Spielberg apparently wanted to end the film, and the 'banal humanization' of his hero.[21] We, in turn, can notice the intensity of Bartov's response, and wonder whether those who denounce melodrama are at some risk of suffering from it themselves. But he is certainly right to see this as a response to the audience expectation that a history film be both 'authentic' and reveal 'a final triumph over the forces of evil'.[22] Unquestionably this *is* a significant moment in the film; and it is not present in the book the film is based on. Williams observes that it is clearly out of character for Schindler, in terms of codes of realistic representation.[23] It is indeed clearly melodramatic, revealing weakness as goodness, mute pathos. And this is its point: whereas heroism is exceptional, tears are the tears of Everyman. 'Suffering gives him the moral recognition that melodrama – not realism – requires. Without it, Schindler is merely heroic.' Williams concludes, controversially, that Schindler thereby 'relieves the rest of us … of the historical burden of guilt',[24] which is certainly *one* possible interpretation of the effect of it all.

Let us take another moment in the film: the Nazi camp commandant, Goeth, is shown taking random pot shots from his office at Jews who happen to cross the exercise yard below. If you happen to be in the wrong place at the wrong time, you get killed; it is death out of the blue, capricious, with no meaning, no rationale, in terms of the individual victim. This appears to contrast with the Schindler example, in that it seems consistent with what we know of Goeth's character. The point here, though, is that in terms of their impact, good and evil actions can be seen as *never* sufficiently 'motivated', rationally explicable. This is where the randomness of Goeth's action works powerfully, because the very capriciousness carries the message that *nothing* here can ever be sufficiently accountable, in terms of rational justification: neither the selection of individual victims in this episode, nor the very selection of the Jews overall, as objects of Nazi denunciation, persecution and hate. And we may recall here a famous episode in Dostoevsky's novel *Crime and Punishment*, where the 'hero', Raskolnikov, murders an old lady and her sister. The murder is essentially unmotivated. She *is* a moneylender, and he resents her, but this is not presented as in any way an adequate explanation. It is, in short, a totally wicked act, an *evil* act, and that reinforces a point already hinted at: that whatever counts as evil is in some sense a challenge to our comprehension, both in terms of causal explanation, and in terms of its moral enormity. It always seems to be in excess of what we can rationally grasp – a fundamental challenge to our imagination. And it is deeply paradoxical: it can serve both as the ultimate explanation, and as the ultimate *failure* of explanation (does 'he is just evil' explain anything at all?).

As a strong believer in the reality of evil in the world, Dostoevsky is significant here. Evil – 'radical' evil, evil for its own sake – is fundamental to the human condition. Charles Guignon suggests that he had little patience with utopian reformers who thought that 'humans are fundamentally good, and that it is only their upbringing or socialization that causes evil', as if 'there is no real evil; there are only dysfunctional families or unfair social conditions'.[25] So if we take the key hate figures of our time – serial killers, mass killers, terrorists, paedophiles – we can point to the simultaneous need to 'explain', in terms of social and psychological problems, 'predisposing factors', and to sense that these explanations are never adequate; indeed, not infrequently these individuals turn out to be relatively 'normal' on most scales of psychological assessment or social upbringing. In the context of cases like that of Jamie Bulger, the toddler killed by two boys in 1993, the journalist Nick Cohen defended the public's attitude: 'If its concept of evil did not exist, it would have to be invented to cover the gaps in all great crimes between understandable causes and inexplicable consequences.'[26] One might add that whether or not there is any useful sense in which the perpetrators of these crimes are 'really' evil, it is as if they must be *made out* to be so; they have to be sufficiently *different*, lest they pollute the 'normal'. If they are 'merely' bad, they become potentially reformable; if they are evil, we can safely condemn them, expel them, or worse. Hence Phillip Cole suggests that when there are thought to be evildoers in the community, *inside* it, 'there can be no negotiation and no compromise ... they can only be hunted down and destroyed'. 'Evil' drives us to understand, just as it makes it imperative that we *not* understand. One can agree with Cole that 'evil closes off all possibility of understanding'.[27] And evil, as that which must not be understood, but only fought and destroyed, is central to melodrama: there is always a gap between our sense of the world as something that can be understood, and our sense of the presence of evil within it; and our very way of posing it in these terms contributes to its perpetual recreation.

Surely, one might reply, there is a real sense in which the Holocaust itself represents some kind of 'absolute evil', a sort of ground zero of evil? Certainly it has been widely discussed in these terms; indeed, this constitutes something of a shared presupposition of 'Holocaust discourse', even when there can be plenty of scope for disagreement within the discourse. Yet, the effect of this is to reconstitute the Holocaust *as melodrama*, as a cosmic battle between the forces of Good and Evil, beyond any conceivable *historically grounded* level of explanation or framework of understanding. Far from being a perversion of Holocaust discourse, *Schindler's List* becomes an appropriate exemplification of it, perpetuating it in the powerful context of film, reinforcing its place as melodrama in the cultural imaginary. Can *any* event have this status, as not only unique but uniquely evil? If its 'uniqueness' is merely the attribute of any event, in its distinctive particularity, then – however horrific it may have been, and undoubtedly was – the Holocaust can be reinserted into history, given a context, related to other events. We can see it, perhaps, as a culmination of the 1930s and 1940s, the decades of the terrible killing fields of Eastern Europe, when millions lost their lives in systematic 'ethnic cleansing' regimes perpetrated by Nazi Germany and the Soviet Union – and, yes, most probably the worst of these cases, the most systematic, the most deliberate, the most thorough; but not 'evil' in some incomparable, absolute sense.[28] And if we are left with a 'gap' in our understanding here, a gap that *disturbs* us, makes us *feel* deeply uncomfortable, this is the gap between cause and effect that we find in so many other contexts too, that does indeed contribute to the powerful emotional drive out of which the melodramatic sense of the world is constructed, and constantly reinforced.

Here we can point to another aspect. Seen by the Nazis as a classic case of the 'enemy within', the Jews were thought to be particularly dangerous, always in principle difficult to identify (like 'terrorists' today), and spreading their tentacles through respectable society, corrupting it. They were, indeed, a *conspiracy*, and conspiracies always have something of the melodramatic about them. In his study of what he calls 'conspiracy culture' in the contemporary West, Peter Knight points to the 'baroque speculations', the 'omnivorous drive to interpretation', evidence that 'The figuration of conspiracy articulates otherwise uncoordinated suspicions that daily life is controlled by larger, unseen forces which cannot be the result of mere coincidence'.[29] But whether we think of society or the self, this can have paradoxical results. By imagining the individual self as threatened by all these invisible forces, conspiracy culture helps bring this about: 'By imagining a self immersed in a global environment of risk, or caught in a vast web of anonymous interconnecting forces, popular paranoia in effect undermines the logical coherence of the very thing it was seeking to defend.'[30]

An important part of our difficulty in locating these 'deep connections', and hence gaining any sense of control, is a crisis of authority. It is not necessarily that we distrust experts in any absolute sense, but that we do not know which experts to trust; and since they, and the politicians who draw on them, can consequently come up with a range of contradictory findings, along with the resulting divergent policies on any given issue that arises, the effect is to cast doubt on the whole notion of 'expertise' in itself. Knight suggests that the Kennedy assassination was a key moment here: not only did it spawn several generations of conspiracy theories, but it produced, arguably for the first time in the era of mass communication, the spectacle of alleged 'experts' endlessly disagreeing about every conceivable aspect of the events in question and the nature of the evidence,[31] and thus contributing strongly to a corrosive effect on popular confidence in the whole notion of an expert – with implications today in the total confusion in the popular consciousness surrounding the 'global warming' debate.

'Connectivity' has become central to our view of the world, and our experience of living in it.[32] This has important ramifications. In complex systems of connectivity, the properties of the systems are not reducible to those of their constituents, nor are causal connections easy to trace. Indeed, cause and effect can appear disparate in scale, or even completely unconnected, just as seemingly random connections can produce ordered interaction in resultant systems that can be in varying degrees self-regulating, while retaining sufficient links with their ecosystems to render them finally unpredictable and uncontrollable in their long-term consequences.[33] And while a lot of this is not new – both the science and the world it attempts to theorize have deep roots in the nineteenth century – we nonetheless have a growing sense that modernity, as the result of our own technological and economic impact on the world, is heavily implicated. Hence the contemporary theorization of risk,[34] together with the salience of debates on accountability and responsibility, the pursuit of someone or something to *blame* when things go wrong – as they do, often or always. David Rodowick suggests that our notions of connectivity imply currents and forces that flow through us, and history is experienced as a wave or tide 'whose energy derives from immense and invisible forces of technological change that are too complex and too enormous for individuals to fathom fully';[35] but if, as individuals, we cannot feel responsible agents in this situation, we tend to assume that someone *else*, somewhere, must play this role, if any sort of satisfactory 'closure' is to be obtained for the manifold tragedies or traumas, large or small, of everyday life, magnified as they readily are through media exposure. None of this guarantees the presence of melodrama as a mode of experiencing all this, or as an inevitable framework of response to it, but it is the necessary backdrop that helps give melodrama its distinctive cultural potential and power.

Melodrama involves dramatizing[36] the sense of a whole, because only by doing so can one 'realize' it, bring it about. It thereby includes 'rationalization', the drive to make the whole intelligible, the search for 'the hidden principle', the key to unlock the secret that reveals the whole *as* whole, as totality, beyond the world of apparent dispersion and distraction. It is not, however, restricted to this, it is not a 'merely' intellectual grasp; it 'realizes' the world as battleground of good and evil in which we are inherently involved as agents; it displays the cosmos as a field of forces, with humans playing the parts of heroes, villains and suffering victims. Hence, again, the 'dialectic of pathos and action',[37] in which the excesses – of action, spectacle and explanation – can never conclusively provide the 'closure' to which they aspire. Indeed, this closure, this appearance of completeness, is necessarily inseparable from simplification, distortion, hence falsity, although this is fully compatible with intense, lively credibility. Melodrama thus aspires to a total closure of meaning, A and not-A together, while avoiding the emptiness of that resolution by instituting a manic fullness; hence the void at its heart is masked by the frantic battle of absolutes and the rapidity and decisiveness of action, reinforcing the sense of excess so central to the melodramatic experience of the world.

And the suffering victims? Bartov and other critics of *Schindler's List* have pointed to the way the film seems to diminish the Jews, making them as anonymous and shadowy as they may perhaps have seemed to their guards. This is an accurate perception, but it is not unique to this film, or inherently to do with the plight of Holocaust victims rather than others in situations of mass suffering: it reveals an aspect of the logic of melodrama itself. Brooks has claimed that we live 'within a system of melodramatic struggle, where virtue and evil are fully personalized'.[38] The latter dimension, clearly present in the film, means that melodrama either has to display suffering in small-scale scenarios, or, where this is not possible, concentrate on exemplars, on 'exemplary instances', to stand in for, figure, mass suffering through their individual 'embodiment' of it. In fiction, Eliza or Tom in *Uncle Tom's Cabin* would of course be classic instances; but the television screen produces instances too, every day, and not just in the frequently parodic excesses of soap opera which can, indeed, distract us from the sense in which little everyday scenes can so easily be presented in, or slide naturally into, the language, emotion and postures of melodrama. Hence we encounter the scenes of parents attempting to articulate distress and despair at the death of a son in Iraq or Afghanistan, or anguish at the sudden murder of a 'loved one' in some meaningless knife or gun attack, coupled with the anger, the demand for answers, for vengeance as 'closure'. Always these little scenes have two features in common: they manifest a standard form, of language and gesture – nothing original is ever said, or shown – and they invade the viewer's space, not always in predictable form. They can engage us emotionally, in a straightforward enough way; or they can make us feel uneasy, as if reacting to the very standardization of these scenes, as if distrusting them, or distrusting our own capacity to be potentially seduced by them. And this reminds us that, at this point, melodrama incorporates the sentimental as an essential dimension of its language of feeling.[39]

Those who suffer evil are always virtuous: the two terms are locked in a mutually affirming embrace. In these everyday scenes, the dead are always described in a language of hyperbole: they are always heroes, wonderful sons and daughters, generous, loving, universally popular; in short, perfect beyond all credibility. This is both intensely understandable, in context, and also an innocent reaffirmation of the language of innocence and virtue in which these issues are cast in the mode of melodrama. Ben Singer notes the pathos, 'a kind of visceral physical sensation triggered by the perception of moral injustice against an undeserving victim'.[40] There is also a subtle universalization here. Everyone is potentially a victim of evil, hence everyone can potentially be enclosed within the community of the virtuous; and since suffering becomes an index of virtue, evidence of it, evil does not just seek it out, but retrospectively constitutes it *as* virtue. Evil indeed *desires* virtue, embraces it as evidence of its own power, its reality; it needs what it must destroy, hence must reconstitute it eternally or face its own oblivion.

In the context of modern culture, it is hardly surprising that this dialectic has become most apparent in the 'child abuse' scenario. Childhood has, after all, been constructed since Romanticism as the heart of innocence and purity, reaching an appropriate apotheosis in Victorian childhood deathbed scenes,[41] coded as the perfect child's departure for the perfection of the hereafter, before the child can be corrupted by the adult world of sexuality and temptation; hence the view that 'the child and the soul are somehow interchangeable, and that consequently children are the keepers and the guarantors of humanity's reputation', as Marina Warner puts it.[42] Despite the best efforts of Freud and the theorization of childhood sexuality, this model has been bizarrely reinforced in the recent decades of media and public panic over paedophiles and the reconstruction of childhood as a zone of endangered, vulnerable purity. So powerful is this model that when children themselves behave badly, they are likely, in extreme cases, to be reclassified as not 'really' children at all (they are 'little monsters' perhaps – certainly evil).[43] 'Childhood' has become a classic site of melodramatic struggle, with good and evil in contention across the hapless body of the child.

It is crucial that this mediated focus on the individual is a focus on the *embodied* individual: melodrama thereby re-enacts the spectacle of suffering in sensational mode, with suffering itself, in the form of the suffering victim, duly sentimentalized. The body becomes the site of violation, the field of battle, both sensational and sensationalized, and it thereby becomes the key subject and resource of the melodramatic framing of the world. Always the victim as embodied self is reinvented, the self as everyman, threatened, violated, yet surviving, with threats to bodily integrity, the body as potentially subject to trauma, becoming central to modern self-identity. From this point of view, the distinctive Christian tradition of the sacred leaves a powerful residue: for the Christian sacred is not just transcendence, disembodied spirituality; it is also the body, the sacrificial abjection of the torn body, the body of Christ on the cross. Melodrama plunges the sublime into the bathos of the abject, forces us to confront this yet also respond in a way that is a choice, the yea or nay of the body in the immediacy of impact being rationalized into the moral, as the outgrowth of the ethical out of the aesthetic, hence facing both ways, towards gesture and language, body and thought. Either way, both ways, 'The melodramatic body is a body seized by meaning', as Brooks puts it.[44]

Gesture and language can be taken as code for nature and culture: and here one might note a final, significant feature of the melodramatic mode. If language is hopelessly enmeshed in particularity, in cultural specificity, always subject to uncertainties of translation and meaning, melodrama yearns for the clarity of meaning as immediacy, manifest in some direct way: gesture as the 'language' of the body, the promise that the universal body of humanity, in its suffering, can be read in its purity, nature transcending the chaotic Babel of multiple tongues. Yet, as has been seen, melodrama is also rationalization. Hadley indicates the conundrum: 'Melodrama attempts to turn all gesture into rational discourse but at the same time to retain within that discourse the passion and simplicity of gesture.'[45] Since the eighteenth century, argues Brooks, gesture has frequently been seen as conveying 'the message of innocence and purity, expressed in an immediate, inarticulate language of presence': whereas language can dissemble, bodily expression reveals truth. Yet the paradox here is never resolved: ultimately, in avoiding the arbitrary conventions of language, truth becomes muteness; nothing must be left unexpressed, yet expression without language is ultimately incommunicable, inarticulate. Brooks concludes that 'the total expressivity assigned to gesture is related to the ineffability of what is to be expressed'.[46] The expressive body is ultimately the silent body.

It is worth pointing here to an intriguing aspect of this: the way this possibility of a 'universal language' beyond or beneath 'languages' resonates in the promise of early, particularly silent film, where the impact of the visual was seen as having a potential for engaging audiences cross-culturally. Miriam Hansen thus observes that the 'seemingly unmediated appeal to sympathy and sentiment was one aspect of the promotion of the film as universal language'.[47] This dimension of melodrama gives it real cultural strength: for if, in the modern world, suffering – in its very 'muteness' – is taken as the mark of our irreducible individuality, by that very fact it can be seen as testifying to our common humanity. The cultural work of suffering, what suffering *does* for us, in its social and ideological implications, is convey this duality, confront us with it, reconciling the modernity of our individualism with the universality of our aspirations. So long as we draw on the twin meanings of 'pathetic', Williams is surely right to observe that 'Virtuous suffering is a pathetic weapon against injustice, but we need to recognize how frequently it has been the melodramatic weapon of choice of American popular culture'.[48]

Moving towards a conclusion, we can note the suggestion by Brooks that 'Perhaps melodrama alone is adequate to contemporary psychic affect', in that it has the flexibility and range 'to dramatize and explicate life in imaginative forms that transgress traditional generic constraints, and the traditional demarcations of high culture from popular entertainment'.[49] We have seen that it also transgresses the demarcations between everyday life, culture and politics. The term itself, of course, is rarely used, doubtless because it does indeed, as Brooks implies, retain these links with disparaged aspects of 'mass culture'. This makes it all the more important to be clear about those patterns, those connections, that do indeed justify invoking 'melodrama' as a key cultural configuration of our times, drawing on its own past incarnations in the modern period while being able to adapt to new challenges.

Melodrama can be characterized as a singularly dynamic version of the Kantian dynamical sublime, not now as experience so much as active appropriation, whereby the aesthetic moment is rationalized to 'make sense' while simultaneously demanding an engagement that is essentially moral. We can map its deep structure by addressing the two gaps it both draws on, reproduces, and attempts to bridge, in the process producing its own distinctive form. There is the gap between cause and effect, the disproportion of one to the other, the unpredictability of the relation, given that the connection depends on the complexity of the whole; and then the gap between action and reflection, the gap that enforces – just as it subverts – the construction of the integrated subject, as self. If sensation is what traverses these gaps, producing feeling, then the sense of the whole, grasped reflectively, is manifested in the image. If the sublime in sensation is what forces us 'beyond' sensation, as has previously been argued, then melodrama can specify, elaborate this 'beyond', taking it through figuration into the dramatization that re-presents the gap as fullness, as excess. This elaboration carries the excess and the rationalization *simultaneously*, the excess *in* or *as* rationalization, conveying a fusion of understanding and involvement. The form this takes is both pictorial and narrative, but here melodrama meets its own distinctive tension, for this simultaneity is difficult or impossible to bring off – hence the 'gap' in melodrama itself, the dynamic tension of tableau and action[50] that drives it on while enforcing 'closure' in the only way possible, as emotional release through climactic excess.

The mediated public sphere

First and foremost, then, melodrama embodies a dramatization of the public sphere in the era of mass media sensation and spectacle, always liable to be traversed by 'currents of feeling', transformations of popular emotion, unpredictable in both origin and outcome. We thereby encounter the distinctive late modern mix of the dramas of media dissemination, political manipulation, and varying degrees of public involvement, with individuals and issues subject to the vagaries of fashion, the rise and fall of celebrities, heroes and villains, and the sentimentalization of suffering. All this seems a long way from the image of the eighteenth-century coffee-house in which men – always men – allegedly sat around sedately debating issues of the day in the terms of an emergent ideal of calm, abstract, disembodied rationality. One can of course point out that this construction already rests on a distinctive structure of feeling and accompanying language of bodily expression, that of sensibility, hardly an *absence* of body,[51] just as we can extend this to point out that women, too, participated in the wider discursive structures opened up by this, as readers and writers of novels, as correspondents, as full agents in this broader – if nonetheless always gendered – conception of the public sphere. And one can further point out that this public sphere was itself traversed, by the turn of the century, by these emerging currents of melodrama, which linked up with the processes of exclusion whereby emergent modernity expelled 'other' patterns of life and culture as inimical to itself, beyond the pale, whether remote or dangerously 'inside'. And in the light of this, and the preceding analysis, one might want to turn this around, and ask: is melodrama so pervasive that it totally subsumes the contemporary public sphere?

This whole distinction between 'public' and 'private' spheres needs examination. The two terms can be seen as mutually interrogatory or interpenetrating. Taking the street as the pre-eminent site of the public, Benjamin thus suggests that '*flânerie* can transform Paris into one great interior', adding that 'the street reveals itself in the arcade as the furnished and familiar interior of the masses'.[52]

Here, Benjamin is setting public and private off against one another, showing that they interpenetrate, or become mutually encompassing. But if the street can become 'interior', how is it that the home, as the classic locus of the private, can also become 'exterior'? If we remain in the 1930s, we can bear in mind that when the *flâneur* – or his successors – returned home, they would be sure to find the radio (the 'wireless') positioned there, and Gillian Beer reminds us that 'Radio produced a new idea of the public, one far more intermixed, promiscuous and democratic than the book could cater for', and that 'intimacy' was central to a radio experience in which 'No secure boundaries prevail between private and public'.[53] Later, of course, there would be a new box in pride of place inside the home: David Morley points out that the television set is 'at the junction of the "inside" and the "outside", the channel through which the news of the public world enters the domestic realm'.[54] This in turn suggests that the media can indeed be positioned as 'mediators' whereby 'public' and 'private' only exist in a constant *process* of dynamic interaction and transformation.

The private could be seen as what, at any time, is *kept from* being public, just as this sets up a contest in which the public seeks to (re)claim, to invade or 'expose' the private and, in so doing, *constitutes* it as such. One might say, with Misha Kavka, that 'privacy only comes into existence when it is on the verge of being lost, extruded in retrospect from its opposing term, publicity'.[55] The core of the private becomes the *secret* – with all its melodramatic potential – just as secrets are always there to be revealed, and are always already known by someone, somewhere, are already in some sense 'open' secrets. Such 'secrets' become endlessly 'negotiable' – selling one's secret, or just exposing it, becomes a route to publicity; indeed, a route we must take, if we seek to gain purchase on the equivalent 'secrets' of others. In her study, Kavka presents 'reality TV' as a core site for exploring this dynamic interrelation between secrets created, shared and exposed, with participants variously sharing or excluded from situations of 'intimate knowledge' of which the viewing public may be – or become – well aware.[56] This also reminds us that intimacy has become an arena where these negotiations over privacy can be particularly intense, with much perceived to be at stake over the fundamentals of self and self-identity. This returns us to the centrality of the body, and its relation to the self, as the heart of the modern notion of the private,[57] and we can see why Kavka argues, *contra* Habermas, that 'the public sphere only *matters* when affective particularity is taken into account', while we need to remember that *neither* pole can be taken as pre-constituted: the very notions of body and self, and the experiences of selfhood and embodiment, cannot escape these criss-crossing fields of force that define the public and the private as currents traversing the terrain of the modern. As she observes elsewhere, of television generally, 'the medium itself works through channels of feeling',[58] though not, one should add, through these alone; or at least, their *effect* brings into play those imaginative acts of reflexive appropriation and figuration that we have already seen as constituting problems for any focus that is too exclusively on sensation and affect.[59]

In her work on the mediated public sphere in relation to perceptions of suffering, Lilie Chouliaraki adds an emphasis on the cosmopolitan, arguing that 'a group of spectators may turn into a cosmopolitan public only if the spectators break with any particular identification'.[60] While unpredictable in its effects, sensationalism can play a role through *disturbing*, breaking down, these existing boundaries.[61] For Kavka, the transmission of affect is crucial here, and since 'affect is a form of knowledge produced from the very movement of crossing a boundary', it is involved not just in embodied person to person relations but in relations between self and other more generally, including relations between the boundaries that both separate and relate different communities. These boundaries, now, are *mediated*: television works through 'the creation of intimate relations across a screen', and the 'across' here refers not just to what is happening on the screen, but *between* screen and viewer. She concludes that 'the public' is 'increasingly a construction of mediated intimacies, a collective performance of private relationality which opens up a space of public interest';[62] it is, in short, more about implicit, affective 'knowledge' than explicit discussion and debate.

One might conclude from all this that while 'community' and 'public sphere' cannot be wholly distinguished – which is why a purely impersonal, universalizing, rationalist approach to the latter cannot work – neither should they be totally assimilated. The mediated public sphere thus emerges as the sphere of endlessly unstable communities, with affect, reflexive awareness and debate, occurring at and through boundaries that are permeable, facing both ways, inside and out; and such communities can thereby be 'mediated' in both senses, in that the media can be said both to 'publicize' and to 'mediate', hence becoming partially *constitutive* of possibilities of communal life. In thus harnessing linguistic, pictorial and sensory resources, the media show how, as Chouliaraki puts it, 'the formation of publics is an aesthetic operation'.[63] Universality exists as process rather than form or content: it designates communities as everemergent and simultaneously in dispersion, in principle porous in relation to each other, and with the media being central agents in these processes. 'Publicness', one might say, is horizontal, structural, involving relations between bodies both as subjects of experience and sources of reflexive thought and imaginative projection, rather than organizing them in more hierarchical and increasingly abstract terms, with each higher level being more disembodied, and contextually disembedded, than the one below.[64]

One can use a historical perspective to suggest another area where the notion of the public sphere requires some revision. Drawing on the work of Benedict Anderson,[65] Burgett suggests that 'print culture seems to trace the circulation of a simultaneity of social time, the homogeneous, empty time that it fills with events',[66] thereby reinforcing the sense of community *in* time and space. For John Thompson, this entails the decline of the 'traditional publicness of co-presence' and makes possible the discovery of 'despatialized simultaneity', as in telephone conversations, signalling the rise of forms of mediated interaction that have, in time, amounted to a 'reinvention of publicness'.[67] The 'modern' perspective on space and time in effect presents them as an abstract framework, imagined simultaneously as a kind of container, divisible into measurable units, *within* which events occur, lives develop, and communities evolve. 'Presence' and co-presence, whatever their precise meaning, are specified relative to this taken-for-granted framework.

The *effect* of modern technologies of media and communication, however, is to subvert this, and it is easy to miss the subtle transition here. In an era when we increasingly find 'face-to-face interaction' occurring via the internet, perhaps we need to think of 'co-presence' as being transformed, rather than replaced. 'Presence' becomes a relative, almost a negotiable concept, no longer tied to any fixed notions of space and time: those I interact with are 'co-present' to me; I might want to 'locate' them, in more conventional spatio-temporal terms, but this isn't essential. 'The present' is what expands to fill the time of interaction, wherever and whenever it occurs. (The internet is a no-place, and, like the city, never sleeps.) Presence can be diffused, and differentiated, just as it can be concentrated; it is not static, a given, but must be seen in terms of relation and process. It also has an element of the vicarious. 'Presence' is what we can carry off as presence; it is *as if* presence, good enough, but not without the element of simulation. Thus we can regard presence as increasingly inseparable from these processes of mediation. As supposed universals, space and time still have their 'place', but are increasingly defined in terms of relation and process, rather than defining them, hence becoming relative to presence. Space and time are not fixed coordinates that uniquely define events; rather, events, as explosive or congealed concentrations of process, become the nodes or markers to which space and time are related. Thus Rodowick can argue that 'digital culture presents us with mixed, layered, and heterogeneous audiovisual images unfolding in a nonlinear space and time', and hence the 'elimination of a felt sense of space and distance as we interact in computer networks'.[68] And Paul Virilio suggests that we live in an age of 'polar inertia', of speeds so frantic that they amount to a virtually instantaneous, 'generalised arrival' of images, messages, and voices, an implosion of space and time.[69]

'Presence' becomes the ever-shifting horizon of experience. In the era of 'mediated experience', both presence and its horizon become transformed. Thompson suggests that mediated experience involves experiencing events which are spatially distant, so that 'experience takes place in a context which is different from the context in which the event actually occurs', adding that this 'recontextualized character of mediated experience is a source both of its charm and of its ability to shock and disconcert'.[70] Taking into account the points just made, we could say that these different contexts do not slide together harmoniously; there is a *jarring* of contexts, a friction as they rub against each other, and it is out of this that sensation emerges. After all, the body itself is subject to this tension: the 'distance' senses (sight, sound) can live in this new regime of co-presence, but the other senses, and, therefore, something of the sense of 'embodiment' itself, are left behind, further emphasizing the potential for sensation to flash across the fissure. Something of this tension is also apparent in Samuel Weber's claim that if television *overcomes* distance and separation, the fact that it is a mode of transmission necessarily also *involves* separation: hence it 'overcomes spatial distance but only by *splitting the unity of place*'. Again the television set as 'Trojan horse', inside yet also outside, is in play here.[71] Yet the result is a new sense of presence as trans-contextual, disjunctive, or perhaps of context as relative to presence, rather than vice versa, and manifest in the affective discontinuities of mediated experience. And one can agree with Thompson that this necessarily transforms our sense of community: 'commonality is no longer linked to the sharing of a common locale'.[72]

Here we can further elaborate the distinctive features of television. Thompson suggests that 'it combines audio-visual presence with spatio-temporal distance', but, as already implied, that doesn't go far enough, and perhaps keeps the experience too close to that of film.[73] For Kavka, it is 'a technology of intimacy' in that there can be 'a collapse of distance and time through the production of affective proximity'; hence we can move 'beyond the semiotics of representation to the affect of presentation'.[74] Jeffrey Sconce makes suggestions that help clarify the tension here. Television is not like film; as an electronic rather than a photographic medium, the television image is in perpetual motion, so the image as the product of a series of electric impulses is necessarily experienced 'as it happens'. He argues that television seems 'live' because 'its scanned images are always in the process of "becoming", hence 'producing a "living" quality that pervades the medium and its programming'. Thus television's distinctive effect – and affect, one might add – 'emanates from this illusion of direct, personalized, and immediate contact with the audience, the medium consistently staging a form of simulated first-person address ... that always seems to be unfolding in the present, the now'.[75] The time of the image and the time of events shown are assimilated, which is different from the 'presence in absence' of film.[76] For Kavka, too, the effect of 'liveness' is to collapse the time of action and the time of viewing; such liveness involves 'belonging to an imagined community of viewers *at the moment of watching*'.[77]

In effect, what we are presented with here is the suggestion that mediated experience, particularly in the context of television, manifests an essential element of the vicarious. As we move away from the classic face-to-face scenario, as experience becomes mediated, so the representational forms become more trans-contextual, and the potential of the vicarious as the mediated experience of otherness intensifies. As experience becomes mediated, it incorporates its own distance from its object; in becoming trans-contextual, it can only do so as other to itself, hence the vicarious as a reflexive distancing from self and other. Thus, one engages with 'reality television' – a category which could, in many ways, be said to incorporate the 'news' – by being aware of the 'performance of reality in a way that *matters*', whatever the elements of simulation and manipulation, of staged event as against actuality, thereby engaging spectacle *as* experience. Hence 'something can *feel real* precisely because it is mediated, because of the affect transmitted to our responsive bodies across a screen', as Kavka puts it.[78] Reality television 'works to catch and represent the reality of watching itself, that is, to catch and represent viewers to themselves; it is they who are more deeply exposed through the affective reality of this "exposure" being relayed back to them'.[79] Between self and other lies the mediated image, with its potential for vicarious identification: the vicarious is the way this transgression of the boundary is 'lived' in experience. One is not really the other – but neither is one really not the other. The vicarious is our mode of experience in spectacle; it corresponds in experience to simulation at the level of representation and reality.[80] And if there is something of the theatrical here, it can remind us of the possibility of an over-identification that can result in both sentimentality and melodrama, the excesses of the subject in the vicarious, escaping into itself as other, through the excesses of feeling and emotion.[81]

Now, however, it is time to incorporate sensationalism more directly. To gain attention, it is necessary to be sensational. To be heard above the hubbub, hold the attention despite all the distractions, even just to convey information in a world of ever-present excess noise, one has to resort to further excess, to eye-catching intensity, or to transgression. This is effect rather than teleology, more like a survival of the fittest, of the sensation with the greatest attention-grabbing power, a response enforced by the exigencies of the modern environment of rapid change and media-inflected experience – in short, life as 'special effects'. In a culture of hyperbole, everything has to be hyped up, sensationalized. Thus do we encounter the anaesthetics of the modern: feelings are numbed, as we live in a cocoon of half-awareness, and shock defence, with 'feeling' itself becoming alien to us; hence, again, sensation has to become sensational, to make an impact, whether external or through our response (in 'feeling'). If this is so, then we can also return to melodrama; for it, too, in its wider ramifications, can be positioned as an extreme point in cycles of sensationalism, whether as the climax of one or the dramatic start of another; and it, too, can never in principle escape the 'fatigue' that marks the excess of the same, desperately though it may try to incorporate even this into its all-encompassing dramas. But just as there are always new opportunities for sensation (and its recuperation in melodrama), due to the very impossibility of an ever-intensifying linear process of uniform sensationalism, so the very *breaks* in this process offer potential for critical and ethical engagement. In short, if all this implies further potential for sensation, for mediated experience as 'sensational', it nonetheless gives no grounds for assuming that these problems *necessarily* have to be seen as somehow inherently threatening any possibility of a meaningful, albeit transformed, public sphere in which communication can 'embody' the sensory and the affective, in the context of mediation, without being *reducible* to these. Least of all does one have to conclude that even a sensationalized pattern of communication must *necessarily* be cast in the mode of melodrama. But this invites further reflection.

Conclusion

We must reflect, one more time, on melodrama, where the supposedly rational world of modernity encounters its nemesis in the dark side of the force, a cosmos of extremes. The obsession with trauma, the identification with the suffering victim, the overflow of pity into sentimentality, the concentration and transformation of the reality of misfortune into the experience of a force of evil, the figuration of evil in human terms, as a person or group: from sensationalism to melodrama, the return of the *theatrum mundi* as nightmare, is a small enough step, though with massive implications. Here we encounter the simultaneous escalation of intensity and sensation into spectacular spectacle, with aesthetics, ethics and politics fused in the battles that rage across the infernal terrain of the world. The great strength of melodrama, after all, is its apparently all-encompassing *openness* to experience, its absorption of the contingencies of the world into a unifying vision that incorporates our own fundamental responses *to* it as part *of* it, our capacity for moral involvement at its most profound. This also is the problem it poses: in being open to the world even to excess, in its frenzy of sense-making, melodrama nevertheless endeavours to close off those disturbing chinks of light, the flickerings of difference, so that they serve merely to generate the enormous energy needed, in putting the *drama* into melodrama. But this very fact reminds us that, as we have seen, the melodrama alternative is not inevitable. It can only succeed at the cost of empty circularity; if that drives it on to renewed efforts, it also opens up a gap for reflexive awareness and the challenging contingencies of experience.

We can recall 'dispersion' here, the 'distracted' experience of the modern world as plethora, representing the irreducibility of the experience of culture to rational, goal-seeking projects and the orientation to control, the irredeemable multiplicity of the world, a world beyond utility and necessity, a world of excess. *This* excess points beyond the excess of melodrama itself, seeing that the latter, too, escapes its own control, cannot but reinforce the diversity of the world it seeks to harness. In the light of this, we can say that modernity swings between two ethical orientations. Firstly, an ethic of degree, a continuum of small differences, varying shades of grey. The drive to knowledge and control, with its ethos of 'reform' and 'improvement', contributes to this relativist continuum. And this is also continuous with the world of everyday life, that of the 'humble narratives', impregnated with moral dimensions that have to be endlessly mediated, finessed in practical situations where right and wrong can only be questions of degree. One can try to live this with integrity or with cynicism, and these dilemmas are central to the moral dimensions of the humble narratives of our lives; but in practice these can slide into each other anyway, for this is also where we encounter the grubby compromises of politics, business and bureaucratic life, the world of rationalization, measurement and money. As for the challenge of integrity, one can further observe that a 'heroism of the everyday' can produce scenarios in which we star in moral dramas where good and bad do have real meaning, even if this is partly a function of our own determination to live our lives in precisely that way, recreating the endless possibility of melodrama, the second orientation. Ultimately, then, this duality of the moral dimension permits us to return to the everyday, but the everyday as a navigational problem, as it were: a problem of negotiating the Scylla of melodrama and the Charybdis of moral squalor, when those two figures of temptation loom uncertainly all around, themselves evading clear definition.

There is hope, then, after all. The murmurings of the world, registered as sensory inputs, as perceptions, always have some priority over subsequent constructions placed on them, even if without these constructions we cannot know just what it is we are registering, and even though these murmurings may themselves be irredeemably marked by previous such constructions, now opaque in their reappearance. The 'sensation' of the image represents this ability to respond to inputs as novel, to revivify our sense of the world, *disturb* our interpretations, even though it can never challenge them directly, for thought (cognition, theory) is as reflexively irreducible to image (aesthetics) as vice versa, albeit rooted in that very domain. Perception, *aisthesis*, retains some independence of the values that can be elaborated out of it, even if the possibility, even the necessity, of such elaboration is there in the very fusion of passive reaction and active orientation, the 'facing both ways' that characterizes the very moment of its occurrence.

The news broadcasts the endless dispersion of the world; sensationalism works as a practice of concentration, breaking into the intimacy of our feelings. This is where everything is at stake, where everything depends on which direction we take. In his thought-provoking discussion of the media, John Peters reminds us that theories of communication are ultimately, in effect, theories of communion, of relationship conceived under the figure of love. Contrasting the Socratic model of dialogue with the Gospel model of dissemination, he writes: 'The fundamental question is whether the epitome of love should be the love that occurs between equals who are present to each other in body and soul or the love that leaps across the chasms.' The former emphasizes unity, even identity; the latter, 'making do with the fragments we find in ourselves and others'. The Socratic dialogues 'figure love as the yearning for oneness; the synoptic Gospels as compassion for otherness'.[82] 'Dissemination' has the effect of taking our attention away from origins and causes, and focusing on outcomes; in the parable of the sower, the seed is 'scattered', so whether it germinates is due largely to the accident of the terrain where it happens to land, and this is not in the control of the sower. Kavka hints at this, referring to the television screen as 'a dispersal mechanism of affect', scattering seeds that can 'take root and generate effects'.[83]

Applied to broadcasting – and one does not really have to *apply* it, since one can already talk of 'broadcasting' the seed over a wide area – this has a radical effect, encouraging us to go beyond the uniformity of the original message and its producer to consider the diversity of outcomes ('reception'). In his account, Peters points out that there can, of course, be potentially totalitarian aspects to this, but is keen to point out that this can be just as true of dialogue: it is not necessarily egalitarian, nor does it necessarily conform to rational ideals, despite the prestige this particular version has had in philosophy and in (Habermasian) theories of the public sphere. The history of sound transmission can be said to incorporate both, with the early priority of dialogue (the telephone, and the years of individual-to-individual 'wireless') giving way to broadcasting ('radio'), but with the latter incorporating elements of the former, rather than eliminating them.[84] And could the internet, too, be said to include both, or incorporate dialogue into dissemination?

So, at the point of sensation, do we continue with the intensity of concentration, incorporate the other into unity with the self in a sphere of intimacy, expelling those others – or aspects of otherness – that fail to fit, with melodrama as *possible* outcome? Or do we make a reflexive move, distancing our self from itself, locating ourselves in the mode of dispersion so as better to encounter the difference of the other, thus liberating feeling, and permitting sympathetic engagement across the gap? For there is to be found here a framework that can make this engagement possible, the possibility of the vicarious immersion and distancing in the otherness of life, a meeting ground in the plane of dispersion, a perspective in the scatter: the spectacle of sympathy, of sympathetic engagement, that distinctive relation between feeling, imagination and judgement that remains in place, that characterizes the cultural imaginary as a space of dissemination that can modify and hence incorporate dialogue. Beyond melodrama, then, we can still encounter moments of intensity, and visions of compassion, in the infinite scatter of the world.

Notes

Sensation and Sensationalism

1. E. A. Poe, 'The Facts in the Case of M. Valdemar', in E. A. Poe, *Tales of Mystery and Imagination* (Everyman, 1984 [1845]), pp. 303–4, 311.
2. Ibid., p. 304.
3. Ibid., p. 307.
4. Ibid., p. 309.
5. J. Elmer, *Reading at the Social Limit: Affect, Mass Culture, and Edgar Allan Poe* (Stanford University Press, 1995), pp. 123, 125, 125.
6. Poe, p. 312.
7. K. Halttunen, *Murder Most Foul: The Killer and the American Gothic Imagination* (Harvard University Press, 1998), p. 70.
8. See M. Bakhtin, *Rabelais and His World* (Indiana University Press, 1984 [1965]), on the 'grotesque body' and Carnival.
9. S. D. Moeller, *Compassion Fatigue: How the Media Sell Disease, Famine, War and Death* (Routledge, 1999), pp. 82, 94; and see the full account, pp. 80–95.
10. W. Smith, *Advertise. How? When? Where?* (Routledge, Warne and Routledge, 1863) pp. 34, 122.
11. Ibid., pp. 108, 108, 110, 83.
12. Both cit. M. Diamond, *Victorian Sensation* (Anthem Press, 2003), pp. 10–11, 253.
13. It is the *conjunction* of these dimensions of 'sensation' that is most important here; any literal-minded search for origins is bound to be never-ending. For example, we find that the invention of the kaleidoscope in 1815 was greeted in these terms by a poet, just a year or two later: 'Need I tell you, indeed, that with such preparation, / So lovely a bauble has caused a *Sensation*?'. This is quoted in H. Groth, 'Kaleidoscopic Vision and Literary Invention in an "Age of Things"', *English Language History* (2007), 74, p. 223. The emphasis in the original again suggests an element of novelty, or fashion, in the use of the word, and the article does suggest that a connection with commercialism is being hinted at.
14. See J. Flanders, *The Invention of Murder* (Harper, 2010), who also examines other famous cases, notably William Corder's murder of Maria Marten in 1827.
15. Rebecca Gowers has written an account of this connection, in fictional form, as *The Twisted Heart* (Canongate, 2009). An original source is B. D. Cousins, *Eliza Grimwood, A Domestic Legend of the Waterloo Road* (c. 1840). The case is outlined

by M. Brown in an article in the *Guardian*, 11 April 2009, p. 15. For the press sensationalism surrounding the 1888 Whitechapel murders, see A. Warwick and M. Willis (eds), *Jack the Ripper: Media, Culture, History* (Manchester University Press, 2007), Chs 2–6; and A. Smith, *Victorian Demons: Medicine, Masculinity and the Gothic at the* Fin de Siècle (Manchester University Press, 2004), Ch. 3.

16 Halttunen, p. 70. See pp. 199–203 for her discussion of the specific case. There is also an account in J. D. Stephens, *Sensationalism and the New York Press* (Columbia University Press, 1991), Ch. 5, confirming the media and popular interest, and presenting it as the first significant case of investigative journalism. He also confirms the general significance of the 1830s in the origins of media sensationalism. Thomas Boyle argues that as late as the 1820s, in the UK, most journalistic accounts of murder trials tended to be relatively brief and restrained, although with quasi-religious moralizing, rather in the eighteenth-century style documented in Halttunen: see his *Black Swine in the Sewers of Hampstead: Beneath the Surface of Victorian Sensationalism* (Hodder & Stoughton, 1990), pp. 42–4.

17 S. Streeby, *American Sensations: Class, Empire and the Production of Popular Culture* (California University Press, 2002), pp. 52, 52, 54.

18 K. Tester, *Compassion, Morality and the Media* (Open University Press, 2001), p. 62.

19 K. Theweleit, *Male Fantasies* (Minnesota University Press, 1987), vol. I, p. 303.

20 O. Barfield, *History in English Words* (Faber and Faber, 1954), pp. 169–70.

21 Elmer, p. 94.

22 A. Cvetkovich, *Mixed Feelings: Feminism, Mass Culture and Victorian Sensationalism* (Rutgers University Press, 1992), p. 2.

23 Halttunen, pp. 3–6, 66–7.

24 W. Wordsworth, Preface to *Lyrical Ballads* (2nd edn, 1800), in D. Wu (ed.), *Romanticism: An Anthology* (Blackwell, 3rd edn, 2006), p. 500.

25 Halttunen, p. 67.

26 T. Gunning, 'The Horror of Opacity: The Melodrama of Sensation in the Plays of André de Lorde', in J. Bratton et al., *Melodrama: Stage, Picture, Screen* (British Film Institute, 1994), pp. 51, 51, 52.

27 B. Singer, *Melodrama and Modernity: Early Sensational Cinema and Its Contexts* (Columbia University Press, 2001), p. 48.

28 Diamond, pp. 218–19.

29 D. Reynolds, *Beneath the American Renaissance* (Harvard University Press, 1988), pp. 171, 183.

30 L. Pykett, *The Sensation Novel* (Northcote House, 1994), p. 4.

31 L. Pykett, *The 'Improper' Feminine: The Women's Sensation Novel and the New Woman Writing* (Routledge, 1992), p. 51. Other sources include N. Daly, *Sensation*

and Modernity in the 1860s (Cambridge University Press, 2009) and, for gender aspects, A. Mangham, *Violent Women and Sensation Fiction: Crime, Medicine and Victorian Popular Culture* (Palgrave, 2007); Ch. 1 gives a useful overall review. On the sensation novel and popular controversy see also Boyle, Chs 12, 14–16.

32 Pykett, *Sensation*, p. 5.
33 Cit. ibid., p. 3.
34 Cvetkovich, p. 13. For further elaboration, see K. Harrison and R. Fantina (eds), *Victorian Sensations* (Ohio State University Press, 2006).
35 Cit. Boyle, p. 188.
36 J. Sloan, *Oscar Wilde* (Oxford University Press, 2003), p. 64.
37 See J. Walkowitz, *City of Dreadful Delight: Narratives of Sexual Danger in Late-Victorian London* (Virago, 1992) p. 86; and, on the Wilde trials, A. Sinfield, *The Wilde Century* (Cassell, 1994).
38 Gunning, p. 52.
39 Cvetkovich, p. 168.
40 N. Rosenthal, 'The Blood Must Continue to Flow', in B. Adams et al., *Sensation: Young British Artists from the Saatchi Collection* (Thames and Hudson, 1998), p. 11.
41 Diamond, p. 288.
42 Elmer, pp. 93, 94.
43 E. K. Sedgwick, *Epistemology of the Closet* (Penguin, 1994), p. 143.
44 R. F. Brissenden, *Virtue in Distress: Studies in the Novel of Sentiment from Richardson to Sade* (Macmillan, 1974), pp. 14–15; R. Williams, *Keywords* (Fontana, 1988), pp. 281–2. For my own more extended discussion of sentimentalism, see *Sympathetic Sentiments: Affect, Emotion and Spectacle in the Modern World* (Bloomsbury, 2014), esp. Chs 2, 8.
45 Williams, p. 281.
46 Streeby, p. 31.
47 These rueful retrospective reflections are actually incorporated into Ch. 11 of *Good Wives*: see L. M. Alcott, *Little Women and Good Wives* (Wordsworth Classics, 2006 [1868–9]). Jo needed money for her charitable aspirations, so 'She took to writing sensation stories, for in those dark ages, even all-perfect America read rubbish' (p. 327); writing, she found herself 'living in bad society, and imaginary though it was, its influence affected her, for she was feeding heart and fancy on dangerous and insubstantial food', losing her 'innocent bloom' (p. 331). Luckily, no lasting damage was done: she came to see that her stories were 'trash', and 'will soon be worse trash if I go on, for each is more sensational than the last' (p. 337), hinting again at the necessity for sensation to become ever more sensational.

48 Halttunen, pp. 160, 140; and see S. Clark, *Sentimental Modernism: Women Writers and the Revolution of the Word* (Indiana University Press, 1991) p. 21.
49 B. Burgett, *Sentimental Bodies: Sex, Gender and Citizenship in the Early Republic* (Princeton University Press, 1998), p. 16.
50 E. Barnes, *States of Sympathy: Education and Democracy in the American Novel* (Columbia University Press, 1997), p. 12.
51 K. Sánchez-Eppler, *Touching Liberty: Abolition, Feminism, and the Politics of the Body* (California University Press, 1993), p. 100.
52 Elmer, p. 14.
53 M. Warner, 'The Mass Public and the Mass Subject', in C. Calhoun (ed.), *Habermas and the Public Sphere* (MIT Press, 1992), p. 394.
54 Elmer, p. 95.
55 Elmer, p. 103.
56 Clark, p. 21.
57 Streeby, p. 54; and see M. Warner, *Publics and Counterpublics* (Zone Books, 2002).
58 B. Anderson, *Imagined Communities: Reflections on the Origins and Spread of Nationalism* (Verso, 1983).
59 D. A. Miller, *The Novel and the Police* (California University Press, 1988), pp. 162, 162, 163.
60 A. Cvetkovich, 'Ghostlier Determinations: The Economy of Sensation and *The Woman in White*', in L. Pykett (ed.), *Wilkie Collins* (Macmillan, 1998), p. 110.
61 M. E. Braddon, *Eleanor's Victory* (Tinsley Bros., 1863), cit. Pykett, *Improper*, p. 83.
62 E. Showalter, 'Family Secrets and Domestic Subversion: rebellion in the novels of the eighteen-sixties', in A. Wohl (ed.), *The Victorian Family: Structure and Stresses* (Croom Helm, 1978), p. 104.
63 See S. Bruhm, *Gothic Bodies: The Politics of Pain in Romantic Fiction* (Pennsylvania University Press, 1994), Chs 1, 2, for useful background on cultural assumptions about pain in the period, particularly in literature and philosophy.
64 Halttunen, pp. 62, 79.
65 B. Singer, 'Modernity, Hyperstimulus and the Rise of Popular Sensationalism', in L. Charney and V. R. Schwartz (eds), *Cinema and the Invention of Modern Life* (California University Press, 1995), p. 87.
66 Cit. Pykett, *Sensation*, p. 4.
67 Singer, 'Modernity', p. 88.
68 Gunning, p. 52.
69 Pykett, *Improper*, p. 35.
70 Cvetkovich, *Mixed Feelings*, pp. 20, 21, 23.
71 J. B. Taylor, *In the Secret Theatre of Home: Wilkie Collins, Sensation Narrative, and Nineteenth-century Psychology* (Routledge, 1988), p. 4.
72 Pykett, *Improper*, p. 97.

73 Cit. J. M. Goulemot, *Forbidden Texts: Erotic Literature and Its Readers in Eighteenth-Century France* (Polity, 1994), p. 56.
74 P. Falk, 'The Representation of Presence: Outlining the Anti-Aesthetics of Pornography', *Theory Culture and Society* (1993), 10:2, p. 10, also reproduced in his book *The Consuming Body* (Sage, 1994), Ch. 7.
75 Goulemot, p. 57.
76 Halttunen, p. 69.
77 S. de Beauvoir, 'Must We Burn Sade?', in her *Marquis de Sade* (Calder, 1962), p. 69.
78 G. S. Rousseau, *Nervous Acts: Essays on Literature, Culture and Sensibility* (Palgrave, 2004), pp. 202–4.
79 Marquis de Sade, *Justine*, cit. and trans. Rousseau, p. 203.
80 *Byron's Letters and Journals*, ed. L. Marchand (Alfred A. Knopf, 1973), vol. III, p. 109. For further discussion, see Bruhm.
81 I. Kant, *Critique of Judgement* (Hafner, 1951 [1790]), trans. J. H. Bernard, p. 155.
82 Miller, p. 147.
83 Cvetkovich, 'Ghostlier', p. 122.
84 Miller, pp. 164, 148.
85 Wolfgang Schivelbusch argues that 'pre-industrial catastrophes were natural events, natural accidents', whereas technology introduces the idea that catastrophes can be 'self-induced', products of the technology itself: see his *The Railway Journey: The Industrialization of Time and Space in the 19th Century* (Berg, 1986), p. 131.
86 This dynamic is of course also apparent in disaster movies, a major Hollywood genre since the 1950s: see S. Keane, *Disaster Movies: The Cinema of Catastrophe* (Wallflower Press, 2001), or the compendious G. Kay and M. Rose, *Disaster Movies: The Ultimate Guide* (Mosaic Press, 2005).
87 M. A. Doane, 'Information, Crisis, Catastrophe', in P. Mellencamp (ed.), *Logics of Television: Essays in Cultural Criticism* (Indiana University Press, 1990), pp. 231, 230.
88 K. Rozario, *The Culture of Calamity: Disaster and the Making of Modern America* (Chicago University Press, 2007), p. 111.
89 See Schivelbusch, Chs 7–9.
90 Rozario, p. 257n. 33.
91 Useful sources on amusement parks are J. F. Kasson, *Amusing the Million: Coney Island at the Turn of the Century* (Hill and Wang, 1978); K. Peiss, *Cheap Amusements: Working Women and Leisure in Turn-of-the-Century New York* (Temple University Press, 1986), pp. 115–38; and D. M. Lubin, *Titanic* (British Film Institute, 1999), pp. 98–108, a brief survey.
92 Rozario, p. 125.
93 Lubin, p. 105.
94 Rozario, p. 224n. 47.

95 Ibid., p. 128; and see Ch. 3.
96 Cit. ibid., p. 102; and see pp. 101–8, for other accounts by survivors.
97 Ibid., pp. 130 and 128–9.
98 S. Kern, *The Culture of Time and Space 1880-1918* (Harvard University Press, 1983), p. 107.
99 R. Howells, *The Myth of the Titanic* (Macmillan, 1997), Ch. 7. See also S. Biel, *Down With the Old Canoe* (Norton, 1996), Chs 2, 4, 7. He documents how, in the Reagan era, the rediscovery and partial salvage of the wreckage was presented as a technological success to redeem the original failure: 'The story of the *Titanic* had to have a happy ending' (p. 225).
100 Kern, pp. 67–8.
101 J. Sconce, *Haunted Media: Electronic Presence from Telegraphy to Television* (Duke University Press, 2000), p. 109. See also pp. 110–18, where he documents the 1938 panic when some listeners thought a broadcast of the H. G. Wells novel *The War of the Worlds* was a news report on a real Martian invasion ...
102 Doane, p. 222, *passim*.
103 Lubin, p. 72. On the film, see also K. S. Sandler and G. Studlar (eds), *Titanic: Anatomy of a Blockbuster* (Rutgers University Press, 1999), and R. Maltby, *Hollywood Cinema: An Introduction* (Blackwell, 2nd edn, 2003), pp. 10–14; and, more generally, T. Bergfelder and S. Street (eds), *The Titanic in Myth and Memory: Representations in Visual and Literary Culture* (I. B. Tauris, 2004).
104 N. Klein, *The Shock Doctrine: The Rise of Disaster Capitalism* (Penguin, 2007), p. 6. On the 'Shock and Awe' document, see pp. 3, 7–9, 329–33. For the 2004 Asian tsunami as an example of how natural disasters can be appropriated in this way, see Ch. 19. Some of this may go back further than she recognizes: see Rozario, for example, on the aftermath of the San Francisco earthquake.
105 Klein, pp. 15–17.
106 For intriguing reflections on the fate of the fragmented 'mass body' in disasters of these kinds, see M. Warner, *Publics and Counterpublics* (Zone, 2002), pp. 177–9.
107 R. L. Hart, in *Atlantic Monthly*, 1907, cit. Rozario, p. 126.
108 S. Sontag, 'The Imagination of Disaster', in *Against Interpretation and Other Essays* (Farrar, Strauss and Giroux, 1966), p. 224.
109 D. Boothroyd, 'Cultural Studies and the Extreme', in G. Hall and C. Birchall (eds), *New Cultural Studies: Adventures in Theory* (Edinburgh University Press, 2006), p. 277.
110 Boothroyd argues that transgression is central to this. Certainly it is important, but perhaps the risk-taking, and the implicit testing of the *reality* of self, in relation to 'the real', is more basic. Transgression is indeed a defining feature of the less usual sexual practices and their representation as pornography, but only a certain range of these, around aspects of sado-masochism, could plausibly count

as sexual 'extreme sports'. For interesting reflections, see J. Benjamin, 'Master and Slave: The Fantasy of Erotic Domination', in A. Snitow et al. (eds), *Desire: The Politics of Sexuality* (Virago, 1984).

111 Doane, p. 233.
112 Lubin, p. 107.
113 Hence Rozario's suggestion that 'the postmodern culture of calamity may well be defined by a collision or collusion between the apocalyptic and the sublime' (p. 188) is very interesting, but we have suggested that the collusion may be the more plausible version, as the two may not be fully distinguishable in the first place.
114 J. Crane, *Terror and Everyday Life: Singular Moments in the History of the Horror Film* (Sage, 1994), pp. 9, 9, 141, 37. See also A. Tudor, 'Why Horror? The Peculiar Pleasures of a Popular Genre', in M. Jancovich (ed.), *The Horror Film Reader* (Routledge, 2001).
115 R. C. Solomon, *In Defence of Sentimentality* (Oxford University Press, 2004), p. 110, from Ch. 5 ('Real Horror').
116 C. J. Clover, 'Her Body, Himself: Gender in the Slasher Film', in J. Donald (ed.), *Fantasy and the Cinema* (British Film Institute, 1989), p. 93, also reproduced in Jancovich.
117 S. de Beauvoir, p. 69.
118 If this suggests self-torture, there is also a parallel with surgery: Marilee Strong, in *A Bright Red Scream: Self-Mutilation and the Language of Pain* (Virago, 2000), suggests the scars 'provide a permanent, physical record not only of pain and injury but also of healing' (p. 150). This is oddly parallel with the logic of 'shock and awe' seen in Klein's argument.
119 See Benjamin, 'Master and Slave', for a view of this that draws on Hegel and Bataille.
120 Z. Bauman, *Postmodernity and Its Discontents* (Polity, 1997), p. 146.
121 All this implies some reservations about the rightly influential account of the rise of modern consumerism in C. Campbell, *The Romantic Ethic and the Spirit of Modern Consumerism* (Blackwell, 1989), esp. Chs 4–5. For Campbell, sensation and emotion are in some sense opposed, and as sensation can only give limited and transient pleasures, the cultivation of emotion as a central feature of the modern self, largely *replacing* sensation, opens up greater scope for the 'imaginative hedonism' essential to modern consumerism. One might reply, however, that this downplays the significance of sensation in two ways: that sensation, *coupled* with emotion and imagination, has the potential for even *greater* pleasure, readily linked to the longings and dreams associated with consumerism; and that sensation can be *symbolically* powerful, engaging the body in intimate relation to the sense of self.

Sensational Processes

1. Cit. A. Cvetkovich, *Mixed Feelings: Feminism, Mass Culture, and Victorian Sensationalism* (Rutgers University Press, 1992), p. 21.
2. C. Campbell, *The Romantic Ethic and the Spirit of Modern Consumerism* (Blackwell, 1989), p. 63.
3. Cvetkovich, *Mixed Feelings*, p. 21.
4. All this is what both contributes to the plausibility of theories of 'compassion fatigue' while yet also contributing to their limitations: the most influential advocate is S. D. Moeller, in her *Compassion Fatigue: How the Media Sell Disease, Famine, War and Death* (Routledge, 1999).
5. S. During, *Modern Enchantments: The Cultural Power of Secular Magic* (Harvard University Press, 2002), pp. 161, 163.
6. Ibid., p. 165.
7. D. A. Miller, *The Novel and the Police* (California University Press, 1988), pp. 150, 146.
8. A. Rabinbach, *The Human Motor: Energy, Fatigue and the Origins of Modernity* (California University Press, 1990), pp. 154, 160, 160.
9. Miller, p. 148.
10. M. Henning, '"Don't Touch Me (I'm Electric)": On Gender and Sensation in Modernity', in J. Arthurs and J. Grimshaw (eds), *Women's Bodies: Discipline and Transgression* (Cassell, 1999), pp. 18, 26.
11. E. Showalter, *The Female Malady: Women, Madness and English Culture, 1830–1980* (Virago, 1987), Chs 6, 7. Following up this recent interest in cultural and gender aspects of hysteria, see S. L. Gilman et al., *Hysteria Beyond Freud* (California University Press, 1993); M. S. Micale, *Approaching Hysteria: Disease and Its Interpretations* (Princeton University Press, 1995); and E. Bronfen, *The Knotted Subject: Hysteria and Its Discontents* (Princeton University Press, 1998). For hysteria, trauma and 'shell-shock', see also my *Sympathetic Sentiments: Affect, Emotion and Spectacle in the Modern World* (Bloomsbury, 2014), Ch. 7.
12. Miller, pp. 154, 163.
13. Henning, pp. 26, 41.
14. R. Sennett, *The Fall of Public Man* (Faber and Faber, 1986), p. 110. For Diderot, great acting is about the simulation of feeling, not the reality.
15. P. Falk, 'The Representation of Presence: Outlining the Anti-Aesthetics of Pornography', *Theory, Culture and Society* (1993), 10:2, pp. 16, 18, also reprinted as Ch. 7 of his *The Consuming Body* (Sage, 1994).
16. S. Connor, *Postmodernist Culture* (Blackwell, 1997), p. 144.
17. M. Fried, 'Art and Objecthood', in G. Bantock (ed.), *Minimal Art* (Dutton, 1968), p. 142.

18   Cvetkovich, *Mixed Feelings*, pp. 23, 6.
19   S. Streeby, *American Sensations: Class, Empire and the Production of Popular Culture* (California University Press 2002), pp. 27, 43.
20   T. Adorno, *Minima Moralia* (Verso, 1978), pp. 235–6, 238, 237.
21   A. Cvetkovich, 'Ghostlier Determinations: The Economy of Sensation and *The Woman in White*', in L. Pykett (ed.), *Wilkie Collins* (Macmillan, 1998), p. 127; and see *Mixed Feelings*, Ch. 7.
22   B. Singer, *Melodrama and Modernity: Early Sensational Cinema and Its Contexts* (Columbia University Press, 2001), p. 9. For his extended discussion of this, see pp. 8–10 and Ch. 4.
23   Ibid., p. 117.
24   R. Crawford, 'A Cultural Account of "Health": Control, Release and the Social Body', in J. B. McKinlay (ed.), *Issues in the Political Economy of Health Care* (Tavistock, 1984); and see A. Young, 'The discourse on stress and the reproduction of conventional knowledge', in *Social Science and Medicine* (1980), 148.
25   Singer, *Melodrama*, p. 119.
26   M. Hansen, *Babel and Babylon: Spectatorship in American Silent Film* (Harvard University Press, 1991), p. 29.
27   Cit. B. Singer, 'Modernity, Hyperstimulus and the Rise of Popular Sensationalism', in L. Charney and V. R. Schwartz (eds), *Cinema and the Invention of Modern Life* (California University Press, 1995), p. 90.
28   Ibid., p. 88.
29   Singer, *Melodrama*, p. 90.
30   G. Simmel, 'The Metropolis and Mental Life', in *The Sociology of Georg Simmel*, ed. K. H. Wolff (Free Press, 1950), p. 414.
31   W. Schivelbusch, *The Railway Journey: The Industrialization of Time and Space in the Nineteenth Century* (Berg, 1986), pp. 159–70.
32   Singer, 'Modernity', p. 93; *Melodrama*, p. 126.
33   Singer, *Melodrama*, p. 105.
34   L. Charney, *Empty Moments: Cinema, Modernity, and Drift* (Duke University Press, 1998), p. 77.
35   Cvetkovich, 'Ghostlier', pp. 111, 111, 116.
36   Charney, p. 8.
37   C. N. Serematakis, *The Senses Still: Perception and Memory as Material Culture in Modernity* (Chicago University Press, 1994), p. 19.
38   Rabinbach, p. 63.
39   Cit. Rabinbach, p. 26.
40   L. Pykett, *The 'Improper' Feminine: The Women's Sensation Novel and the New Woman Writing* (Routledge, 1992), p. 53.
41   W. B. Carpenter, *Principles of Mental Physiology* (1876), cit. J. L. Matus, 'Emergent

Theories of Victorian Mind Shock', in A. Stiles (ed.), *Neurology and Literature, 1860–1920* (Palgrave, 2007), p. 174.
42 Rabinbach, p. 66.
43 E. Mach, *Analysis of Sensations* (1886), cit. C. Asendorf, *Batteries of Life: On the History of Things and Their Perception in Modernity* (California University Press, 1993), p. 170. The echoes of Hume's work in these claims by Mach are unmistakeable … For the sources in Hume etc. see my *Sympathetic Sentiments*, Ch. 5.
44 Henning, p. 32.
45 Asendorf, p. 176.
46 Rabinbach, p. 4.
47 T. Gunning, 'Phantom Images and Modern Manifestations: Spirit Photography, Magic Theater, Trick Films, and Photography's Uncanny', in P. Petro (ed.), *Fugitive Images: From Photography to Video* (Indiana University Press, 1995); and T. Gunning, 'An Aesthetic of Astonishment: Early Film and the (In)Credulous Spectator', in L. Williams (ed.), *Viewing Positions: Ways of Seeing Films* (Rutgers University Press, 1994). Gunning's work is an invaluable resource for 'sensational' aspects of early film and popular culture.
48 P. Thurschwell, *Literature, Technology and Magical Thinking, 1880–1920* (Cambridge University Press, 2001), pp. 2, 4, 7.
49 R. Kaye, 'Sexual Identity at the *fin de siècle*', in G. Marshall (ed.), *The Cambridge Companion to the* Fin de Siècle (Cambridge University Press, 2007), p. 63.
50 J. Crary, *Suspensions of Perception: Attention, Spectacle and Modern Culture* (MIT Press, 2001), pp. 170, 13, 13; and see pp. 164–72, *passim*.
51 Crary, *Techniques of the Observer: On Vision and Modernity in the Nineteenth Century* (MIT Press, 1990), pp. 24, 92.
52 Ibid., pp. 145, 147, 92.
53 Crary, *Suspensions*, pp. 17–19, 27; and see H. Ferguson, *The Science of Pleasure: Cosmos and Psyche in the Bourgeois World View* (Routledge, 1990), pp. 178–84. Crary adds that 'sensation became an effect or set of effects that were technologically produced and were used to describe a subject who was compatible with those technical conditions' (pp. 26–7), which, as I shall argue, goes rather too far towards technological determinism.
54 E. Meyerson, *Identity and Reality* (Allen and Unwin, 1930 [1908]), pp. 291, 297–8.
55 Ibid., p. 298.
56 Crary, *Suspensions*, p. 27; *Techniques*, p. 72.
57 Rabinbach, p. 41.
58 Crary, *Suspensions*, p. 169.
59 Cit. Ferguson, pp. 179, 180. There is reference to the 'vibrations' of sensations in these earlier accounts (Hartley, Hume), but this is rather static in relation to the emphasis in nineteenth-century science.

60 Henning, p. 19.
61 From *Contre Sainte-Beuve* (Pléiade, 1971) p. 154, cit. and trans. M. R. Finn, *Proust, The Body and Literary Form* (Cambridge University Press, 1999), p. 23.
62 G. S. Rousseau, *Nervous Acts: Essays on Literature, Culture and Sensibility* (Palgrave, 2004), p. 54.
63 Cit. Asendorf, p. 171.
64 Asendorf, p. 177. One might add here that it was only late in the century that psychological causation came to rival 'nerves' as an explanation of mental stresses and illness, nor were they seen as necessarily incompatible. Overall, as Athena Vrettos claims, 'nervousness … was used to describe emotional exhaustion as well as unexplained physical pain and to define evolutionary progress as well as the debilitating effects of modern civilization': see her *Somatic Fictions: Imagining Illness in Victorian Culture* (Stanford University Press, 1995), p. 12.
65 Rabinbach, p. 4.
66 Ibid., pp. 153–61; Finn, pp. 38–41.
67 Asendorf, p. 173.
68 Rabinbach, p. 40.
69 Finn, p. 1.
70 Finn, pp. 4, 179; and see p. 8.
71 W. Benjamin, *Charles Baudelaire: A Lyric Poet in the Era of High Capitalism* (Verso, 1983), p. 175.
72 W. Benjamin, 'On Some Motifs in Baudelaire', in his *Selected Writings*, vol. 4: 1938–40 (Harvard University Press, 2003), p. 328, also in *Illuminations* (Fontana, 1992), p. 171.
73 On Eisenstein, particularly in relation to Deleuze, see G. Lambert, 'Cinema and the Outside', in G. Flaxman (ed.), *The Brain is the Screen: Deleuze and the Philosophy of Cinema* (Minnesota University Press, 2000); D. Frampton, *Filmosophy* (Wallflower Press, 2006), Ch. 4; and Charney, pp. 128–38.
74 G. Deleuze, *Cinema 2: The Time-Image* (Athlone, 1989), pp. 161, 161, 156. The shock thus *induces*, but cannot *control*, the reflective process; there is a disjunction here, the further implications of which will be explored in the later chapters of this book.
75 *The Diary of Beatrice Webb*, vol. 4: 1924–43, *The Wheel of Life* (Virago, 1985), p. 1, cit. J. Seaton, *Carnage and the Media: The Making and Breaking of News about Violence* (Allen Lane, 2005), p. 248.
76 J. Sconce, *Haunted Media: Electronic Presence from Telepathy to Television* (Duke University Press, 2000), pp. 21, 14, and see Ch. 1, *passim*.
77 Cit. ibid., p. 47.
78 S. Kern, *The Culture of Time and Space, 1880-1918* (Harvard University Press, 1983), p. 183.

79 'On Action at a Distance', in *Scientific Papers* (Cambridge University Press, 1890), 2: 322, cit. J. D. Peters, *Speaking into the Air: A History of the Idea of Communication* (Chicago University Press, 2000), p. 102. For discussion, see B. Clarke, *Energy Forms: Allegory and Science in the Era of Classical Thermodynamics* (Michigan University Press, 2001), Ch. 7. See also Kern, p. 154.
80 Cit. Peters, p. 102.
81 *Shorter Oxford Dictionary*, entry for 'ether'.
82 Sconce, p. 63.
83 Ibid., p. 28.
84 Peters, pp. 160–4.
85 L. Rickels, *Aberrations of Mourning: Writing on German Crypts* (Wayne State University Press, 1988).
86 For accounts that emphasize gender, see A. Braude, *Radical Spirits: Spiritualism and Women's Rights in Nineteenth-Century America* (Beacon press, 1989); A. Owen, *The Darkened Room: Women, Power, and Spiritualism in Nineteenth-Century England* (Virago, 1989); and Sconce, pp. 12–14 and Ch. 1.
87 S. Connor, 'The Machine in the Ghost: Spiritualism, Technology, and the "Direct Voice"', in P. Buse and A. Stott (eds), *Ghosts: Deconstruction, Psychoanalysis, History* (Palgrave, 1999). On the relation to science, see also Thurschwell. On spiritualism, the telegraph, and contacting 'others' generally, see Peters, Chs 2, 6. In this context, one might just observe, in passing, that W. T. Stead, as responsible as anyone for developing newspaper sensationalism in the 1880s and later, went down with the *Titanic*, but – sensational to the last, and beyond – subsequently made contact with his daughter through a medium: see Connor, 'Machine', p. 213.
88 E. d'Esperance, *What I Know of Materialisations from Personal Experience* ('Light' Publishing Co., London, 1904), cit. Connor, p. 209.
89 R. Kipling, 'Wireless', in *Traffics and Discoveries* (Macmillan, 1908 [1902]).
90 Ibid., p. 229.
91 Ibid., p. 239.
92 G. Beer, '"Wireless": Popular Physics, Radio and Modernism', in F. Spufford and J. Uglow (eds), *Cultural Babbage: Technology, Time and Invention* (Faber, 1996), p. 156. See also the discussion in Sconce, pp. 69–70.
93 Kipling, p. 230.
94 Ibid., p. 219.
95 As an appropriate postscript, one can note that as late as the 1960s Konstantin Raudive used various recording techniques, including receivers tuned to the 'white noise' between channels, enhanced playback, and microphones in silent rooms, to capture voices, sounding like a fragmentary, jammed overload, that were, he claimed, the voices of the dead. Not surprisingly, this caused a minor media sensation. See Connor, 'Machine', pp. 217–18, and Sconce, pp. 85–90.

96 J. Donald, 'As It Happened ... *Borderline*, the Uncanny and the Cosmopolitan', in J. Collins and J. Jervis (eds), *Uncanny Modernity: Cultural Theories, Modern Anxieties* (Palgrave, 2008), p. 97.

97 M. Cuddy-Keane, 'Virginia Woolf, Sound Technologies, and the New Aurality', in P. L. Caughie (ed.), *Virginia Woolf in the Age of Mechanical Reproduction* (Garland, 2000), pp. 85, 85 (my italics), 90.

98 J. Joyce, *Finnegans Wake* (Faber and Faber, 1975 [1939]), p. 407, cit. J. Lewty, '"What They Had Heard Said Written": Joyce, Pound and the Cross-Correspondence of Radio', in D. R. Cohen et al. (eds), *Broadcasting Modernism* (Florida University Press, 2009).

99 Peters, p. 23. One might add that if Marshall McLuhan, in the 1960s, saw telecommunications media as extensions of the 'nervous system', that might seem a rather nineteenth-century preference; for a version that seems to reverse this – more in tune, perhaps, with 'posthuman' fashion – see the comments in F. Kittler, *Optical Media* (Polity, 2010), Ch. 1.

100 Peters, p. 24.

101 Sconce, p. 8. Since he suggests that the postmodern, also, is concerned with 'the transmutability of electricity, information and consciousness within electronic telecommunications' (p. 18), this might imply that the postmodern might better be seen as an aspect or mode of the modern, rather than deeply antithetical to it, a possibility that will be hinted at elsewhere in this book.

102 On the history of radio, see Peters, pp. 206–25, and Sconce, Chs 2, 3.

103 Peters, p. 211.

104 See, for example, Sconce (pp. 206–25) on the episode in 1938 when a broadcast of the H. G. Wells novel *The War of the Worlds* on the radio led to panic among sections of the audience; and Ch. 4, on television as an 'alien' medium.

105 S. Jonsson, 'Masses, Mind, Matter: Political Passions and Collective Violence in Post-Imperial Austria', in P. Meyer (ed.), *Representing the Passions: Histories, Bodies, Visions* (Getty Research Institute, 2003), p. 79. Most influential of these early theorists were Gustave Le Bon, particularly for *The Crowd: A Study of the Popular Mind* (1895, and much reprinted since),and Gabriel Tarde.

106 S. Moscovici, *The Invention of Society: Psychological Explanations for Social Phenomena* (Polity, 1996), pp. 20, 21.

107 T. Brennan, *The Transmission of Affect* (Cornell University Press, 2004).

108 Peters, p. 218.

109 *Shorter Oxford Dictionary*, entry for 'live'.

The Aesthetics of Sensation

1. J. Crary, *Suspensions of Perception: Attention, Spectacle, and Modern Culture* (MIT Press, 2001), pp. 174, 344.
2. P. Cézanne, *Letters*, ed. J. Rewald (Cassirer, 1941 [1906]), p. 262.
3. W. Pater, *Studies in the History of the Renaissance* (Oxford University Press, 2010 [1873]), p. 3. (Other editions may be entitled *The Renaissance*, with different pagination. Quotes given are from the Preface, Conclusion and the page preceding the latter.)
4. Ibid., p. 117.
5. Ibid., pp. 118, 119, 119.
6. Ibid., pp. 119, 120, 121.
7. J. Loesberg, *Aestheticism and Deconstruction* (Princeton University Press, 1991), pp. 20, 22, 23, 24. See also the whole of Loesberg's invigorating discussion: Ch. 1, esp. sec. II. The claim of J. Matz, in his *Literary Impressionism and Modernist Aesthetics* (Cambridge University Press, 2001), Ch. 2, that Pater aestheticizes the empiricist tension between impression and idea, thus constituting literary Impressionism's 'moment of genius' (p. 64), is also pertinent here.
8. It is evident enough that the rigorous separation of art from other 'passions' is highly problematical; and even before the trial of Pater's best-known follower, Oscar Wilde, with the intensifying homophobia, Aestheticism as a whole had come under suspicion. Pater himself had removed these passages from the second edition of the book, lest they 'might possibly mislead some of those young men into whose hands it might fall' (ibid., p. 177). Recent scholarship has suggested some young women might have been led astray, too: discussing Pater, Ruth Vanita identifies the gem as a clitoral image, giving other examples, such as Clarissa describing her love for Sally Seton in Virginia Woolf's *Mrs Dalloway* as a 'burning diamond' (Granada, 1977 [1925], p. 164), thus neatly linking Pater's two images. Vanita concludes that this conjunction constitutes 'an immensely influential trope for homoerotic and ... lesbian love'; see her *Sappho and the Virgin Mary: Same-sex Love and the English Literary Imagination* (Columbia University Press, 1996), p. 69. See also R. Dellamora, *Masculine Desire: The Sexual Politics of Victorian Aestheticism* (North Carolina University Press, 1990). That Aestheticism influenced early modernism is evident enough, as is the modernist disavowal of all this. One can also note that an early, hostile review compared Pater's attitude to that of housemaids addicted to 'sensation fiction'; see M. Beaumont's introduction to Pater, p. xx.
9. V. Shklovsky, 'Art as Technique', in *Russian Formalist Criticism: Four Essays*, trans. L. T. Lemon and M. J. Reis (Nebraska University Press, 1965), p. 12.
10. L. Charney, *Empty Moments: Cinema, Modernity and Drift* (Duke University Press, 1998), p. 8.

11 G. Deleuze and F. Guattari, *What Is Philosophy?* (Verso, 2004), pp. 164 (italics in the original), 164, 176, 176. (Cited henceforth as *WP*.)
12 Deleuze, *WP*, p. 176.
13 Cit. Charney, p. 22, page ref. not given.
14 J. Rajchman, *The Deleuze Connections* (MIT Press, 2000) p. 133; and see G. Deleuze, *Difference and Repetition* (Athlone Press, 1994), pp. 222–4 (henceforth *DR*).
15 D. W. Smith, 'Deleuze's Theory of Sensation: Overcoming the Kantian Duality', in P. Patton (ed.), *Deleuze: A Critical Reader* (Blackwell, 1996), p. 41.
16 Deleuze, *WP*, p. 177.
17 J. Williams, *Gilles Deleuze's* Difference and Repetition: *A Critical Introduction and Guide* (Edinburgh University Press, 2003) p. 199.
18 D. Polan, 'Francis Bacon: The Logic of Sensation', in C. V. Boundas and D. Olkowski (eds), *Gilles Deleuze and the Theater of Philosophy* (Routledge, 1994), p. 231.
19 G. Deleuze, *Francis Bacon: The Logic of Sensation* (Continuum, 2003), p. 45 (henceforth *FB*).
20 C. Colebrook, *Gilles Deleuze* (Routledge, 2002), pp. 39, 106, 106.
21 Deleuze, *FB*, p. 85.
22 G. Flaxman, 'Cinema Year Zero', in G. Flaxman (ed.), *The Brain Is the Screen: Deleuze and the Philosophy of Cinema* (Minnesota University Press, 2000), p. 94.
23 Smith, p. 49.
24 B. Massumi, *Parables for the Virtual: Movement, Affect, Sensation* (Duke University Press, 2002), p. 13.
25 Deleuze, *DR*, pp. 46, 251; and see Williams, pp. 187–9.
26 S. Shaviro, *The Cinematic Body* (Minnesota University Press, 1993), pp. vii, 255.
27 B. M. Kennedy, *Deleuze and Cinema: The Aesthetics of Sensation* (Edinburgh University Press, 2000), pp. 3, 4, 5, 5.
28 R. Newman, '(Re)Imaging the Grotesque: Francis Bacon's Crucifixion Triptychs', in D. Andrew (ed.), *The Image in Dispute: Art and Cinema in the Age of Photography* (Texas University Press, 1997), p. 217.
29 M. Leiris, *Francis Bacon: Full Face and In Profile* (Phaidon, 1983), pp. 24, 27.
30 Deleuze, *FB*, p. 56; and see *WP*, pp. 182–3.
31 Deleuze, *FB*, pp. xiv, 34; and see p. 58. One can add that Deleuze's concept of figure is indebted to the Lyotard of *Discours, Figure* (Klincksieck, 1971).
32 Smith, p. 44.
33 Deleuze, *FB*, p. 36.
34 Kennedy, p. 110.
35 Interview in D. Sylvester, *The Brutality of Fact: Interviews with Francis Bacon* (Thames and Hudson, 1975), p. 17.

36 Deleuze, *FB*, p. xiv.
37 Interview in H. M. Davies, *Francis Bacon: The Papal Portraits of 1953* (Museum of Contemporary Art, San Diego, and Lund Humphries, 2002), pp. 40, 59.
38 Newman, pp. 212, 214. Not surprisingly, Newman finds the concept of abjection useful here: see pp. 209–11, 215.
39 Deleuze, *WP*, pp. 178, 179, 183.
40 In Sylvester, pp. 105–7.
41 Deleuze, *WP*, p. 213.
42 Deleuze, *FB*, Ch. 7.
43 Ibid., p. 45; and see pp. 45–9. See also my discussion of hysteria in *Sympathetic Sentiments: Affect, Emotion and Spectacle in the Modern World* (Bloomsbury, 2014), Ch. 7.
44 Deleuze, *FB*, pp. 51, 51–2, 51, 50, 51.
45 David Morris articulates this perspective, while moving somewhat towards Bacon, in his claim that 'the scream might serve as a potent image for the metaphorical silence at the heart of suffering. A scream is not speech but the most intense possible negation of language: sound and terror approaching the limits of absolute muteness.' The continuation of the quote, implying continuity with conventional film, would, however, doubtless have been rejected by both Bacon and Deleuze: 'A typical Hollywood scream, while it often shatters a preceding silence or calm, also deepens the silence it shatters, as if gesturing toward something radically inexpressible.' See. D. B. Morris, 'About Suffering: Voice, Genre, and Moral Community', *Daedalus* (1996) 125:1, p. 27.
46 In Sylvester, pp. 82, 48.
47 L. Ficacci, *Francis Bacon* (Taschen, 2003), p. 16.
48 Deleuze, *FB*, p. 60.
49 Deleuze, *DR*, p. 260.
50 Williams, p. 208. 'Ideas' in Deleuze are conditions for changes in our actual ideas, 'relations between things in the virtual' (Williams, p. 112), hence not 'transcendental' in any Kantian sense.
51 Smith, p. 42.
52 Deleuze, *FB*, pp. 45, 38.
53 A. Brighton, *Francis Bacon* (Tate, 2001) p. 65.
54 In Sylvester, pp. 56, 62.
55 C. Greenberg, interview with E. Lucie-Smith, in *Clement Greenberg: Collected Essays and Criticism* (Chicago University Press, 1993), vol. IV, p. 278.
56 In Sylvester, pp. 60, 126; and see p. 40.
57 Brighton, pp. 65, 67, 67.
58 Newman suggests that a tension between 'grotesque as narrative form' and 'grotesque as cognitive disruptor' runs through Bacon's work (p. 207); and

Ernst van Alphen sees Bacon's work as a struggle against Western traditions of representation, and, referring to the triptychs, claims that 'it is the inevitable consequence of representation, the tearing apart of the body, the destructive effect of reproductive mimesis, which the crucifixion betokens': see his *Francis Bacon and the Loss of Self* (Harvard University Press, 1993), p. 93.

59 Ibid., p. 67.
60 Deleuze, *WP*, p. 193.
61 Deleuze, *FB*, pp. 97, 98, 115.
62 Deleuze, *DR*, Ch. VIII. See also *WP*, pp. 144–6, for a critique of everyday 'opinion', linked through the hold over it of 'recognition' to the critique of representation.
63 Deleuze, *FB*, pp. 39, 34.
64 Ibid., p. 87.
65 Ibid., pp. 87, 93–4, 100–2.
66 Ibid., p. 89. This obsession with cliché continues in his work on film: see, for examples and commentary, G. Flaxman, 'Introduction', pp. 11, 17, 35–9, and G. Lambert, 'Cinema and the Outside', pp. 264–5, 273, 275, 278, 287–8, in Flaxman, *Brain*; and R. Bogue, *Deleuze on Cinema* (Routledge, 2003), pp. 108–11, 170–1. Parallel with his analysis of Bacon, one reason for his concerns comes out clearly in his acknowledgement, in *Cinema 2: The Time-Image* (Athlone, 1989), that 'modernist shock' might not have the desired effect: 'The shock would be confused, in bad cinema, with the figurative violence of the represented instead of achieving that other violence of a movement-image developing its vibrations in a moving sequence which embeds itself within us …' (p. 157).
67 J. Rancière, *The Emancipated Spectator* (Verso, 2009), p. 66.
68 Polan, pp. 245, 254.
69 V. Woolf, *To the Lighthouse* (Penguin, 1992 [1927]), p. 209.
70 *The Eye's Mind: Bridget Riley, Collected Writings 1965–1999*, ed. R. Kudielka (Thames & Hudson, 1999), p. 66. Unless otherwise indicated, all Riley quotes are from this source.
71 F. Follin. *Embodied Visions: Bridget Riley, Op Art and the Sixties* (Thames & Hudson, 2004), p. 9. For further discussion, see also J. Houston, *Optic Nerve: Perceptual Art of the 1960s* (Merrell, 2007).
72 Riley, pp. 76, 76, 78.
73 Ibid., pp. 118, 120.
74 Ibid., pp. 120, 128, 130. Riley is aware of Proust, and glosses his insight as the paradox that 'you must give up that which you love in order to recreate it'; see Riley, *Dialogues on Art*, ed. R. Kudielka (Zwemmer, 1995), p. 89.
75 M. Merleau-Ponty, *The Phenomenology of Perception* (Routledge, 1962 [1945]), p. 68; and see Riley, p. 122.

76 Riley, pp. 118, 88, 99, 123, 116.
77 Ibid., pp. 95, 127.
78 This implies a certain parallel to the constitution of the cinematic experience, explored later in this book.
79 Riley, pp. 132, 132, 134, 118 (and see p. 188).
80 'Modernist Painting' (1960), from Greenberg, vol. IV, p. 86.
81 Riley, p. 83.
82 Follin, pp. 83, 18.
83 Riley, p. 122.
84 Cit. H. Spurling, Review of Bridget Riley exhibition, *Guardian Review*, 27/11/10, p. 17.
85 Riley, pp. 122, 190, 125.
86 Ibid., p. 116.
87 Ibid., p. 147. Riley uses the term 'plastic' here, in a sense influenced by Mondrian: 'By plastic I mean that which hangs between the cognitive reading of an image and its perceptions' (p. 147; see also pp. 116–18, 147, 154, 188–90).
88 For discussion, see Follin, esp. pp. 66–7 and Chs 1, 2, 5, 6, *passim*.
89 Riley, p. 122.

The Distractions of the Modern

1 See J. D. Stevens, *Sensationalism and the New York Press* (Columbia University Press, 1991), esp. Part 2, for background.
2 New York *World* magazine, 15 November 1914, in D. Barnes, *New York* (Sun & Moon Press, 1989), p. 187 (a collection of her newspaper articles, ed. Alyce Barry). For general accounts of Barnes's journalism see D. Warren, *Djuna Barnes' Consuming Fictions* (Ashgate, 2008), Ch. 2, and D. Parsons, *Djuna Barnes* (Northcote House, 2003), Ch. 1.
3 Appropriately, Daniela Caselli suggests that her journalism shows that, for Barnes, 'any form of representation is … inherently spectacular'; see *Improper Modernism: Djuna Barnes's Bewildering Corpus* (Ashgate, 2009), p. 39.
4 6 September 1914, in Barnes, pp. 174–9.
5 Ibid., pp. 175, 176, 177.
6 Ibid., pp. 178, 178, 179.
7 Ibid., pp. 174–5, 178, 178.
8 L. Boltanski, *Distant Suffering: Morality, Media and Politics* (Cambridge University Press, 1999), p. 30, and see pp. 21–32. One might indicate a reservation about Boltanski's 'pure' spectator, 'without ties and prior commitments' (p. 29), which makes it sound as though 'absolute' impartiality is possible. These issues are

discussed further in my *Sympathetic Sentiments: Affect, Emotion and Spectacle in the Modern World* (Bloomsbury, 2014), Ch. 4.

9   For sources on the US, see S. A. Glenn, *Female Spectacle: The Theatrical Roots of Modern Feminism* (Harvard University Press, 2000), Ch. 5, and A. Auster, *Actresses and Suffragists: Women in the American Theater, 1890-1920* (New York, 1984). On the UK, see L. Tickner, *The Spectacle of Women: Imagery of the Suffrage Campaign, 1907-14* (Chicago University Press, 1988), and V. Gardner and S. Rutherford (eds), *The New Woman and Her Sisters: Feminism and Theatre, 1850-1914* (Michigan University Press, 1992).

10 Boltanski, pp. 186-7.

11 Glenn, pp. 128, 12, 13.

12 Ibid., p. 147, and see pp. 145-8.

13 W. Benjamin, 'The Work of Art in the Age of Its Technological Reproducibility', in *Selected Writings,* vol. 4: 1938-40 (Harvard University Press, 2003), p. 282. (*Selected Writings* henceforth cited as SW.) The earlier translation, in *Illuminations* (Fontana, 1992) p. 244, gives 'mechanical equipment'.

14 In I. Kant, *Political Writings* (ed. H. Reiss), 2nd edn (Cambridge University Press, 1991 [1798]).

15 J. and S. Donald, 'The Publicness of Cinema', in C. Gledhill and L. Williams (eds), *Reinventing Film Studies* (Arnold, 2000), p. 116.

16 M. Hansen, *Babel & Babylon: Spectatorship in American Silent Film* (Harvard University Press, 1991), pp. 116-17. See also Ch. 3, on cinema as an alternative public sphere.

17 M. Hansen, 'America, Paris, the Alps: Kracauer (and Benjamin) on Cinema and Modernity', in L. Charney and V. R. Schwartz (eds), *Cinema and the Invention of Modern Life* (California University Press, 1995), p. 366.

18 Hansen, *Babel*, p. 1.

19 New York *World* magazine, 23 August 1914, in Barnes, p. 171.

20 B. Green, 'Spectacular Confessions: "How It Feels To Be Forcibly Fed"', *Review of Contemporary Fiction* (1993), 13:3, pp. 85, 71, 71.

21 Tickner, pp. 81, 38. Laura Hinton explores the sado-masochistic undertones of contemporary popular culture – particularly television – in her *The Perverse Gaze of Sympathy* (New York State University Press, 1999).

22 Glenn, p. 82.

23 Green actually implies that Barnes *intended* the article as critique (pp. 80-3), but I could not find any grounds for this. It is, however, true that the overall pattern of her life does not make Barnes seem to be a natural supporter of causes ... One might add that the relative distance Barnes adopts here could *enhance* her appeal as a 'witness', given the significance of the appearance of witness impartiality as a condition of the transition from spectator to activist.

24 Glenn, p. 162; and see Ch. 6.
25 There is, of course, a strand of feminist theory – and, in particular, feminist film theory – that would argue to the contrary, usually developing out of a reading of Freud. The *locus classicus* remains L. Mulvey, 'Visual Pleasure and Narrative Cinema', *Screen* (1975), 16:3; see also her later collection, *Visual and Other Pleasures* (Indiana University Press 1989).
26 W. James, *Principles of Psychology* (Dover, 1950 [1890]), vol. I, p. 424.
27 Cit. G. Bennington, *Lyotard: Writing the Event* (Manchester University Press, 1988), p. 73.
28 J. Crary, *Suspensions of Perception: Attention, Spectacle, and Modern Culture* (MIT Press, 2001), pp. 1–2, *passim*.
29 J. Seaton, *Carnage and the Media: The Making and Breaking of News About Violence* (Penguin, 2005), p. 247, and see pp. 247–50.
30 Crary, pp. 35–7.
31 E. Titchener, *Experimental Psychology* (Macmillan, 1901), p. 186, cit. Crary, p. 21.
32 Crary, pp. 4, 18.
33 L. Charney, *Empty Moments: Cinema, Modernity, and Drift* (Duke University Press, 1998), p. 6.
34 T. Armstrong, 'Two types of Shock in Modernity', *Critical Quarterly* (2000), 42:1, pp. 65, 66.
35 Charney, p. 7.
36 James, pp. 402, 402, 288, 288.
37 Ibid., p. 444, cit. Crary, p. 101.
38 Charney, pp. 8, 20.
39 Crary, pp. 45–6, 49.
40 Ibid., pp. 288, 288, 78.
41 L. Sass, *Madness and Modernism* (Harvard University Press, 1992), p, 66, *passim*.
42 Charney, p. 82.
43 I. Kant, *Critique of Pure Reason*, trans. N. K. Smith (Macmillan, 1979/1929 [1781]), A96, p. 129.
44 Ibid., A112, p. 139. Note that 'perceptions', in Kant's terminology, are conscious representations.
45 L. Aragon, *Paris Peasant* (Exact Change, Boston, 1994 [1926]), p. 7.
46 On dissociation, see Crary, pp. 67–8, 96, and the discussion in my *Sympathetic Sentiments*, Ch. 7.
47 *Illustrated Guide to Paris* (Cassell, 1884), p. 111, cit. V. R. Schwartz, *Spectacular Realities: Early Mass Culture in* Fin-de-Siècle *Paris* (California University Press, 1998), p. 1.
48 It can be related to aspects of sound, for example: see G. Beer, '"Wireless":

Popular Physics, Radio and Modernism', in F. Spufford and J. Uglow (eds), *Cultural Babbage: Technology, Time and Invention* (Faber, 1996); and S. Connor, 'The Modern Auditory I', in R. Porter (ed.), *Rewriting the Self: Histories from the Renaissance to the Present* (Routledge, 1997). The term can also be related to others, notably 'dissipation', which also manifests a range of connotations, positive and negative. For a fascinating account, see M. H. Whitworth, *Einstein's Wake: Relativity, Metaphor and Modernist Literature* (Oxford University Press, 2001), pp. 64–71.

49   V. Woolf, 'Sketch of the Past', from *Moments of Being: Autobiographical Writings* (Pimlico, 2002 [1939–40]), p. 86. On this theme, see also R. Barthes, 'The Reality Effect', in his *The Rustle of Language* (California University Press, 1989), where he explores 'narrative *luxury*' (p. 141), and the 'significance of this insignificance' (p. 143).

50   W. Benjamin, *The Origin of German Tragic Drama* (Verso, 1985 [1928]), p. 188.

51   Ibid., pp. 185–9. See also the illuminating discussion in S. Weber, 'Mass Mediauras, or: Art, Aura and Media in the Work of Walter Benjamin', in his *Mass Mediauras: Form, Technics, Media* (Stanford University Press, 1996).

52   W. Benjamin, *The Arcades Project* (Harvard University Press, 1999), Convolute R2, 3, p. 540. See also the 'Work of Art' essay, on the tactile appropriation of architecture as a form of distraction, and how distraction can become habit: SW 4, p. 268, and in *Illuminations*, pp. 232–3.

53   Benjamin, *Arcades*, H4a, 1, p. 211. On 'distraction' in Benjamin and other writers, see T. Armstrong, *Modernism, Technology and the Body* (Cambridge University Press, 1998), Ch. 7, and p. 293n. 118.

54   Ibid., H5, 1, p.211. For further discussion of 'involuntary memory' in Benjamin and Proust, see my *Sympathetic Sentiments,* Ch. 6.

55   H. Eiland, 'Reception in Distraction', in A. Benjamin (ed.), *Walter Benjamin and Art* (Continuum, 2005), p. 11.

56   Benjamin, *Arcades*, M1a, 2, p. 418. See also D. Boothroyd, *Culture on Drugs: Narco-Cultural Studies of High Modernity* (Manchester University Press, 2006), Ch. 5.

57   Benjamin, *Arcades*, R2, 3, p. 540.

58   W. Benjamin, 'On Some Motifs in Baudelaire', in SW 4, sec. X. (Also in *Illuminations*.)

59   Eiland, p. 11.

60   Benjamin, *Origin*, p. 28.

61   Ibid., p. 29. See also the discussion by D. S. Ferris, 'Introduction: Reading Benjamin' in D. S. Ferris (ed.), *The Cambridge Companion to Walter Benjamin* (Cambridge University Press, 2004).

62   Eiland, p. 11.

63 Benjamin, 'Work of Art', SW 4, p. 269 (first sentence in italics), and in *Illuminations*, p. 233 (no italics).
64 W. Benjamin, 'Theory of Distraction', *Selected Writings*, vol. 3: 1935-8 (Harvard University Press, 2002), p. 141.
65 Benjamin, 'Work of Art', SW 4, p. 267. The translation in *Illuminations*, p. 232, is slightly but intriguingly different, giving 'should be cushioned by heightened presence of mind', a formulation that implies an element of protectiveness, and an element of doubt over *Geistesgegenwart*, raising the issue of the relation between 'presence of mind', attention and consciousness – all discussed in the following paragraphs.
66 S. Shaviro, *The Cinematic Body* (Minnesota University Press, 1993), p. 47.
67 Cit. S. Kracauer, *Theory of Film: The Redemption of Physical Reality* (Princeton University Press, 1977 [1960]), p. 159.
68 Charney, p. 82.
69 T. Gunning, 'An Aesthetic of Astonishment: Early Film and the (In)Credulous Spectator', *Art and Text* (1989), 34, and in L. Williams (ed.), *Viewing Positions: Ways of Seeing Films* (Rutgers University Press, 1994). See also Hansen, *Babel*, pp. 76-86, on spectatorship, cinema and film between early and classical cinema.
70 Charney, pp. 77, 77, 7.
71 H. Münsterberg, *The Photoplay: A Psychological Study* (D. Appleton, New York, 1916), cit. D. Frampton, *Filmosophy* (Wallflower Press, 2006), p. 162.
72 Frampton, p. 150. This Deleuze-inflected account is useful on the way the filmgoer engages actively with the film; see Ch. 8.
73 Kracauer is the less subtle thinker, and some of his formulations tend towards the crude, but a good case for his significance is made by T. Y. Levin's introduction to S. Kracauer, *The Mass Ornament: Weimar Essays* (Harvard University Press, 1995); Hansen, 'America, Paris'; and D. N. Rodowick, *Reading the Figural, or, Philosophy After the New Media* (Duke University Press, 2001), Ch. 5.
74 Kracauer, *Theory*, p. 159. This is a reason why film can be powerful propaganda; see pp. 160-3.
75 Ibid., p. 165.
76 Ibid., p. 166.
77 For interesting background on 'shock' see J. Matus, 'Emergent Theories of Victorian Mind Shock: From War and Railway Accident to Nerves, Electricity and Emotion', in A. Stiles (ed.), *Neurology and Literature, 1860-1920* (Palgrave, 2007).
78 On the notion of trauma, and its ambiguities, see my discussion in *Sympathetic Sentiments*, Ch. 7.
79 Benjamin, 'Work of Art', sec. XIII; and 'Little History of Photography', in *Selected Writings*, vol. 2: 1927-34 (Harvard University Press, 1999). See also C. Lury, *Prosthetic Culture: Photography, Memory and Identity* (Routledge, 1998),

pp. 204–12, and, for critical discussion and a different perspective, R. Krauss, *The Optical Unconscious* (MIT Press, 1994).

80 S. Buck-Morss, 'Aesthetics and Anaesthetics: Walter Benjamin's Artwork Essay Reconsidered', *October* (1992), 62.

81 See S. Bruhm, *Gothic Bodies: The Politics of Pain in Romantic Fiction* (Pennsylvania University Press, 1994), pp. 4–7, 17–20, 124–8.

82 W. Benjamin, 'The Author as Producer', in SW 2, p. 775.

83 W. Benjamin, 'This Space for Rent', from *One-Way Street*, in *Selected Writings*, vol. 1: 1913–26 (Harvard University Press, 1996), p. 476. One might add that in his own explicit discussion of distraction, along similar lines to Benjamin, Kracauer, too, mentions sentimentality: see 'Cult of Distraction' [1926], in his *Mass Ornament*, p. 327.

84 Benjamin, 'Work of Art', SW 4, p. 269, and *Illuminations*, p. 234 (using 'critical' and 'absent-minded' respectively). Benjamin adds that we find, in audience response, an 'immediate fusion of pleasure' with 'expert appraisal' (ibid. p. 264 and *Illuminations*, p. 227), which seems to fit Frampton's claim that 'Even when we are "losing ourselves" in the film we are still thinking with and against the film', hence our 'particularly filmic mode of attention' (p. 163).

85 M. Jennings, 'Walter Benjamin and the European avant-garde', in Ferris, p. 30.

86 J. Mieczkowski, 'Art Forms', in Ferris, p. 42.

87 Weber, p. 96.

88 Benjamin, 'Work of Art', SW 4, p. 268, and *Illuminations*, p. 232.

89 Ibid., p. 264, and *Illuminations*, pp. 227–8, which gives 'individual reactions are predetermined by the mass audience response they are about to produce', a translation that retains the sense of anticipatory response that is central to the suggestion of the reflexive here.

90 Ibid., p. 262, in italics, and *Illuminations*, p. 225, no italics.

91 Kracauer, *Theory*, pp. 71, 168.

92 Ibid., p. 169.

93 Benjamin, 'Work of Art', SW 4, p. 265, and *Illuminations*, p. 229.

94 Ibid., p. 263, and *Illuminations*, p. 226, which gives 'orchid' here, a translation that comprehensively misses the allusion; see M. Hansen, 'Benjamin, Cinema and Experience: "The Blue Flower in the Land of Technology"', *New German Critique* (1987), 40, pp. 204–5, and SW 4, n. 30, pp. 278–9.

95 Benjamin, 'Work of Art, SW 4, p. 264, and *Illuminations*, p. 227; and see sec. XI, *passim*.

96 Ibid., p. 273n. 14, second part in italics; and *Illuminations*, p. 237n. 14, no italics.

97 Ibid., p. 254, and *Illuminations*, p. 215, respectively.

98 Weber, p. 84.

99 Benjamin, 'Work of Art', SW 4, p. 267, and *Illuminations*, p. 232.

100 Ibid., p. 282n. 47, first quote in italics; and *Illuminations*, p. 243n. 21, no italics.
101 Ibid., p. 277n. 27, and *Illuminations*, p. 240n. 12. The classic case of the potential for propaganda in all this is doubtless Leni Riefenstahl's film of the Nuremberg rallies, *Triumph of the Will*. For discussion, see S. Sontag, 'Fascinating Fascism', in *A Susan Sontag Reader* (Penguin, 1983).
102 Weber, p. 90.
103 See Benjamin, 'Work of Art', sec. IX, SW 4, esp. pp. 260–2, and *Illuminations*, pp. 223–4.
104 For discussion, see C. Gledhill (ed.), *Stardom: Industry of Desire* (Routledge, 1991), esp. C. Gledhill, 'Signs of Melodrama'.
105 For a fascinating exploration of this, see J. Elmer, *Reading at the Social Limit: Affect, Mass Culture, and Edgar Allan Poe* (Stanford University Press, 1995); and for further aspects of 'mass culture' as the denounced other of modernism in the arts, see A. Huyssen, *After the Great Divide: Modernism, Mass Culture and Postmodernism* (Macmillan, 1986), esp. Chs 1–3.

Cinematic Sensation: The Sublime and the Spectacle

1 For a general account, see M. Myrone, 'John Martin: art, taste and the spectacle of culture', in M. Myrone (ed.), *John Martin: Apocalypse* (Tate, 2011). Useful also are M. Meisel, *Realizations: Narrative, Pictorial and Theatrical Arts in Nineteenth-Century England* (Princeton University Press, 1992), and M. D. Paley, *The Apocalyptic Sublime* (Yale University Press, 1986).
2 On the conflict between catastrophists and uniformitarians in early nineteenth-century science, see D. Bindman, 'Deep time, dragons and dinosaurs', in Myrone.
3 S. Morley, 'Staring into the Contemporary Abyss', *Tate Etc.* (2010), 20, p. 72. See also his more extended account, in *The Sublime: Documents of Contemporary Art* (Whitechapel Art Gallery, 2010).
4 Highly pertinent here is Scott Lash's suggestion that, in considering the sublime, as the source of our deepest experiences, we should, *pace* Kant, circumvent imagination and understanding, since judgements of the sublime spring 'direct from the sphere of sensation', where subjectivity finds its ground. Hence sensation, as ground, lies 'beyond the discourse of reason and the figure of the imagination'. See *Another Modernity: A Different Rationality* (Blackwell, 1999), p. 233. Leaving aside Lash's ambitious attempt to locate this 'ground' in terms of social theory, one might argue that sensation cannot be adequately located 'beyond' discourse and imagination, even if irreducible to them; indeed, 'figuration' is an important mode of its manifestation (see Ch. 3 above).
5 Cit. J. Griffin, 'John Martin I', *Tate Etc.* (2011), 23, p. 34.

6   J. Milne, 'The abyss that abides', in Myrone, p. 53.
7   Indeed, the large Tate Britain exhibition of his work (2011–12), testifying to the revival of interest, featured a light and sound spectacle around the *Last Judgement* triptych, in the spirit of the nineteenth-century popular appropriation of his work.
8   In S. Kracauer, *The Mass Ornament: Weimar Essays* (Harvard University Press, 1995), pp. 78, 84.
9   Hence self-harming as 'cutting': see Ch. 2, above.
10 J. Derrida, *The Truth in Painting* (Chicago University Press, 1987), from 'Parergon', sec. IV, p. 120.
11 G. Bennington and I. McLeod, in ibid., p. 120n. 32.
12 Derrida, pp. 122, 123.
13 Derrida proceeds to subsume the sublime into his theory of the parergon, the frame that appears to be 'outside' but is actually constitutive of the (art) work, hence is as much 'inside'; but one might respond that this does not *exhaust* the sublime, in that a necessary condition for the experience of the sublime is nonetheless not constitutive of it. For a useful account, see D. Carroll, *Paraesthetics: Foucault, Lyotard, Derrida* (Routledge, 1989), Ch. 6:1.
14 R. Maltby, with I. Craven, *Hollywood Cinema: An Introduction* (Blackwell, 1995), p. 210.
15 C. Colebrook, *Gilles Deleuze* (Routledge, 2002), p. 31.
16 G. Deleuze, *Cinema 1: The Movement-Image* (Minnesota University Press, 1986), p. 40; and see Chs 2, 3, for useful reflections on cutting, framing and montage. Deleuze is influenced here by the Soviet film-maker and theorist Dziga Vertov, for whom the movement of the camera eye could adapt to or even merge with the movement of matter; for further discussion, see F. Zourabichvili, 'The Eye of Montage: Dziga Vertov and Bergsonian Materialism', in G. Flaxman (ed.), *The Brain Is the Screen: Deleuze and the Philosophy of Cinema* (Minnesota University Press, 2000).
17 G. Deleuze, *Cinema 2: The Time-Image* (Minnesota University Press, 1989), p. 156, in italics from 'producing …'.
18 I. Kant, *Critique of the Power of Judgment*, trans. P. Guyer and E. Matthews (Cambridge University Press, 2001 [1790]), §24, p. 131. For the full discussion of the sublime, see §§23–9.
19 Ibid., §27, p. 141.
20 See my *Sympathetic Sentiments: Affect, Emotion and Spectacle in the Modern World* (Bloomsbury, 2014), Ch. 5.
21 Deleuze, *Cinema 2*, p. 110. In his cinema books, Deleuze distinguishes the 'classic' cinema of the 1920s and 1930s, committed to film as an 'expressive totality', and 'modern' cinema, centred on the French 'New Wave' of the 1950s, with its self-conscious exploration of the relationship between gap and image, manifested

in 'irrational' cuts and bizarre juxtapositions, a contrast which arguably downplays the continuities between innovative strands in both. Indeed, narrative coherence and expressive totality might be more appropriately located in the mainstream Hollywood tradition – but this, of course, for Deleuze, is not worth serious consideration ... For a thorough account, see R. Bogue, *Deleuze on Cinema* (Routledge, 2003), and the discussions in Flaxman.

22 G. Lambert, 'Cinema and the Outside', in Flaxman, pp. 261, 285, and see pp. 259–63, on the Kantian sublime in relation to Deleuze. Lambert points out that what in Kant is seen as an impasse of the imagination is reconfigured by Deleuze, following Bergson, by seeing the brain itself as an interval or gap that opens onto a 'virtual whole' (p. 285). In his discussion, Ronald Bogue suggests (p. 173) that 'The images cannot be integrated within the concept of an internal self-consciousness, nor can they be treated as differentiations of a whole within a coherent external world'; and see his account in Ch. 2.

23 Deleuze, *Cinema 2*, p. 181.

24 And this is one area where one might have reservations about Deleuze, who tends – as in the quotes given above – to subsume the latter under the former.

25 *Critique of Practical Reason* [1788], in I. Kant, *Practical Philosophy* (Cambridge University Press, 1996), p. 269.

26 Ibid., p. 270.

27 G. Deleuze, *Kant's Critical Philosophy: The Doctrine of the Faculties* (Minnesota University Press, 1984), p. 51 (and see pp. 50–2).

28 Ibid., p. 50.

29 Kant, *Judgment*, §25, p. 133; §28, p. 144; §28, p. 144.

30 See Deleuze, *Cinema 1*, pp. 49–55 for discussion of the mathematical sublime and the dynamical sublime in the context of film, and Bogue, Ch. 2. One further area of comparison, in relation to this distinction, is the part played by the contrast of light and dark: Deleuze uses German expressionism (Fritz Lang, F. W. Murnau) as exemplifying the dynamical sublime, where we find that light and shadow become warring forces, clashing intensities, hence distorting perspectives, coming alive in the very objects they constitute, producing eerie, charged atmospheres ...

31 Kracauer, p. 76.

32 Kant, *Judgment*, §26, p. 136.

33 See S. Bordo, 'Reading the Slender Body', in M. Jacobus et al. (eds), *Body/Politics: Women and the Discourses of Science* (Routledge, 1990); and A. Synnott, *The Body Social: Symbolism, Self and Society* (Routledge, 1993), Ch. 3.

34 Given the stigmatization of the sentimental, this could also be a contribution to the meaning of that expression 'from the sublime to the ridiculous': your experience of being 'moved' by the sublime can seem bathos, self-indulgence, to me ...

35 L. Berlant, 'Poor Eliza', *American Literature* (1998) 70:3, p. 645, and in her *The Female Complaint* (Duke University Press, 2008), Ch. 1.
36 S. Cubitt, 'Introduction. *Le réel, c'est l'impossible*: the sublime time of special effects', *Screen* (1999), 40:2, p. 129.
37 See J. Baudrillard, 'The Precession of Simulacra', in his *Simulacra and Simulation* (Michigan University Press, 1994 [1981]), esp. p. 3, distinguishing simulation from pretence. For discussion, see R. Butler, *Jean Baudrillard: The Defence of the Real* (Sage, 1999), Ch. 1.
38 F. Léger, 'The Spectacle', in *Functions of Painting* (Viking, 1973), p. 35. For a history of the concept of spectacle, see J. Crary, 'Spectacle, Attention, Counter-Memory', *October* (1989), 50.
39 N. Abercrombie and B. Longhurst, *Audiences: A Sociological Theory of Performance and Imagination* (Sage, 1998), p. 97.
40 D. Kellner, *Media Spectacle* (Routledge, 2003), p. 11.
41 See my discussion in *Sympathetic Sentiments*, Ch. 3, and, for later issues raised by spectacle, Ch. 8.
42 S. Neale, '*Triumph of the Will*: notes on documentary and spectacle', *Screen* (1979), 20:1, p. 66.
43 V. R. Schwartz, *Spectacular Realities: Early Mass Culture in* Fin-de-Siècle *Paris* (California University Press, 1998), pp. 157, 16.
44 Ibid., p. 130, and Ch. 3. See also T. J. Clark, *The Painting of Modern Life: Paris in the Art of Manet and His Followers* (Thames and Hudson, 1990), Introduction, for an account of the origins of Parisian spectacle that draws on Debord; and J. Drucker, *Theorizing Modernism* (Columbia University Press, 1994), Ch. 2, for discussion of simulation and spectacle in relation to modern art.
45 T. Brown, 'Spectacle/gender/history: the case of *Gone With the Wind*', *Screen* (2008), 49:2, p. 159.
46 T. Richards, *The Commodity Culture of Victorian England: Advertising and Spectacle 1851–1914* (Verso, 1991), pp. 111–12.
47 S. Buck-Morss, *The Dialectics of Seeing: Walter Benjamin and the Arcades Project* (MIT Press, 1991).
48 Aspects of this are discussed in S. Stewart, *On Longing: Narratives of the Miniature, the Gigantic, the Souvenir, the Collection* (Duke, University Press, 1993).
49 Richards, p. 203.
50 Schwartz, p. 190.
51 J. Rancière, *The Emancipated Spectator* (Verso, 2009), p. 14.
52 G. Debord, *Society of the Spectacle* (Black & Red, Detroit, 1970), ¶¶1, 8, 30. (There are several translations, none authorized, so Debord's numbered paragraphs are given.)
53 Ibid., ¶29.

54 For discussions of Debord in this wider context, see Rancière, pp. 6–7, 44–6, and S. Cubitt, *Simulation and Social Theory* (Sage, 2001), Ch. 3:1.
55 Debord, ¶1.
56 Ibid., ¶¶69, 66, 68.
57 And, indeed, more speculatively, Adam Smith: see my *Sympathetic Sentiments*, Ch. 4. Overall, Debord's theory is surely more subtle and insightful than many summaries or rival accounts that over-emphasize the abstraction, positing an abstract spectacle, reduced to an effect of power, that positions and confronts a subject, passive and featureless save as object of power – an analysis that also manages to reify spectacle, detaching it from the relations in which it is embedded.
58 Debord, ¶65, and see ¶¶63–5 overall.
59 Abercrombie and Longhurst, p. 84.
60 Kellner, p. 11.
61 G. Debord, *Comments on the Society of the Spectacle* (Verso, 1990).
62 *New York Times*, 3 April 2003, cit. E. A. Kaplan, *Trauma Culture: The Politics of Terror and Loss in Media and Literature* (Rutgers University Press, 2005), p. 99. Paul Virilio would of course answer Boxer's question with an unequivocal affirmative; see his *War and Cinema: The logistics of Perception* (Verso, 1989).
63 J. Seaton, *Carnage and the Media: The Making and Breaking of News About Violence* (Penguin, 2005), p. 140.

Sensational Affect

1 W. E. Connolly, *Neuropolitics: Thinking, Culture, Speed* (Minnesota University Press, 2002), p. 67. Elsewhere (notably Ch. 3) this book offers some useful insights.
2 It should be added that much of the recent discussion of 'affect' oddly echoes earlier discussions, from the eighteenth century, and some of the controversies have recognizable continuities. On this, and for a critique of efforts by affect theorists to reposition Spinoza as an ancestor, see my *Sympathetic Sentiments: Affect, Emotion and Spectacle* (Bloomsbury, 2014), Ch. 5.
3 T. Brennan, *The Transmission of Affect* (Cornell University Press, 2004), pp. 5, 116.
4 L. Grossberg, 'Is There a Fan in the House? The Affective Sensibility of Fandom', in L. A. Lewis (ed.), *The Adoring Audience: Fan Culture and Popular Media* (Routledge, 1992), pp. 60, 57, 57.
5 M. Kavka, *Reality Television, Affect and Intimacy: Reality Matters* (Palgrave, 2008), pp. xii, 34.
6 M. Wetherell, *Affect and Emotion: A New Social Science Understanding* (Sage, 2012), p. 45. This is a useful survey of the field, critical but fair-minded.

7   Brennan, p. 183n. 5.
8   Kavka, p. 35.
9   Lisa Blackman argues that the affect/cognition distinction is difficult to sustain if one accepts that the two hemispheres of the brain disclose 'interdependency and parallelism, rather than separation and hierarchy'. See her *Immaterial Bodies: Affect, Embodiment, Mediation* (Sage, 2012), p. 181, and the further references given there. For this issue, and more discussion of 'feeling' and 'emotion', see *Sympathetic Sentiments*, Ch. 4.
10 B. Massumi, *Parables for the Virtual: Movement, Affect, Sensation* (Duke University Press, 2002), p. 4.
11 B. Massumi, 'Introduction: Like a Thought', in B. Massumi (ed.), *A Shock to Thought: Expression after Deleuze and Guattari* (Routledge, 2002), p. xxiv.
12 Wetherell, p. 87.
13 Massumi, 'Introduction', p. xxiv.
14 G. Deleuze, *Difference and Repetition* (Continuum, 2004 [1968]), p. 144.
15 Ibid., p. xxx.
16 Brennan, p. 157.
17 Massumi, *Parables*, pp. 28, 29, 30.
18 One might insert another example, from a latter-day Zeus. Demanding the execution of Louis XVIII, Robespierre claimed that 'the people' do not judge like a court of law: 'they do not hand down sentences, they throw thunderbolts …'. See M. Robespierre, *Virtue and Terror* (Verso, 2007), p. 129.
19 Massumi, 'Introduction', p. xxv. In his book *Violence* (Profile, 2009) Slavoj Žižek, coming from a different direction (Hegel, Lacan), shows an intriguingly similar hostility to language: it 'dismembers the thing, destroys its organic unity'. If we take 'gold', for example, with the very name 'we violently extract a metal from its natural texture, investing into it our dreams of wealth, power, spiritual purity', which have nothing to do with its 'immediate reality' (p. 52). As with Massumi, the effect of this is to disregard any imaginative or creative powers of language itself in favour of reducing language to the power of something external, whether affect (Massumi) or the master-signifier as exercise of the paternal law (Žižek, Lacan). The difference is that, for Massumi, language, as representation, becomes conservative, inert, whereas for Žižek, it inherently manifests the 'violent imposition' of the master-signifier (p. 53), hence is violent in itself – a sweeping perspective that proves far too broad to make a useful contribution to a theory of violence, and leaves Žižek (like Massumi) unable to account for the non-violent *metaphorical* power of his own language.
20 Massumi, *Parables*, p. 7.
21 Ibid., p. 98. Massumi often uses 'sensation' and 'affect' interchangeably (e.g. p. 98), sometimes using sensation more narrowly, as the affective contrast to perception.

22 G. Seigworth, 'From affection to soul', in C. J. Stivale (ed.), *Gilles Deleuze: Key Concepts* (Acumen, 2005), p. 161.
23 P. T. Clough, 'The Affective Turn: Political Economy, Biomedia, and Bodies', in G. J. Seigworth and M. Gregg (eds), *The Affect Theory Reader* (Duke University Press, 2010), p. 209. See also her introduction to P. T. Clough and J. Halley (eds), *The Affective Turn* (Duke University Press, 2007).
24 Massumi, *Parables*, p. 30.
25 Wetherell, p. 59.
26 Massumi, *Parables*, pp. 28, 35.
27 Ibid., p. 123.
28 This is the title of the particularly influential first chapter of *Parables*; it was published, in an earlier form, in *Cultural Critique* (1995) 31.
29 Massumi, *Parables*, p. 25.
30 Ibid., pp. 58–61; 265–6n. 13; 266n. 16.
31 One can cite here the increasingly influential work of Silvan Tomkins, spanning the period from the 1960s onwards, providing detailed studies of the workings of affect and drawing out the implications. Claiming to separate out nine different affects, in all their embodied and emotional complexity, along with 'affect scripts' to show how these unfold in relation to one another and the problems they raise, he derives a critique of the over-valuation of Western rationality and its dependence on the priority of consciousness, concluding that there can be no cognition purified of affective content. See S. S. Tomkins, *Exploring Affect: The Selected Writings of S. S. Tomkins* (Cambridge University Press, 1995), esp. Parts I and IV; and see also the introduction by V. Demos to Part I, surveying his theory.
32 G. J. Seigworth and M. Gregg, 'An Inventory of Shimmers', in Seigworth and Gregg, p. 1.
33 Massumi, *Parables*, pp. 43, 217, 35.
34 Wetherell, p. 59.
35 Massumi, *Parables*, pp. 138, 139. It should be added that, in practice, Massumi frequently offers more wide-ranging analyses than his theoretical presuppositions would seem to allow, suggesting an implicit awareness that his ostensible framework of assumptions is too restrictive.
36 Anyway, as we saw earlier, 'heartbeat' is only tenuously 'affect' at all – it is not quite autonomic enough.
37 Wetherell, pp. 46, 47. Her criticisms of Massumi are developed in Ch. 3, pp. 54–67. For critique, see also C. Hemmings, 'Invoking Affect: Cultural Theory and the Ontological Turn', *Cultural Studies* (2005) 19:5, and, for a particularly wide-ranging discussion, R. Leys, 'The Turn to Affect: a critique', *Critical Inquiry* (2011) 37:3.
38 In an excellent overview, written from *within* the 'affective turn', Anna Gibbs

registers something of this tension, telling us that 'Whether an affect is coming or going is information that is then conscripted into semiotic systems of meaning', and agreeing that language 'enables a reflective handle on experience'. Elsewhere, unsurprisingly, a rather cruder approach can be apparent: for example, she refers to 'corporeally based forms of imitation, both voluntary and involuntary (and on which literary representation ultimately depends)', where the claim in brackets could range from the completely vacuous to the implausibly reductionist, cutting out any relative autonomy of language altogether. See A. Gibbs, 'After Affect: Sympathy, Synchrony, and Mimetic Communication', in Seigworth and Gregg, pp. 192, 201, 186.

39 Controversies in the sociological theorizing of charisma do indeed run intriguingly parallel here: does the 'charismatic authority' of the revolutionary leader reside in his personal, psychological qualities, hence his affective powers, or in the transformations he proclaims in established doctrines? In the light of this discussion, we might want to say that it lies in the awkward disjunction of both. For the classic source, see M. Weber, 'The Nature of Charismatic Domination' [1922], in *Max Weber: Selections in Translation*, ed. W. G. Runciman (Cambridge University Press, 1978), Ch. 11.

40 Deleuze, p. 176.

41 C. Colebrook, *Gilles Deleuze* (Routledge, 2002), pp. 111, 115. In keeping with her conscientious exposition of Deleuze, Colebrook makes some contentious statements, such as: 'Language is not about representation, naming or propositions, but rather about creating worlds of sense that interact with other material worlds ...' (p. 111). Surely it is about *all* of these?!

42 An interesting account that brings this out well is B. J. Gold, *ThermoPoetics: Energy in Victorian Literature and Science* (MIT Press, 2010).

43 D. Stern, 'Applying Developmental and Neuroscience Findings on Other-Centred Participation to the Process of Change in Psychotherapy', in S. Braten (ed.), *On Being Moved: From Mirror Neurons to Empathy* (John Benjamin's, 2007), p. 37. For sympathetic accounts of the mirror neurons evidence, see G. Rizzolatti and C. Sinigaglia, *Mirrors in the Brain: How Our Minds Share Actions and Emotions* (Oxford University Press, 2007); and, ranging more widely, J. Decety and W. Ickes (eds), *The Social Neuroscience of Empathy* (MIT Press, 2011). For short critical assessments, see Wetherell, Ch. 2, and Blackman, Ch. 7; and, for a thorough critique, J. Coulter et al., *Brain, Mind, and Human Behaviour in Contemporary Cognitive Science: Critical Assessments of the Philosophy of Psychology* (Edwin Mullen Press, 2007). We might also note that in these 'scientific' usages, 'empathy' is shifting in meaning, becoming de-moralized, anaesthetized, losing its remaining links to 'sympathy'.

44 It has also been taken up elsewhere, notably in N. Thrift, *Non-Representational*

45 R. Terada, *Feeling in Theory: Emotion after the 'Death of the Subject'* (Harvard University Press, 2001), pp. 17, 29.
46 Massumi, *Parables*, pp. 14, 16, 36. Massumi describes this relational, rather than substantive, conception of the self as an instance of the 'incorporeal materialism' he espouses (p. 16). He adds that this conception of the self, involving the 'doubling' implied by the 'feeling of having a feeling', does not necessarily involve being self-reflexive, or the splitting and distancing this involves (pp. 13, 14), but this again leaves us unable to theorize the intervention of language and concept, and the very fact of *intervention* here.
47 Massumi uses 'resonation' more frequently than 'resonance', but there does not seem to be any difference between them; since the latter is in wider use, and is also used in the translations of Deleuze, it is adopted here.
48 Massumi, *Parables*, p. 14.
49 Ibid., p. 33.
50 G. Deleuze, *Francis Bacon: The Logic of Sensation* (Continuum, 2003 [1981]), pp. 65, 66. For Deleuze's treatment and use of resonance elsewhere, see, for example, *Difference*, pp. 144–5, 148–9, 151, 281, 363–4, where resonance between levels, systems or series is emphasized; and *What Is Philosophy?* (Verso, 1994 [1991], with F. Guattari), p. 211, where the link between sensation, vibration and resonance is explicit.
51 In the context of language, indeed, 'evocation', with its hint of temporal depth, might be a term that overlaps significantly.
52 Thus Adam Phillips and Barbara Taylor remind us that Hume compared the transmission of feelings with the vibration of violin strings, 'with each individual resonating with the pains and pleasures of others': see *On Kindness* (Penguin, 2010), p. 29.
53 Kavka, p. 29.
54 In his early *Empiricism and Subjectivity* (Columbia University Press, 1991 [1953]), on Hume, Deleuze offers intriguing reflections on how the mind's two characteristics, resonance and vividness, come to constitute it as *subject* when the part containing vivid impressions communicates with the part containing less vivid ideas, and when '*all the parts taken together resonate in the act of producing something new*' (p. 132, italics in the original). Belief and invention are hence 'modes of transcendence' whereby mind rises above itself.
55 Terada, p. 156.
56 Gibbs, p. 186.
57 Not surprisingly, there has been some revival of interest in 'crowd psychology' as part of these developments; see Blackman, Chs 2, 3, and Wetherell, Ch. 7, for

discussion. Blackman shows an interest in the 'power of suggestion', and theories of porous boundaries and 'multiple selves' and calls for a revival of nineteenth-century 'subliminal psychology'.

58 F. Jameson, *Postmodernism, or, the Logic of Late Capitalism* (Duke University Press, 1991), pp. 10, 15.

59 Again, one sometimes suspects another revival here, that of nineteenth-century evolutionism. Thus Gibbs argues that movement, sound and rhythm are not 'vestigial', superfluous to language and its modes: 'they also inhabit and actively shape them' (p. 199). Indeed so; but the use of 'vestigial' here is interesting. It was a favourite of evolutionary discourse: 'vestiges' of previous stages could linger on, possibly presenting dangers. And the article is much preoccupied with mother–infant interaction, clearly seen as fundamental to the affect paradigm: do we see here a revival of 'ontogeny recapitulates phylogeny', the idea that the history of evolution can be mapped onto the development of the child? Certainly the cultural politics of the affective turn is intriguing, caught between a dubious repetition of old cultural motifs and a reflection of more contemporary, green ones, a willingness to accept the necessary immersion of the human in a broader conception of organic nature (even though, as argued here, 'culture' – whatever it is – can get somewhat lost in the process).

The Melodrama of the Modern

1 Kevin Rozario points out that 'Within a week, indeed, the spectacular and the sentimental had been woven into an ethical and aesthetic hybrid entirely familiar to audiences of disaster movies'; see his *The Culture of Calamity: Disaster and the Making of Modern America* (Chicago University Press, 2007), p. 193, and see pp. 180, 193–5. See also N. Klein, *The Shock Doctrine: The Rise of Disaster Capitalism* (Penguin, 2007), Ch. 14, and, for an emphasis on the representational dynamics of 9/11, S. Žižek, *The Desert of the Real* (Verso, 2002), Ch. 1.

2 L. Williams, 'Melodrama Revised', in N. Browne (ed.), *Refiguring American Film Genres: History and Theory* (California University Press, 1998), p. 52.

3 It is important to remember that we are doing cultural history or cultural theory here, not philosophy or theology. From the viewpoint of Christian theology, Manichaeism – the dualism of good and evil as cosmic forces – is heresy, seeming to elevate Satan to equal status with God, and was driven out by St Augustine in the earliest phase of Christian institutionalization. This doesn't alter the fact that, in popular belief and practice, Christian culture has always been deeply dualist, as has the church itself, when persecuting 'heretics'.

4 And pornography can emerge as the excess of this in representation itself,

pushing representation into the real, even as it reveals the excess of the real in its transgression of the distinction itself. This also shows the inseparable link between Enlightenment thought and its 'other side', from Sade to Bataille; see S. Sontag, 'The Pornographic Imagination', in *A Susan Sontag Reader* (Penguin, 1982).

5   It is important to emphasize that what matters here is not a critique of 'reason' as such, in any conceivable use of the term, but an examination of the implications, in practice, of a particular, universalizing model of reason that has been particularly important in Western philosophy and culture. One should add that appeals to universal notions of 'human rights' do, of course, have their place, when embedded in *particular* contexts of liberation struggles.

6   See the reflections in J. Baudrillard, *The Spirit of Terrorism* (Verso, 2012 [2002]), where he claims that 'Good and Evil advance together, as part of the same movement', and that, ultimately, 'Good could thwart Evil only by ceasing to be Good since, by seizing for itself a global monopoly of power, it gives rise, by that very act, to a blowback of a proportionate violence' (pp. 10, 11). He adds that universalizing value makes it self-subverting (pp. 67–70). Elsewhere, he adds a further possible consequence, namely that Evil can be positioned as what resists hegemonic domination, the 'non-unification of things …'; see his *Passwords* (Verso, 2003), p. 33. Despite their contrasting overall frameworks, there is a convergence here with Badiou, for whom Good is only such if it accepts self-limitation: 'Every absolutization of a power of truth organizes an Evil.' See A. Badiou, *Ethics: An Essay on the Understanding of Evil* (Verso, 2012 [1993]), p. 85.

7   Postmodern readings of Kant, stemming from Lyotard, have perhaps distracted attention from the link here by portraying the sublime as a crisis of representation in the arts, separate from an account of the fate of reason in the 'collapse of grand narratives'. See J.-F. Lyotard, *The Postmodern Condition: A Report on Knowledge* (Manchester University Press, 1984), and 'Answering the Question: what is Postmodernism?', in ibid., and re-translated in his *The Postmodern Explained: Corrrespondence 1982-85* (Minnesota University Press, 1992).

8   A. MacIntyre, *After Virtue: A Study in Moral Theory* (Duckworth, 1985), Ch. 2 (see also Chs 4, 5). Coming from a different tradition, Lyotard's concept of the differend attempts to grapple with similar issues; see J.-F. Lyotard, *The Differend: Phrases in Dispute* (Manchester University Press, 1988).

9   Cit. D. J. Denby, *Sentimental Narrative and the Social Order in France, 1760-1820* (Cambridge University Press, 1994), p. 160, my trans.

10 P. Brooks, *The Melodramatic Imagination: Balzac, Henry James, Melodrama, and the Mode of Excess* (Yale University Press, 1995 [1976]), p. 101. This is the founding text of modern melodrama studies, still indispensable. For another insightful literary treatment, see C. Williams, 'Moving Pictures: George Eliot

and Melodrama', in L. Berlant (ed.), *Compassion: The Culture and Politics of an Emotion* (Routledge, 2004).
11 M. Gluck, *Popular Bohemia: Modernism and Urban Culture in Nineteenth-Century Paris* (Harvard University Press, 2005), pp. 44, 45. See Ch. 2, *passim*.
12 E. Hadley, *Melodramatic Tactics: Theatricalized Dissent in the English Marketplace, 1800–1885* (Stanford University Press, 1995), pp. 211, 225. Hadley is concerned to display melodrama as basically a reactionary form (pp. 3, 11), but here as elsewhere her examples don't always seem to confirm this; she concedes that it is not easily categorized (p. 12). On the 'Maiden Tribute' episode, see also J. R. Walkowitz, *City of Dreadful Delight: Narratives of Sexual Danger in Late-Victorian London* (Chicago University Press, 1992), Chs 3, 4; and, for a comparable American experience, in the context of the politics of anti-semitism, anti-immigration and implicit racism, see R. Maltby, 'The Social Evil, the Moral Order, and the Melodramatic Imagination, 1890–1915', in J. Bratton et al. (eds), *Melodrama: Stage, Picture, Screen* (BFI, 1994).
13 Williams, 'Melodrama', p. 42. See also the useful discussion in B. Singer, *Melodrama and Modernity: Early Sensational Cinema and Its Contexts* (Columbia University Press, 2001), esp. Ch. 2. Singer's identification of 'moral polarization and sensational action and spectacle' (p. 58) as the two essential elements of melodrama would command general assent.
14 See C. Gledhill (ed.), *Home is Where the Heart Is: Studies in Melodrama and the Woman's Film* (BFI, 1987).
15 One might note here that in the two Gulf Wars, George Bush, Senior and Junior, both battled the Satanic Saddam, and it was as if the Son took it on himself to carry on (avenge or upstage) the work of the Father, who had not won the ultimate victory, thus presenting us with a scenario that the protagonists, and the media alike, already presented in melodramatic terms, as a battle of good and evil – but now re-imagined as a sort of ghastly 'domestic melodrama' beyond Hollywood's wildest imaginings, projected onto the political stage. The reader can pursue the psychoanalytical/theological complexities here, if so inclined …
16 Williams, 'Melodrama', p. 51.
17 See discussion of these themes in S. Jeffords, *The Remasculinization of America: Gender and the Vietnam War* (Indiana University Press, 1989).
18 Williams, 'Melodrama', p. 59.
19 This also reveals continuities with the tableau of nineteenth-century stage melodrama, and its eighteenth-century predecessors; see Williams, 'Melodrama'.
20 See the exploration of this in C. Gledhill, 'Signs of Melodrama', in C. Gledhill (ed.), *Stardom: Industry of Desire* (Routledge, 1991), emphasizing the role of 'excess' both in stardom and in the modern construction of personality.
21 O. Bartov, 'Spielberg's Oskar: Hollywood Tries Evil', in Y. Loshitzky (ed.),

Spielberg's Holocaust: Critical Perspectives on Schindler's List (Indiana University Press, 1997), pp. 44, 45, 45.
22 Ibid., p. 49.
23 Williams, 'Melodrama', p. 54.
24 Ibid., pp. 62, 61. One might add that Jean Seaton argues that the tragic hero, and tragedy generally, should be distinguished from melodrama, the lazy use of 'tragic' in the media obscuring this; see her *Carnage and the Media: The Making and Breaking of News about Violence* (Penguin, 2005), pp. 241–5.
25 C. Guignon, Introduction to F. Dostoevsky, *The Grand Inquisitor* (Hackett, 1993, an extended excerpt from *The Brothers Karamazov* [1879]), p. xx.
26 *Observer*, 18 January 2004, cit. P. Cole, *The Myth of Evil* (Edinburgh University Press, 2006), p. 126.
27 Cole, pp. 93, 8. The conclusion of his thoughtful account is that 'evil' constitutes 'a highly dangerous and inhumane discourse and we are better off without it' (p. 21). See Chs 4, 5, on the 'enemy within'.
28 What has sometimes happened, to reinforce the uniqueness case, is the presentation of the Holocaust itself as 'traumatic' – which seems fair enough in itself – and to link this with a specific *theory* of trauma whereby it 'infects' those who later attempt to debate, reflect on, or represent it, obliterating the gap between reality and representation in the literalness of repetition. This trauma theme is discussed in my *Sympathetic Sentiments: Affect, Emotion, and Spectacle in the Modern World* (Bloomsbury, 2014), Ch. 7, and I will merely observe here that it can, in some ways, be seen to *reinforce* the melodrama perspective. For discussions that shows an awareness that Holocaust studies do indeed constitute a *discourse*, and an awareness of trauma issues, see D. LaCapra, *Writing History, Writing Trauma* (Johns Hopkins University Press, 2001), and his earlier *Representing the Holocaust: History, Theory, Trauma* (Cornell University Press, 1994). See also T. Snyder, *Bloodlands: Europe between Hitler and Stalin* (Bodley Head, 2010), an important account of the wider context.
29 P. Knight, *Conspiracy Culture: From Kennedy to* The X-Files (Routledge, 2000), p. 117.
30 Ibid., p. 244.
31 Ibid., Ch. 2.
32 Knight points out that 'everything is connected' could be a slogan in a wide range of fields, beyond conspiracy theory: epidemiology, ecology, systems theory, risk theory, globalization theory, the internet, theories of intertextuality (p. 205). One might add that it features as a symptom of mental illness …
33 Intriguing ramifications of all this can be traced in the horror film. Jonathan Crane argues that the 'nihilism' of these films reveal 'overt codes that explicitly deny the possibility of knowledge or collective action producing a remotely viable

future'; indeed, the eternal return of the 'menace' seems to be part of the spectacle of pleasure here. Expertise is no use when the potential for disaster is omnipresent and we can all potentially be monsters ... See his *Terror and Everyday Life: Singular Moments in the History of the Horror Film* (Sage, 1994), pp. 8, 10.

34 See U. Beck, *Risk Society* (Sage, 1992).
35 D. N. Rodowick, *Reading the Figural, or, Philosophy After the New Media* (Duke University Press, 2001), p. 209. Influenced by the Deleuze and Guattari of *A Thousand Plateaus*, Rodowick presents this language of 'flows', 'tides', 'waves' and 'currents' as the appropriate language of contemporary societies of 'control' (rather than of earlier 'disciplinary' societies); but as we have seen in previous chapters, since the eighteenth century this figuration of energy as flow or current has been just as central as the more mechanical language of impact or atom.
36 Dramatization can involve a kind of 'realization', a 'making real' through an intensification of the process of enactment discussed above (Ch. 3). This has some relation to Deleuze's use of the term: 'Intensity is the determinant in the process of actualisation. It is intensity which *dramatises*.' See his *Difference and Repetition* (Continuum, 2004 [1968]), pp. 306–7. In Deleuze, however, it is linked to his theory of Ideas and the critique of representation.
37 Williams, 'Melodrama', p. 42.
38 Brooks, p. 203. See also J. Gripsrud, 'The Aesthetics and Politics of Melodrama', in P. Dahlgren and C. Sparks (eds), *Journalism and Popular Culture* (Sage, 1992), arguing that personalization and sensationalism are two defining attributes of melodrama in popular journalism.
39 Keith Tester suggests that 'Sentimentality is an emotion which requires that the world become melodrama', an interesting observation that might even imply that 'sentimentality', as supposedly distinct from sensibility or 'sentiment' more generally, can only ever be identified as such in relation to melodrama; see his *Moral Culture* (Sage, 1997), p. 68. For a more extended discussion of sentimentality, see my *Sympathetic Sentiments*, Chs 2, 8.
40 Singer, p. 44.
41 For examples from literature, see S. Thornton, 'The Vanity of Childhood: Constructing, Deconstructing, and Destroying the Child in the Novel of the 1840s', in M. Lesnik-Oberstein (ed.), *Children in Culture: Approaches to Childhood* (Macmillan, 1998).
42 M. Warner, *Managing Monsters* (Vintage, 1994), p. 35.
43 For a historical overview of the modern Western construction of childhood, see A. Higonnet, *Pictures of Innocence: The History and Crisis of Ideal Childhood* (Thames & Hudson, 1998); and, for a controversial comparison of past and present, J. R. Kincaid, *Child-Loving: The Erotic Child in Victorian Culture* (Routledge, 1992). For recent controversies, particularly the James Bulger case, see

Cole, Ch. 6; K. Farrell, *Post-Traumatic Culture* (Johns Hopkins University Press, 1998), Ch. 7; and Warner, Ch. 3.

44 P. Brooks, 'Melodrama, Body, Revolution', in Bratton, p. 18.
45 Hadley, p. 73.
46 Brooks, *Melodramatic Imagination*, pp. 72, 11. On the eighteenth-century cult of the (universal) 'language of the body' see also my *Sympathetic Sentiments*, Ch. 3.
47 M. Hansen, *Babel & Babylon: Spectatorship in American Silent Film* (Harvard University Press, 1991), p. 80. See also pp. 76–81.
48 Williams, 'Melodrama', p. 80. She adds that the 'paradoxical power of the victim' has become important in other areas, such as litigation (p. 83n. 15).
49 Brooks, *Melodramatic Imagination*, preface to 2nd (1995) edn, p. xii. He adds that psychoanalysis, too, can be seen as an example of melodrama (p. xi).
50 For elaboration, see *Sympathetic Sentiments*, Ch. 3, also relevant to the discussion of the public sphere in the following section.
51 See M. Warner, *Publics and Counterpublics* (Zone, 2002), p. 176, where he points out that 'Part of the bad faith of the *res publica* of letters was that it required a denial of the bodies that gave access to it', a principle of abstraction seen as differentially distributed by class and gender. See also, on broadly similar lines, B. Burgett, *Sentimental Bodies: Sex, Gender, and Citizenship in the Early Republic* (Princeton University Press, 1998). It needs to be added that the work of Habermas remains indispensable for understanding the foundations of the public sphere, and he is more aware of problems than his critics acknowledge; it is perhaps his 'narrative of decline' that is most in need of revision, closing off as it does the possibility that *some* of the subsequent changes, at least, could be said to transform rather than corrupt the public sphere, just as they may require that we rethink it. See J. Habermas, *The Structural Transformation of the Public Sphere* (Polity, 1992).
52 W. Benjamin, *The Arcades Project* (Harvard University Press, 1999 [1930s]), M3, 2, p. 422, and M3a, 4, p. 423.
53 G. Beer, '"Wireless": Popular Physics, Radio and Modernism', in F. Spufford and J. Uglow (eds), *Cultural Babbage: Technology, Time and Invention* (Faber, 1996), pp. 150, 166.
54 D. Morley, 'Television: Not so much a visual medium, more a visible object', in C. Jenks (ed.), *Visual Culture* (Routledge, 1995), p. 181.
55 M. Kavka, *Reality Television, Affect and Intimacy: Reality Matters* (Palgrave, 2008), p. 67.
56 Ibid., pp. 67–74, and see the thoughtful discussion of related themes elsewhere in the book. One might add that internet sites like Facebook reveal further evidence of this dynamic.
57 This body focus suggests a sense in which the private is indeed a private *sphere*,

with the local, spatial connotations of the latter, whereas the public 'sphere' always points beyond this. The German term *Öffentlichkeit*, used by Habermas, could perhaps, therefore, be better seen as 'publicness', the public *aspect* of something.
58 Kavka, pp. 55, x.
59 The emphasis here on intimacy could become problematical, as it does, arguably, in Lauren Berlant's ongoing exploration of what she has called the 'intimate public sphere', based on the idea that 'Publics presume intimacy'. When she argues that 'What makes a public sphere intimate is an expectation that the consumers of its particular stuff *already* share a worldview and emotional knowledge that they have derived from a broadly common historical experience', one might suspect a certain conservatism here, an emphasis on identity as pre-given, and on a closed circuit of mutual identification as the basis of community. However, she adds that if, from a theoretical angle, 'an intimate public is a space of mediation in which the personal is refracted through the general', then 'what's salient for its consumers is that … it flourishes as a porous, affective scene of identification among strangers that promises a certain experience of belonging'; and here, the emphasis on mediation, porous boundaries, and relations among 'strangers' seems to redress the balance. See *The Female Complaint: The Unfinished Business of Sentimentality in American Culture* (Duke University Press, 2008), pp. vii, viii.
60 L. Chouliaraki, *The Spectatorship of Suffering* (Sage, 2006), p. 190.
61 Chouliaraki's category of 'emergency news' comes close to this; see Ch. 6.
62 Kavka, pp. 35, x, 51.
63 Chouliaraki, p. 39.
64 This is not to deny the significance of verticality in other contexts, notably that of power in relation to surveillance, but, however important, this cannot suffice to furnish an adequate account of the public sphere and its role in Western culture and ideas.
65 B. Anderson, *Imagined Communities* (Verso, 1991), Ch. 2, from p. 22.
66 Burgett, p. 15.
67 J. Thompson, *The Media and Modernity: A Social Theory of the Media* (Polity, 1995), pp. 125, 32 (in italics), 244. See Chs 3, 4, 7, 8, for further exploration; and also A. Giddens, *Modernity and Self-Identity: Self and Society in the Late Modern Age* (Polity, 1991), pp. 16–27.
68 Rodowick, p. 212.
69 P. Virilio, *Polar Inertia* (Sage, 1999). For discussion, see J. Armitage, *Virilio and the Media* (Polity, 2012), Chs 3, 4; and S. Lash, *Another Modernity, A Different Rationality* (Blackwell, 1999), pp. 302–7.
70 Thompson, p. 228.
71 S. Weber, 'Television: Set and Screen', in his *Mediauras: Form, Technics, Media* (Stanford University Press, 1996), pp. 116, 117, 122.

72 Thompson, p. 231. One might add that this suggests an element of truth in Marshall McLuhan's much-derided 'global village'; for discussion, see J. Marchessault, *Marshall McLuhan* (Sage, 2005), Ch. 12.
73 Ibid., p. 98.
74 Kavka, p. 7. Weber makes a similar claim: television 'does not transmit *representations* but rather *the semblance of presentation as such*' (p. 117).
75 J. Sconce, *Haunted Media: Electronic Presence from Telepathy to Television* (Duke University Press, 2000), p. 173.
76 See S. Heath and G. Skirrow, 'Television: A World in Action', *Screen* (1977) 18:2, esp. pp. 53–4.
77 Kavka, p. 17.
78 Kavka, p. 23. And this fits the case of the father who cries at his daughter's wedding – but does so when he sees the video *subsequently*, rather than at the time (p. 1). It could also be that if we know in advance that there will be a video, this could distance us from the experience of the event itself (pp. 5–6) – though it might be more appropriate to suggest that the whole notion of 'the event itself' is what comes into question here. The event is what becomes present in its effects; it is the 'presence' of the experience as vicarious that makes the event what it is, in its significance.
79 Kavka, pp. 29, 48; and see Chs 1, 4, *passim*. For other discussions of reality television that touch on these issues, see A. Fetveit, 'Reality TV in the Digital Era: A Paradox in Visual Culture?', in J. Friedman (ed.), *Reality Squared: Televisual Discourse on the Real* (Rutgers University Press, 2002); A. Biressi and H. Nunn, *Reality TV: Realism and Revelation* (Wallflower Press, 2005), which discusses the wider context (therapy culture, narcissism); and the introduction to S. Holmes and D. Jermyn (eds), *Understanding Reality Television* (Routledge, 2004), which surveys the field.
80 One might note, in passing, that all this might seem to exemplify what Rousseau detested about emergent modernity: above all, the betrayal of the authenticity of face-to-face communal presence. But it could be argued that this is not the most basic dimension of his critique, and that one can harness the notions of extended co-presence and mediated spectacle being developed here to pinpoint its continued power as a critique of the narcissistic self, under the sway of a self-serving but self-deluded pursuit of identity as entailing identification with the appearance of others under the aegis of fashion and consumerism, encouraging deceit and hypocrisy and a lack of autonomy that ultimately subverts the reflexive, self-constituting basis of communal life and leaves us subservient to the reified abstractions of state and market (reflected, for Rousseau, in the 'theatre' as an institution where an 'entertainment' is imposed on passive spectators). This is the Rousseau who can denounce the modern city, where each of us 'shows himself

only by his reputation and is esteemed only for his riches', but who can also see beyond this: 'The heart of man is always right concerning that which has no personal relation to himself. In the quarrel at which we are purely spectators, we immediately take the side of justice … But when our interest is involved, our sentiments are soon corrupted. And it is only then that we prefer the evil which is useful to us to the good that nature makes us love.' (From the *Letter to M. d'Alembert on the Theatre* [1758], translated by A. Bloom as *Politics and the Arts*, Cornell University Press, 1968, pp. 59, 24.)

81 This can also, though, open up possibilities of irony, parody, and distancing, as 'postmodern' modes of experiencing this otherness of experience to itself.

82 J. D. Peters, *Speaking into the Air: A History of the Idea of Communication* (Chicago University Press, 2000), pp. 60, 60–1, 61; and see the extended discussion in Ch. 1.

83 Kavka, p. 30.

84 Peters, Ch. 5, esp. pp. 206–25; and see Sconce, Ch. 3.

Index

Note: authors of single, short quotes are not generally listed here.

abjection 17, 27, 132
Adorno, T. W. 48
advertisements 18, 116 *see also* commodity
Aestheticism 196n. 8 *see also* Pater
aesthetics 32, 46–7, 67–73, 83, 85–6, 88–93 *passim*, 98, 116, 124, 175, 182
    cultural 8–9, 67, 87–8
    see also anaesthetics; art; sublime
affect 4, 16, 26, 66, 141–2, 145, 152, 152–3, 155–6, 175
    theory 145–52, 154–5, 212n. 31
    theory, critique of 9, 147–52, 156, 157, 215n. 59
    see also feeling
Alcott, L. M. 24, 185n. 47
allegory 108–9
amusement parks 35–6, 38, 39, 98 *see also* entertainment
anaesthetics 94, 115, 179
Anderson, B. 27, 176
Aragon, L. 107
art 1–2, 86–7, 88–93, 105, 111, 123
Artaud, A. 47, 76
Asendorf, C. 54, 58
attention 5, 55, 101–6, 111–14, 116, 118, 136
    contributes to distraction 104–5, 106
    see also concentration; distraction; focus
aura 121
awareness 88, 92–3, 102, 103, 106, 142, 153, 155 *see also* consciousness

Bacon, F. 73–82, 86
Badiou, A. 216n. 6
Barnes, D. 95–7, 98–101
baroque 108–10, 122
Bartov, O. 164, 169

Baudrillard, J. 216n. 6
Bauman, Z. 42
Beer, G. 63, 174
Benjamin, W. 51, 97–8, 136, 173–4
    on distraction 108–13, 114–17
    on film, shock, mass culture 59, 111–21, 125
Bergson, H. 70
Berkeley, B. 100, 131
Berlant, L. 132–3, 221n. 59
Bishop, W. I. 44–5
body, the 4, 25–6, 41, 47–8, 125, 132, 170–1
    abstract versus corporeal 25–8
    deformation of (Bacon) 74–5, 86
    private 25, 26
    reading and 26, 31
    spectacle of 29, 38, 99–100
    without organs (Deleuze) 76
    see also gender; senses; sex
body-horror 17, 29, 32 *see also* film, horror; body, deformation of
Boltanski, L. 96–7
Boothroyd, D. 39, 188–9n. 110
Boxer, S. 139–40
Brennan, T. 66, 141, 142, 144
broadcasting 65, 181–2 *see also* wireless
Brooks, P. 163, 171, 172
Burgett, B. 25, 176

camera 59, 119–20, 126–7
Campbell, C. 43, 189n. 121
catastrophe 35–8, 39, 123–5, 187n. 85
cause and effect 10–11, 56, 63–4, 143–4, 150–1, 168, 172
celebrity 121–2, 139, 164
Cézanne, P. 67, 105
chance *see* fate
charisma 213n. 39
Charney, L. 51, 102, 103, 105, 112

child abuse 170
Chouliaraki, L. 175
Christianity 160, 171
cinema 59, 73, 98–9, 111–13, 116–17, 207–8n. 21
   cinematic experience 73, 126–9, 130, 133–4
   cinematic space 126–7, 133–4
   film experience, relation to 126–9
   see also film
civilizing process 17, 25, 29
cliché 69, 74, 83–5
Colebrook, C. 71–2, 126
collecting 108–9
commodity (fetishism) 49, 136, 138–9 *see also* advertising; consumerism
communication theory *see* information
community 57, 175, 177
concentration 5–6, 93, 94, 101, 107, 117–18, 139 *see also* attention; distraction; focus
connectivity, systems of 167–8
Connor, S. 62
consciousness 5, 87–8, 102–6, 113–16, 144, 145, 152 *see also* awareness; self, proactive and reactive; shock defence
conspiracy, culture of 167
consumerism 42, 109, 139, 156 *see also* advertising; commodity
contemporary, the *see* modernity
Crane, J. 41
Crary, J. 55–7, 67, 101–2, 103, 104–5
cultural configuration 9, 38, 172
cultural imaginary 10, 61
culture, mass and popular 7, 8, 13, 18, 22, 85–7, 117–18, 121, 123–4 *see also* entertainment
cutting 41–2, 120, 125–6
Cvetkovich, A. 21, 22, 23, 29, 31, 34, 44, 47, 49

death, the dead 15–17, 24, 38–40, 61, 65, 66, 169, 194n. 95 *see also* murder
Debord, G. 137–9
Deleuze, G. 59, 142, 143, 154, 214n. 54, 219n. 36
   and aesthetics, Bacon 69–81, 82–3, 87

   and affect theory 148, 149–50, 152
   and film 127–8, 130–1
   sensationalism, critique of 80–1, 83–6
depth and surface 16, 17, 92, 103, 113–14, 129
Derrida, J. 125–6, 153
desire 33–4, 42, 170
Diamond, M. 21, 23
Dickens, C. 19, 163
diffusion 6, 11, 64, 94, 120, 133, 139, 161, 180, 181 *see also* concentration; dissemination
disaster *see* catastrophe; movies, disaster
disease 15, 17
disgust 32, 33
dispersion *see* diffusion
dissemination (and dialogue) 181–2
dissociation, states of 107, 114
distraction 5–6, 101, 103–11, 153, 180
   distracted gaze 107, 112–13
   and film 111–17, 117–18, 126
   reception in 111, 116–17
Doane, M. A. 35, 37, 39
Dostoevsky, F. 165–6
drama 36, 37, 98, 162, 163–4 *see also* melodrama; theatre
dramatization 44–6, 71, 72–3, 136, 143, 168, 173, 219n. 36
During, S. 44, 45

Ebola virus 17
Eisenstein, S. 59, 78
electricity, electromagnetism 1, 30, 60, 63, 64, 89, 143
Elmer, J. 16, 24
emotion
   and sensation 189n. 121
enactment 44–7 *see also* dramatization
energy 1, 13, 53–4, 60, 66, 91, 141, 168
Enlightenment *see* modernity, ethical choices in
entertainment 3, 5–6, 18, 40, 44–5, 50, 98–100, 107, 123–5, 131 *see also* amusement parks
enthusiasm (Kant) 98
ether 60–1
evil 159–61, 162, 165–7, 169–70 *see also* film, horror; melodrama

Index

evolutionism 215n. 59
excess 16–17, 25, 27–8, 78, 117, 124, 136, 160, 172, 179, 180
experience
  extreme 39
  mediated 31, 37, 40, 112–19, 126–7, 135–6, 177–8
  modern 6, 30–1, 115–17
  see also immediacy; vicarious

'Facts in the Case of M. Valdemar, The' (Poe) 13–17
Fascism 48
fate 52, 53, 157
Fechner, G. 53, 55, 76
feeling 89–91, 124, 141, 145, 147, 149, 154, 175
  structure of 24
  see also affect; sensation, two meanings of
femininity, masquerade of 99–100 *see also* gender
figuration, figure 10, 26, 27–8, 47–8, 53, 59, 88, 136, 142, 153, 155, 175, 180, 219n. 35
  in Deleuze, Bacon 74, 81–3, 128
  see also cultural configuration; representation
film 2, 111, 117–20, 125, 163–5
  horror 41, 218–19n. 33
  see also cinema
flâneur (stroller) 106, 109, 173–4
focus 87, 92, 94, 102–4 *see also* concentration; periphery
Follin, F. 88, 92
force *see* energy
frame, framing 127, 134, 136–7
Freud, S. 51, 115

gender 4, 17, 46, 48, 61–2, 95–100, 163–4, 173, 196n. 8, 221n. 59
Gibbs, A. 155, 215n. 59
Glenn, S. 97, 99, 100
Gold Diggers of 1933 (LeRoy) 131
Gone With the Wind (Cukor et al.) 136
Gothic 4
Green, B. 99, 100
Greenberg, C. 81, 92
Grossberg, L. 141–2

Gulf War *see* Iraq War
Gunning, T. 21, 23, 30

Habermas, J. 220n. 51
Hadley, E. 163, 171
Halttunen, K. 17, 19, 21, 24, 29–30, 32
Hansen, M. 50, 98–9, 171
Henning, M. 46, 57
history 11
Holocaust 164–5, 166–7
horror 16–17, 24, 27 *see also* body-horror; film, horror
'How It Feels To Be Forcibly Fed' (Barnes) 95–6
hysteria 26, 46, 58, 76–8, 83

ideology 1, 8, 47–9, 129, 156–7, 161–2
imagination *see* cultural imaginary
information (theory) 65
intensity 6, 33, 37, 39, 41–2, 42, 47, 50, 56–7, 180
  in affect theory, Massumi 143, 146–8 *passim*, 153–4, 219n. 36
  in Deleuze 71–2, 72–3, 75, 83
  see also sensation; shock; vibration
interest (self and group) 1, 8
Iraq War (2003) 37–8

James, W. 36, 56, 101, 102–3
Jameson, F. 156
Joyce, J. 64

Kant, I. 32, 33, 70, 83, 98, 105–6, 161
  on the sublime 125–6, 128, 129–30, 131–2, 161, 172
Kavka, M. 142, 174–5, 177, 178, 181–2
Keats, J. 62–3
Kennedy, B. 73, 74
Kennedy, J. F., assassination of 167
Kipling, R. 62–4
Klein, N. 37–8
Knight, P. 167
Kracauer, S. 51, 113, 118–19, 125, 131

language 70–1, 148–51, 171–2, 211n. 19, 212–13n. 38 *see also* meaning; sensation, language of
Lash, S. 206n. 4
leisure *see* entertainment

Lighthouse, To The (Woolf) 87
lightning 142–5
London Dungeon 40
Lubin, D. 36, 37, 39–40

Mach, E. 54
MacIntyre, A. 161–2
Martin, J. 123–5
mass, the masses, mass public 13–14, 51, 87, 100, 117–18, 121–2, 131, 135
   mass reproduction 119–21
   see also culture, popular; media technology; public sphere
mass media 5–6, 14, 36–7, 65, 97, 107–8, 173 *see also* media technology
Massumi, B. 72, 142–9, 150, 152, 154–5
meaning 8, 17, 34, 93–4, 137, 141, 144, 148–9, 151, 162, 164–5, 168–9 *see also* language; sign
media technology, impact of 59–66, 174–8, 182 *see also* mass media (and specific technologies)
melodrama 2, 7, 21, 22, 52, 156, 163–73, 179–80
Merleau-Ponty, M. 91
mesmerism 15
Mexican-American War (1846–8) 19, 27
Meyerson, E. 56
Miller, D. A. 28, 34, 45, 46
modernism 69, 81, 84, 85–6, 87–8, 92, 115, 199n. 66
modernity 5, 6, 49, 101, 179, 222–3n. 80
   as background to sensation 49–51, 94, 98–101, 105, 106, 113–15
   and the contemporary 10–11
   critique of (Rousseau) 222–3n. 80
   ethical choices in 161–2, 180
   as progress 44, 162
   project of 35, 162, 168, 180
   see also experience, modern
monstrous, the 122, 131–2
montage 120, 125, 127, 129, 207n. 16
movement
   in film 126–8
   see also energy; sensation, as process
movies, disaster 125, 131 *see also* film
murder 4, 19, 30, 165, 166, 169
   staged 44–5

nerves 1, 30, 33, 45, 60, 193n. 99
   nervous system 67–8, 70–1, 76, 128, 146–7, 195n. 99
   see also neurasthenia
neurasthenia ('nervous exhaustion') 5, 45, 46, 58
neurons, mirror 151
neuroscience 9, 151–2, 157 *see also* affect, theory
Newman, R. 73, 75
news 14, 100–1, 181
newspapers 18–19, 22–3, 34, 95, 101, 184n. 16
9/11 3, 37, 159
novel, the 28, 108
   sensation 22, 28–9, 30, 45–6, 54
   see also reading

Oliver Twist (Dickens) 19
Op art 92
otherness, the other 7, 122, 160–1, 181

pain 29, 32–3, 96, 115 *see also* suffering
Pater, W. 67–9, 88, 196n. 8
pattern *see* structure
perception *see* attention; vision
periphery 103, 105, 106, 113 *see also* focus
personality *see* celebrity
Peters, J. D. 65, 66, 181
phonograph 61
photograph 85, 127 *see also* camera
pleasure *see* sensation, pleasures of
plethora, world as 135, 180
Poe, E. A. 13–17, 28, 86–7
pornography 32–3, 215–16n. 4
posthuman, the 157
presence 15, 37, 66, 73–4, 77–8, 102, 176–8 *see also* sensation, immediacy of
project, modern *see* modernity
proprioception 146–7, 153 *see also* senses
Proust, M. 57, 58
public/private 26, 27, 173–5
public sphere 24–5, 98–9, 173–9, 182
   mediated 173–9
Pykett, L. 22, 31, 54

Rabinbach, A. 45, 53, 54, 56, 58
race 48

radio *see* wireless
Rancière, J. 137
reading 16, 25, 26, 28–9, 31–2, 148
reception *see* distraction; spectator
recognition 83, 149–50
reflexivity 10–11, 68, 87–8, 93, 99, 118, 128, 140, 153, 155, 175, 182
repetition 21, 34, 35–6, 43–4, 91–2
representation 31–3 *passim*, 47, 55, 56–7, 73–4, 136, 136–7, 143–5 *passim*, 198–9n. 58, 200n. 3
  Deleuzian critique of 72, 76–8, 82–3, 148, 152
resonance 72, 154–5, 214n. 54
Riley, B. 88–94
risk 38–40, 168
Robespierre, M. 163
Rodowick, D. 168, 177
Rosario, K. 35, 36
Rousseau, J.-J. 222–3n. 80

Sade, Marquis de 32–3
Schwartz, V. 135–6, 136–7
science 53–6, 60–1, 65 *see also* media technology; neuroscience
Sconce, J. 37, 60, 61, 65, 177–8
scream, the 40, 78–80, 198n. 45
screen 126, 133–4, 175, 178, 182
Seaton, J. 101, 140
secrecy, the secret 2, 28–9, 174
Seigworth, G. 145, 147
self 20, 31, 39, 41, 42, 64, 68, 113, 121, 152–4, 155, 214n. 46
  as interior space 56, 57, 153
  proactive and reactive 112–14
sensation
  as boundary-crossing 27–8, 51–2, 54, 56–7, 74, 91–2, 134, 155
  circuit of 1, 4, 9, 11, 26, 43, 51–8, 66, 76, 90–1, 93–4, 114, 128, 150–1, 155–6
  contrast to everyday, mundane 6, 52–3, 69, 83–4, 87, 94, 180–1
  culture of 1–2, 7, 13, 18, 22–3, 43, 46, 48, 85–6, 134, 155–7
  cycles of 43–4, 179
  early uses of 20–1, 22, 183n. 13
  field of, web of (Riley) 90–4
  immediacy of 30, 34, 48, 51, 102

  language of 1, 10, 17, 54
  modes of manifestation 44–8, 179
  pleasures of 23, 38–42, 68, 189n. 121
  as process 43–4, 53, 71–2, 91
  subject of 2–3, 152–5
  two meanings of 1, 3, 13, 20, 52
  see also affect; excess; experience, extreme; intensity; melodrama; modernity, as background; novel, sensation; public sphere, mediated; resonance; shock; spectacle; vibration
Sensation (Young British Artists) 23
sensationalism 1, 6, 13, 14–15, 18–19, 22–3, 27–31 *passim*, 34, 37–8, 48, 49, 88–9, 99, 116, 163, 179
  critique of 31, 48–51, 80–1, 83–6
  original meanings of 21–2
  and sentimentalism 24–8
  see also mass media; sensation; spectacle
senses, the 15, 17, 91, 146–7, 177 *see also* proprioception; vision
sensibility 4, 24
sentimentalism, the sentimental 4, 24–5, 26–7, 116, 132–3, 169–70, 219n. 39
sex 22–3, 54–5 *see also* pornography
Shaviro, S. 73, 111
shock 5, 22, 37–8, 50, 59, 84, 111–12, 116–17, 127, 128, 135, 199n. 66
  defence 113–14
sign, the 72, 75, 138 *see also* meaning
Simmel, G. 51
simulation 39–40, 120, 127, 134
Singer, B. 21, 30, 49–51, 170
Smith, D. 71, 72, 74
space 6, 64, 92, 176 *see also* cinema; time
special effects 41, 133, 159
spectacle 3, 5–6, 29, 33, 36, 37–8, 45, 94, 95–100, 118, 200n. 3
  culture of 97
  and process 139–40
  and sensation 133, 134–5, 162, 173
  theory of 134–40
  see also body, spectacle of; sympathy, spectacle of
spectator 38, 98, 126, 137, 140, 178
Spinoza, B. 70
spiritualism 61–2, 63

stardom *see* celebrity
Stead, W. T. 22, 163
stimulus 50, 53, 115
   shield 5, 51
Streeby, S. 19, 24, 27, 48
stress 50
structure 10–11, 24–5, 38, 65, 91, 140
   see also connectivity; cultural configuration
subject *see* sensation, subject of
sublime 33, 123–4, 125–6, 133–4, 159, 161, 189n. 13
   cinematic 127–8, 128–9
   filmic 129–32
   mathematical and dynamical (Kant) 130–2, 133, 159, 172, 208n. 30
   technological 36–7
suffering 36, 96, 160, 162, 169, 170–1 *see also* pain
suffragettes 95–7, 99–100
sympathy 3, 21, 96–7, 181
   spectacle of 4, 97, 100, 135

technology *see* media technology
telegraph 59–60
television 139–40, 174–5, 177–8, 181–2
Terada, R. 153, 155
text 26, 31 *see also* reading
theatre 21, 96, 100, 163 *see also* drama
theatricality *see* dramatization
thermodynamics 58, 60
Thompson, J. 176, 177
Tickner, L. 99
time 127, 133, 140, 176–7 *see also* cinema; space

Titanic (Cameron) 36, 37, 39
Titanic, sinking of 36–7
Tomkins, S. 212n. 31
torture 38
transgression 6, 17, 22–3, 160, 188–9n. 110 *see also* sensation, boundary-crossing; pornography; sex
trauma 2, 41, 46, 114, 179, 218n. 28
Twin Towers *see* 9/11

uncanny, the 63–4
Uncle Tom's Cabin (Stowe) 132
unconscious, the 5, 103–4, 114, 142
   optical 114–15

Vampyr (Dreyer) 24
vibration 62, 72, 128, 154
vicarious, the 27, 31, 36, 38, 39–40, 96, 116, 178
violation 28–34 *see also* transgression
violence 29–30, 41, 74 *see also* murder; pain
Virilio, P. 177
virtual 71, 75–6, 145, 147, 149
vision 55, 89–91, 92–3, 102, 103, 181

Webb, B. 59, 65
Weber, S. 117, 121, 177
Wetherell, M. 142, 143, 145, 147, 148
Williams, L. 159, 163–4, 165, 172
wireless 37, 59, 62–4, 65, 66, 174, 182
'Wireless' (Kipling) 62–4
Woolf, V. 64, 87, 108

Žižek, S. 211n. 19